WATER
MATTERS

WATE

MAT

AlterNet Books

Why We Need to Act Now to Save
Our Most Critical Resource

Edited by Tara Lohan

Table of Contents

Section Two: **SAVING OUR MOST
CRITICAL RESOURCE**

Introduction Tara Lohan

Southern Utah's sandstone is soft, and the rock here has been worked by wind and water like clay in the palms of an artist. This handiwork has resulted in a secret labyrinth of slot canyons, deep crevices that allow the nimble to slip between the folds of the rock and shimmy into the belly of the earth.

At least, that's what it feels like to me.

With the help of a climbing harness, belay device, and rope I've lowered myself through a slit into a cold chamber of red rock, where only a sliver of sunlight scrapes through. My companions and I will walk, crawl, swim, and climb our way through this canyon—over boulders and down steep drops. We'll pass through holes in the rock that are barely bigger than our bodies, we'll test the sandstone's smoothness against the sticky grip of our shoes.

And the whole time our mouths will be agape. This is Zion National Park, but it feels more like a museum. Each room of rock we find ourselves in is more beautiful than the last. If you want to get a sense of time, of the slow scalpel that water has taken to the region over the last, say, 170 million years, this is the place. Looking out at the Grand Canyon and imagining the carving of that monument is too enormous to fully comprehend. But in here, where icy cold water pools up to my knees, and I can put my cheek against the cold rock and listen, water's patience is palpable. It has hieroglyphed the rock—been both poet and soothsayer—leaving a line behind to mark the good times, the high times. This line now reads like a warning.

I think of the stark photos that appeared in the *New York Times Magazine* a few years back showing the massive bathtub rings, 100 feet high, of receding Lake Mead. The dwindling pool behind Hoover Dam is a catastrophe in the making, especially for Las Vegas, which relies on the lake for 90 percent of its drinking water. But it goes much further. Lake Mead is fed by the Colorado and the 1,400-mile-long river is struggling to quench the thirst of the 30 million people in seven states who depend on it, not to mention our neighbors in Mexico. It turns out when folks got together in 1922 to divvy up water rights to the Colorado it was the wettest 12 months in the last 1,200 years. Consequently, the mighty Colorado has never been able to live up to our lofty expectations. There is simply not enough water.

It's a story repeated across the Western U.S., especially the Southwest where scarce water resources are straining to meet the needs of bulging cities, and resort communities and golf courses seem to be cloning themselves across the desert. The word "drought" is familiar in these parts. New to the lips may be "permanent drought." And parsing those words with "climate change" is fast becoming part of our new lexicon.

A recent report from the Natural Resources Defense Council found that one-third of counties in the lower 48 states will face high risks of water shortage in the next 40 years because of global warming. The areas likely to be hardest hit are the Great Plains, California, and the Southwest. But even the South, especially Florida, could be in trouble, as well as the Midwest. Higher temperatures could significantly reduce water levels in the Great Lakes. It's not just surface water that's at risk; we're also using groundwater in many areas faster than nature can replenish it. Of particular concern is the Ogallala Aquifer, which Plains states are overdrafting with astounding speed.

This may affect not just how much water we have to drink and clean with, but also how much is available for us to grow food, produce energy, drive industry, and of course, maintain a healthy environment. This problem is nationwide—it's exacerbated in many places by climate change, but our water resources are also threatened by unchecked development, agricultural and industrial pollution, privatization, increasing population, and aging infrastructure. The crisis is made worse by a lack of consciousness about water conservation and efficiency—by a sheer blindness to the fact that our very lives depend on something we take for granted daily.

Our blue planet may be mostly water, but 97 percent of it is too salty for us to drink. Of the 3 percent that is freshwater, most of it is frozen away in glaciers and ice caps or out of reach in deep underground aquifers. Less than 1 percent is left for all freshwater life. "Deprive any plant or animal of water, and it dies," renowned water expert Sandra Postel wrote. "Our decisions about water—how to use, allocate, and manage it—are deeply ethical ones; they determine the survival of most of the planet's species, including our own."

Not only is the scale of the problem vast, it's also urgent. Globally a crisis is already in full swing.

The World Health Organization tells us that 2.6 billion people do not have access to adequate sanitation, a condition that kills a child every 20 seconds. These are the numbers that keep me up at night. One-sixth of the world's population, nearly a billion people, don't have a reliable source of clean drinking water to meet their minimal daily requirements of 13 gallons a day—literally the same amount we flush down the drain in two trips to the loo. By 2025 the number of people without access to drinkable water is likely to reach 3 billion. In some cases it's an issue of true scarcity, but in many cases it's an issue of access.

Living in the U.S., I haven't had to think about access too much, although I know there are those in my country who aren't nearly so lucky. By any standard I've got a privileged life. When I turn on the tap, clean water comes out and I pay far less for it than I do for nonessential stuff like my cell phone bill. When I lived in the high desert of New Mexico several years ago, I thought about water a lot. People talked about it in town. The weather was not just polite conversation. How much would it snow, when would it melt, would the rains come in the summer—all that was critical. The local economy depended on it. My neighbors worked to maintain the *acequias*, or earthen irrigation ditches, to fun-

PHOTOGRAPHS BY BOWE ELLIS

Exploring Ordeville Canyon, and the Subway and Das Boot on the Left Fork of North Creek in Zion National Park.

Introduction

nel the snowmelt to their fields. My friend Paul ran an entire farm based on what fell from the sky that he could catch and store.

I got my desert initiation on a hike that was too long with too little water. I learned how quickly you can lose your mind and lose your way when your mouth sticks with thirst. I also learned the value of water and came to revel in the theater of its arrival—the sky changing from bright blue to bruised in the moments before a summertime burst of monsoon. It's one of the reasons I'm perpetually drawn to the desert; it's a not-so-subtle reminder of the things that matter most in life—like water.

My hiking trip through Zion National Park in Utah was another lesson. In the belly of that slot canyon, I thought about having too little water, even as I heard the slosh inside my overweighted pack. Park bulletins said the region was suffering from drought, the rivers were low, we were in pools of water up to our knees that could easily have been over our head. Just a day after my trip ended, a flash flood tore through one of the canyons, catching three canyoneers by surprise and washing them over 40- and 60-foot drops. They survived, but across the world at the same time rising waters in Pakistan had just claimed over 1,500 lives and the disaster was still in the making. That's the thing about water, sometimes you have too little and other times too much.

We've spent thousands of years trying to figure out how to engineer our way out of that problem. Over 50,000 large dams worldwide stand as a testament to the effort. They've provided us with electricity and a place to store our drinking water. They've also given us an environmental nightmare, ruined ecosystems, and displaced millions of people. I think about that tradeoff every day: The water I drink in San Francisco is courtesy of the O'Shaughnessy Dam snuggled up against Yosemite; a dam environmental activists have spent decades trying to remove so the Hetch Hetchy Valley—which John Muir called "one of nature's rarest and most precious mountain temples"—can be restored to its natural splendor. We've rolled the dice. Taken our

chances. Mortgaged our future, perhaps, for fleeting moments of prosperity.

In the 20th century we went big—big infrastructure, big farms, big houses, big cars. I'm hoping the 21st century is about building smaller and smarter and more holistically. "As the limitations of big infrastructure strategies have become more apparent, a vanguard of citizens, communities, farmers, and corporations are thinking about water in a new way," wrote Postel in a 2010 issues of *Yes!* magazine. "The upshot of this shift in thinking is a new movement in water management that is much more about ideas, ingenuity, and ecological intelligence than it is about big pumps, pipelines, dams, and canals."

I'm putting my money on Postel's vision. We have to begin imagining a new water future, and then working to make it happen. Right now the U.S. is attempting to recover from one of the worst environmental disasters we've ever seen. Just as that rogue Gulf of Mexico oil gusher was being plugged, nearly a million gallons of crude oil spilled into Michigan's Kalamazoo River. Once again we found ourselves in a head-on collision between our energy and water crises. Building a new water future will need to go hand-in-hand with a new energy revolution—one the world badly needs.

The trouble we've seen in the Gulf of Mexico is not just confined to oil slicks and tar balls. For decades, the Mississippi River and its tributaries have teamed up to deliver a toxic dose of nitrogen pollution, mostly from farms, which has created a dead zone in the Gulf that is now about the size of Massachusetts. As we begin to use water more wisely, we'll need to grow food more wisely. This is especially pertinent because global warming is already impacting water resources in some agricultural regions and things are likely to get worse.

Time is of the essence. In July 2010 news sources reported that about 60 million people who live around the Himalayas are predicted to run short on food in the next 20 years because glaciers are shrinking and there won't be enough water for agriculture. At the same time, drought in

Russia has crippled crops and ignited over 500 fires across the country. Australia is reeling from over a decade of drought and Maude Barlow, a U.N. adviser on water, has warned that California is following in Australia's footsteps.

As for the precious water resources we have left, well, they're not in such great shape either. In the U.S. 40 percent of our rivers and 46 percent of our lakes are too polluted for fishing, swimming, or to support aquatic life. It's time to clean up our act. Recently, environmental groups were urging the Israeli government to close down a baptism site on the Lower Jordan River because of concern that the river had become too polluted for those who bathe at the holy site. Friends of the Middle East reported that Israel, Syria, and Jordan had diverted 98 percent of the famous river and were dumping agricultural runoff, untreated sewage, and fishpond effluent into the water. Is nothing sacred any more?

We may have reserved a place for water in ceremony, but what about holding it in high esteem each and every day? Thankfully, there are reasons to be hopeful. Here's one of the best: On July 29, 2010, the United Nations General Assembly declared that access to clean water and sanitation is a fundamental human right. This is a victory over powerful corporate interests and wealthy countries, including my own (the U.S. abstained from voting, along with Canada, the United Kingdom, Australia, and New Zealand). The victory should also be celebrated as a testament to a growing grassroots movement.

It's all part of a mass of critical work being done in communities all over the world—folks are protecting wetlands and rivers, taking on corporate polluters, working for public control of water resources, developing water-efficient technologies, increasing literacy about conservation, advocating for water justice, and drawing the connection between energy, food, and water systems. These things are happening where we live and the severity of this crisis begs us to pitch in—in every way we can.

Here's how I got hooked; Years ago, I fell in love with the writing of Terry Tempest Williams, who has made her home in the red rock desert of Utah that I've come to love. It was there that I understood for the first time the power of water to give and to take life, to make myths, to move mountains. She wrote, "For those who have not experienced the sublime nature of Utah's canyon country, I invite you to imagine what it might be like to see and feel the world from the inside out. If you do come visit, be prepared to be broken open like a rock fallen from a once-secure place."

I took her advice literally. I went to her desert and it brought me to my knees. It also put me on a "water path"— now I get to read and write about water for a living and talk to people who are working to protect water resources and make sure everyone has access to clean water. I've ditched bottled water and take shorter showers, but it's not enough. We need change on a Titanic scale. When Williams writes, "be prepared to be broken open like a rock," I think of it as a metaphor for change. We need to change ourselves and the world and it's not going to be easy. We're going to need to crack the exterior of our collective complacency. Dislodge ourselves from where we've always felt comfortable. Fall out of our old habits.

Deserts may be patient, they may have all the time in the world, but we don't. We have to act now.

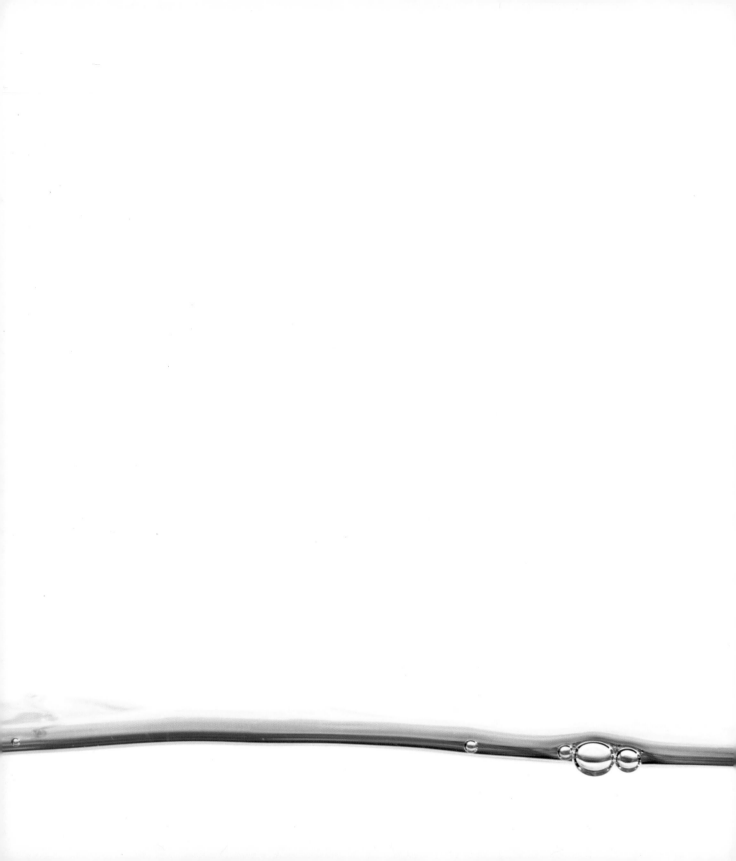

Section One **A WORLD IN CRISIS**

Water Is Life

BARBARA KINGSOLVER

We keep an eye out for wonders, my daughter and I, every morning as we walk down our farm lane to meet the school bus. And wherever we find them, they reflect the magic of water: a spider web drooping with dew like a rhinestone necklace; a rain-colored

heron rising from the creek bank. One astonishing morning, we had a visitation of frogs. Dozens of them hurtled up from the grass ahead of our feet, launching themselves, white-bellied, in bouncing arcs, as if we'd been caught in a downpour of amphibians. It seemed to mark the dawning of some new aqueous age. On another day we met a snapping turtle in his primordial olive drab armor. Normally this is a pond-locked creature, but some murky ambition had moved him onto our gravel lane, using the rainy week as a passport from our farm to somewhere else.

The little, nameless creek tumbling through our hollow holds us in thrall. Before we came to southern Appalachia, we lived for years in Arizona, where a permanent runnel of that size would merit a nature preserve. In the Grand Canyon State, every license plate reminded us that water changes the face of the land, splitting open rock desert like a peach, leaving mile-deep gashes of infinite hue. Cities there function like space stations, importing every ounce of fresh water from distant rivers or fossil aquifers. But such is the human inclination to take water as a birthright that public fountains still may bubble in Arizona's town squares and farmers there raise thirsty crops. Retirees from rainier climes irrigate green lawns that impersonate the grasslands they left behind. The truth encroaches on all the fantasies, though, when desert residents wait months between rains, watching cacti tighten their belts and roadrunners skirmish over precious beads from a dripping garden faucet. Water is life. It's the briny broth of our origins, the pounding circulatory system of the world, a precarious molecular edge on which we survive. It makes up two-thirds of our bodies, just like the map of the world; our vital fluids are saline, like the ocean. The apple doesn't fall far from the tree.

Even while we take Mother Water for granted, humans understand in our bones that she is the boss. We stake our civilizations on the coasts and along the mighty rivers. Our deepest dread is the threat of having too little moisture—or too much. We've lately raised the Earth's average temperature by 0.74°C (1.3°F), a number that sounds inconsequential. But these words do not: flood, drought, hurricane, rising sea levels, bursting levees. Water is the visible face of climate and therefore, climate change. Shifting rain patterns flood some regions and dry up others as nature demonstrates a grave physics lesson: Hot air holds more water molecules than cold.

The results are in plain sight along pummeled coasts from Louisiana to the Philippines as superwarmed air above the ocean brews superstorms, the likes of which we have never known. In arid places the same physics amplify evaporation and drought, visible in the dust-dry farms of the Murray-Darling River Basin in Australia. On top of the Himalaya, glaciers whose meltwater sustains vast populations are dwindling. The snapping turtle I met on my lane may have been looking for higher ground. Last summer brought us a string of floods that left tomatoes blighted on the vine and our farmers needing disaster relief for the third consecutive year. The past decade has brought us more extreme storms than ever before, of the kind that dump many inches in a day, laying down crops and utility poles and great sodden oaks whose roots cannot find purchase in the saturated ground. The word "disaster" seems to mock us. After enough repetitions of shocking weather, we can't remain indefinitely shocked.

How can the world shift beneath our feet? All we know is founded on its rhythms: Water will flow from the snow-capped mountains, rain and sun will arrive in their proper seasons. Humans first formed our tongues around language, surely, for the purpose of explaining these constants to our children. What should we tell them now? That "reliable" has been rained out, or died of thirst? When the Earth seems to raise its own voice to the pitch of a gale, have we the ears to listen?

A world away from my damp hollow, the Bajo Piura Valley is a great bowl of the driest Holocene sands I've ever gotten in my shoes. Stretching from coastal, northwestern Peru into southern Ecuador, the 14,000-square-mile Piura Desert is home to many endemic forms of thorny life. Profiles of this eco-region describe it as dry to drier, and Bajo Piura on its southern edge is what anyone would call driest. Between January and March it might get close to an inch

was an innovative reforestation project. Peruvian conservationists, partnered with the NGO Heifer International, were guiding the population into herding goats, which eat the protein-rich pods of the native mesquite and disperse its seeds over the desert. In the shade of a stick shelter, a young mother set her dented pot on a dung-fed fire and showed how she curdles goat's milk into white cheese. But milking goats is hard to work into her schedule when she, and every other woman she knows, must walk about eight hours a day to collect water.

Their husbands were digging a well nearby. They worked with hand trowels, a plywood form for lining the shaft with concrete, inch by inch, and a sturdy hand-built crank for lowering a man to the bottom and sending up buckets of sand. A dozen hopeful men in stained straw hats stood back to let me inspect their work, which so far had yielded only a mountain of exhumed sand, dry as dust. I looked down that black hole, then turned and climbed the sand mound to hide my unprofessional tears. I could not fathom this kind of perseverance and wondered how long these

WHEN THE EARTH SEEMS TO RAISE ITS OWN VOICE TO

of rain, depending on the whims of El Niño, my driver explained as we bumped over the dry bed of the Río Piura, "but in some years, nothing at all." For hours we passed through white-crusted fields ruined by years of irrigation and then into eye-burning valleys beyond the limits of endurance for anything but sparse stands of the deep-rooted *Prosopis pallida*, arguably nature's most arid-adapted tree. And remarkably, some scattered families of *Homo sapiens*.

They are economic refugees, looking for land that costs nothing. In Bajo Piura they find it, although living there has other costs, and fragile drylands pay their own price too, as people exacerbate desertification by cutting anything living for firewood. What brought me there, as a journalist,

beleaguered people would last before they'd had enough of their water woes and moved somewhere else.

Five years later they are still bringing up dry sand, scratching out their fate as a microcosm of life on this planet. There is nowhere else. Forty percent of the households in sub-Saharan Africa are more than a half hour from the nearest water, and that distance is growing. Australian farmers can't follow the rainfall patterns that have shifted south to fall on the sea. A salmon that runs into a dam when homing in on her natal stream cannot make other plans. Together we dig in, for all we're worth.

Since childhood I've heard it's possible to look up from the bottom of a well and see stars, even in daylight. Aristotle wrote about this, and so did Charles Dickens. On many a dark night the vision of that round slip of sky with stars has comforted me. Here's the only problem: It's not true. Western civilization was in no great hurry to give up this folklore; astronomers believed it for centuries, but a few of them eventually thought to test it and had their illusions dashed by simple observation.

Civilization has been similarly slow to give up on our myth of the Earth's infinite generosity. We pumped aquifers and diverted rivers, trusting the twin lucky stars of unrestrained human expansion and endless supply. Now water tables plummet in countries harboring half the world's population. Rather grandly, we have overdrawn our accounts.

In 1968 the ecologist Garrett Hardin wrote a paper called "The Tragedy of the Commons," required reading for biology students ever since. It addresses the problems that can be solved only by "a change in human values or ideas of morality" in situations where rational pursuit of individual self-interest leads to collective ruin. Cattle

New Mexico's antique irrigation codes to the UN Convention on International Watercourses, communities have studied water systems and redefined wise use. Now Ecuador has become the first nation on Earth to put the rights of nature in its constitution so that rivers and forests are not simply property, but maintain their own right to flourish. Under these laws a citizen might file suit on behalf of an injured watershed, recognizing that its health is crucial to the common good. Other nations may follow Ecuador's lead. Just as legal systems once reeled to comprehend women or former slaves as fully entitled, law schools in the U.S. are now reforming their curricula with an eye to understanding and acknowledging nature's rights.

On my desk, a glass of water has caught the afternoon light, and I'm still looking for wonders. Who owns this water? How can I call it mine when its fate is to run through rivers and living bodies, so many already and so many more to come? It is an ancient, dazzling relic, temporarily quarantined here in my glass, waiting to return to its kind, waiting to move a mountain. It is the gold standard

THE PITCH OF A GALE, HAVE WE THE EARS TO LISTEN?

farmers who share a common pasture, for example, will increase their herds one by one until they destroy the pasture by overgrazing. Agreeing to self-imposed limits instead, unthinkable at first, will become the right thing to do. While our laws imply that morality is fixed, Hardin made the point that "the morality of an act is a function of the state of the system at the time it is performed." Surely it was no sin, once upon a time, to shoot and make pies of passenger pigeons.

Water is the ultimate commons. Watercourses once seemed as boundless as those pigeons that darkened the sky overhead, and the notion of protecting water was as silly as bottling it. But rules change. Time and again, from

of biological currency, and the good news is that we can conserve it in countless ways. Also, unlike petroleum, water will always be with us. Our trust in Earth's infinite generosity was half right, as every raindrop will run to the ocean, and the ocean will rise into the firmament. And half wrong, because we are not important to water. It's the other way around. Our task is to work out reasonable ways to survive inside its boundaries. We'd be wise to fix our sights on some new stars. The gentle nudge of evidence, the guidance of science, and a heart for protecting the commons: These are the tools of a new century. Taking a wide-eyed look at a watery planet is our way of knowing the stakes, the better to know our place.

THE
VALUE OF WATER

The Rev. Canon Thomas Miller

THE 18TH CENTURY PHILOSOPHER Novalis wrote, "Our bodies are molded rivers." Such poetic sentiment is easy to appreciate even in the less-than-poetic age in which we live. We are generaly aware of our bodies as organic compositions attuned to the dynamics of nature. It is more difficult, perhaps, to think of buildings as organic bodies in quite the same way. Imagine, for instance, streams of water coursing through the seemingly solid stones of The Cathedral of St. John the Divine in New York; water rising up through the pillars like sap in a soaring forest.

Outside, the Gothic-styled Cathedral seems impressively massive, built to withstand the tempering of time. Inside, the breathtaking view from the Bronze Doors to the far end of the building presents an even more compelling vision: stone, wood, and glass, all hard materials of the Earth that have been molded into an architectural body of wondrous dimension. So, where's the water—that element that makes it a living cathedral rather than just a pile of stones?

The simple answer is that there's water, water everywhere, as the imagination might fashion it, since none of the stone, wood or glass would exist without the presence and power of water over geological time. As biblical tradition has it, human beings bear the image of their Creator. Perhaps in like manner, all the materials in the Cathedral bear the mark of water, that basic element of Creation through which all things were made.

Another simple answer is that water is at the very foundation of the Cathedral. The land on which it stands is dotted with wells, springs, and underground streams. So, even while we look at the stones and think of the building as the solid monumental body it surely is, we can also envision the water-laced land from which it rises.

Shortly there will be yet another answer to the question, "Where's the water in the Cathedral?" "The Value of Water," an ambitious installation of art opens in September, 2011. Works by painters, sculptors, and media artists, including the seven presented in the following pages, will be installed in bays of the nave, in various chapels, and along the walls of the Great Crossing. As interpreters of the unseen, artists will help us to see what has been there all along; to strengthen our awareness of water, and to prompt our imaginations in the contemplation of water, from wells and underground springs to surging seas and mighty rivers. With this collection of powerful presentations, there really will be water, water everywhere.

APRIL GORNIK
Sun, Storm, Cloud, 2004
Oil on linen, 72" x 96"
Courtesy: The artist and Danese, New York

THE
VALUE OF WATER

An Art Exhibition 2011-2012
CATHEDRAL OF ST. JOHN THE DIVINE, NEW YORK CITY

Poisoning the Well

BILL MCKIBBEN

It's common knowledge that you can survive for weeks without food. But how long can you survive without water? A few days, at most. Human beings are mostly water and our planet is mostly water—indeed Earth is often called the "water planet," its blue

seas and white cloudy mists forming the dominant features we see from space.

Yet in many ways water is scarce. Ninety-seven percent of the planet's water is undrinkable seawater, and most of the rest is locked up in glaciers and ice caps, or falls in remote places. Even so, we'd have enough water if we hadn't invented a staggering list of ways to pollute and squander our birthright.

The most obvious examples loom large in our collective memory. Forty years ago, America awoke one morning to discover that the Cuyahoga River in Cleveland was on fire. When a river catches fire, that gets our attention. One would think that billions of dead fish bobbing to the surface of ponds, lakes, and rivers all over the world would be a clear sign that something was seriously wrong, but in most places those warning signs are still being ignored.

These are examples of our collective failure to see what is right before our eyes. But the subterranean, slow-moving and subtle water disasters—many of them occurring literally beneath our feet —should frighten us even more.

Consider, for instance, the ways the United States has managed to overpump the invisible, deep aquifers beneath its fields and cities. This might have been a warning to other nations, but greed and short-term gains have a curious ability to blind us to the bigger picture. Unfortunately, all of the major grain-producing countries adopted deep-water pumping in the years right after World War II. The United States implemented this technology quicker, and thus encountered its problems first—but not by much, and by then, the rest of the world was already deeply committed.

The result is that China, India, and the United States, as well as scores of other countries, are all starting to pump their reservoirs dry at the same time, which is right now. Over the last decade the water table beneath the North China Plains and the Indian Punjab has been dropping by meters each year—in some places, tens of meters. These deep aquifers took millions of years to fill, and we are draining them in less than a century.

One result of this unconscionable draining of humanity's lifeblood is that a once-invisible disaster is surfacing. Travel the countryside north of Beijing and you'll meet scores of people who are in despair because the same wells their families have been using for generations have suddenly run dry. China's crisis is so severe that the country is re-routing entire rivers in the south through thousands of miles of aqueduct in a desperate attempt to serve the needs of the north.

But that diversion, in turn, is creating its own crisis. To deal with the water shortage, large regions of China are now switching from growing wheat, a notoriously thirsty grain, to corn, which uses less water but also produces lower yields. The impact of that shift is depressingly predictable: With small harvests, China has been forced for the first time to import grain from the West. In effect, China, for the very first time in its long history, is importing "virtual water" in the form of goods.

The world has become too small in the 21st century for any nation to export its problems. And if you think these problems are simply those of the developing world, then visit Las Vegas. Or Phoenix. Or ....

This is just the beginning. When it comes to water, disasters cluster. Already, there are places on Earth where water-based crises are mounting so fast it is hard to know where to begin to solve them. The solution to one problem exacerbates another.

Take Bangladesh, home to 150 million people and one of the wettest places on earth. It's the delta of the great sacred rivers of Asia—the Ganges and the Brahmaputra both reach the ocean here, finishing their descent from the high Himalayas in slow and stately fashion. One might think water would be the least of the country's problems—indeed, Bangladesh has so much water that travel in many seasons is easier by ferry than by bus.

But because Bangladesh's water sits on the surface, it is vulnerable to many kinds of pollution—some from industry, some from the spread of human waste. From the latter, for example, waterborne cholera has become an endemic problem.

The United Nations thought it had a solution to the polluted surface water: Go underground. Mile-deep wells were dug across much of the nation, and people were urged to stop drinking surface water. Unfortunately, the U.N. forgot to check the underlying geology or even to test the underground water. Only when entire communities of Bengalis fell sick did scientists determine that the new deep wells were bringing massive quantities of arsenic to the surface, slowly poisoning the people.

Bangladesh is the canary in the coal mine for an impending water crisis that may well engulf us all: climate change. Mankind, without much forethought, has been conducting the largest and most extensive hydrological experiment in history—and, like the sinking cities and drying wells of the world, the disastrous results are only now beginning to reveal themselves.

Consider the Ganges and the Brahmaputra, both now fed by ever-faster melting glaciers. The two rivers in turn pour into the Bay of Bengal in the Indian Ocean, an ocean that has now begun to rise. That higher sea acts as a kind of fluid dam, forcing the rivers to spread out in a devastating flood. By mid-century, according to some estimates, much of Bangladesh will be underwater.

Raising the planet's temperature, in fact, will disrupt almost everything aquatic on earth. The salient scientific fact is that warm air holds more water vapor than cold. Thus in arid areas, one can expect more evaporation: Computer models show that virgin flows along the Colorado River may drop by half as the century proceeds. That's bad news for a West that already strains that river to slake its thirst.

But if humanity always seems to ignore problems until they reach crisis proportions, so too does it have the capacity, once mobilized, to bring vast amounts of energy and ingenuity to solving those problems. So it is good news that we've at least begun early experiments in water-saving agriculture, such as new, less-thirsty varieties of plants, drip irrigation, and water recycling. In the United States, 35 years of the Clean Water Act means that we can swim in and drink from far more of our lakes and rivers in the first years of the 21st century than we could in the last years of the 20th.

But will our solutions be efficient and sweeping enough to deal with what is now a rapidly intensifying worldwide water crisis? Can our experiments spread fast enough to keep up with the pace of expanding consumer life, a life that, by its very nature, uses more and more water?

Perhaps the only real hope is a change in mindset toward valuing clean, fresh water at its true worth. Some of that new valuation will be, for lack of a better word, spiritual—learning to once again see water not as a commodity, in infinite supply, but as something precious, to be preserved and not taken for granted.

The most spiritual human moments involve water, whether it is baptism in the Christian church or the ritual bathing by Hindus in Mother Ganges. Pious Muslims wash before prayer; pious Jews before marriage. Water has cleansed us—cleansed us literally, cleansed us of our sins, cleansed our minds and hearts. We must learn how to return the favor, to wash water free of the thousand stains we've inflicted on it in our heedless rush toward prosperity.

Previous page, Rapid economic growth has brought new industrialization and new pollution to rural parts of China. 150 million people live in the Huai River Basin in the Henan Province, one of the most polluted stretches of water in the country. *This page*, In January and February 2007, extreme rainfall triggered by El Niño caused the worst flooding in 25 years in Bolivia. Here, a young girl bathes with black, contaminated water following the floods.

Shortage in the Land of Plenty

CYNTHIA BARNETT

The Chattahoochee River begins as a small spring in North Georgia and widens as it travels south, creating pebbled mountain streams and hidden waterfalls that delight southernmost hikers on the Appalachian Trail. As it winds down Georgia, the river

meanders through oak and pine forests set off with red maples and white dogwoods, rushing over rocks it has flattened smooth over thousands of years.

The Creek Indians gave the Chattahoochee its name, which means River of Painted Rocks.[1] Southerners just call it the Hooch.

Considering its size and all that it has to do, the Hooch may be the hardest-working river in America. Its northernmost streams are nurseries to native brook trout, its lower shoals and pools stocked with rainbows and browns. Come summer, it carries thousands of tourists in tubes or rafts who "shoot the Hooch" through the faux-Bavarian town of Helen and other North Georgia mountain retreats.

From here, the sweet burden of recreation gives way to heavier demands. The Chattahoochee cools sixteen power-generating plants. It's constrained by fourteen dams.[2] Fifty miles above Atlanta, the Army Corps of Engineers built Buford Dam in the 1950s, dug a huge blue reservoir and christened it Lake Sidney Lanier in honor of the poet. Lanier saw in the river a moral duty to complete its journey without folly:

> I hurry amain to reach the plain,
> Run the rapid and leap the fall,
> Split at the rock and together again,
> Accept my bed, narrow or wide,
> And flee from folly on every side[3]

Apparently, Georgia's engineers never read the poem. From Helen in the north to a dam called West Point 85, miles south of Atlanta, hundreds of cities and industries have permits to discharge pollution into the Chattahoochee. Metro Atlanta's sewage-treatment plants dump 500 million gallons of treated wastewater into the river every day. They regularly spill raw sewage illegally, as well; Atlanta is under federal consent decree to complete a massive, $4 billion overhaul of its sewer system to stop the spills.[4]

Flowing on to southern Georgia, Alabama, and Florida, the Chattahoochee's basin helps irrigate 780,000 acres of corn, cotton, peanut, and other crops each year.[5]

In Florida's Panhandle, the Hooch joins another Georgia river, the Flint, to become the powerful Apalachicola. It flows through bluffs, then thick tupelo and cypress swamps. The journey that began at tiny Chattahoochee Spring ends at Florida's huge Apalachicola Bay. There, 16 billion gallons of fresh water a day mix with the Gulf of Mexico to create the last unspoiled bay in Florida.[6]

Apalachicola's estuary teems with numbers of fish and shellfish absent from the bays of south and central Florida for more than five decades. The bay's shrimpers pull in six million pounds of crustaceans a year. Its oystermen tong up 90 percent of the oysters slurped down in Florida, 10 percent of those consumed in the United States. This productivity requires just the right blend of Hooch and Gulf: high salinity in the bay brings ocean-side predators that stalk young marine creatures in their sea-grass nurseries.[7]

But of all these grave responsibilities, the Chattahoochee carries one all-but-impossible burden. It is the smallest river in the country to supply water to a major metropolitan area—Atlanta. In the early years of the 21st century, the sprawling capital of the New South added more residents than any other in the United States, pushing past five million people. [8] The river must irrigate their lawns (the top residential use of water in Atlanta). The river must flush their toilets (the second-greatest use, at about 20 gallons a person every day).[9] The Hooch must even convert itself to cash: The Chattahoochee ends up in millions of bottles of Dasani water that roll off Coca-Cola's production line in Marietta.[10]

By the late 1980s, it was clear the Chattahoochee couldn't do it all, particularly during times of drought. In 1988, federal environmental officials declared Apalachicola Bay a disaster area when weakened flow devastated the oyster harvest. But the Army Corps' allegiance was to the sprinklers rather than the shellfish. In 1989, the Corps came up with a new dam and reservoir plan to harness even more of the Chattahoochee in dry times. A year later, Alabama filed a lawsuit to stop the dam, worried dwindled flow would hamper the state's ability to grow and develop. Florida joined the suit, arguing further upstream withdrawals would destroy Apalachicola Bay and the region's signature seafood industry.

Those were the first punches in a water fight that has slogged on for twenty years. In 1998, Congress passed a water compact for the three states. But their officials failed so miserably in negotiating the compact—they missed a total of fourteen deadlines—that it was terminated five years later. The match-up then moved on to courthouses across the South. The lawyers fared no better than the politicians figuring out how to share the Hooch, but they did manage to bill the taxpayers of Florida and Georgia alone more than $28 million in legal fees.

It's not surprising to see Americans slugging it out over who gets how much water. We expect such conflicts in water-scarce regions of the West, where some states have been duking it out for more than a century. What's astonishing is to watch water scarcity and strife emerge in the Southeast—the wettest region in the lower 48.

And what's maddening is that we did it to ourselves.

In 1876, Major John Wesley Powell, the adventuresome, one-armed explorer who then headed the U.S. Geological Survey, declared that the 100th Meridian, a longitudinal line down the middle of Oklahoma, North and South Dakota, Nebraska, Kansas, and Texas, divided a wet East from an arid West. To the west of the line, he reported to Congress, a lack of rainfall would require cooperative irrigation and an equitable system of water rights to ensure scarce water would be used for the greatest good.

But to the east of the line, the major said, more than 20 inches of rainfall a year meant that people could settle and grow anything they wanted—without irrigation.

Powell, the first non-native American to explore the wild Colorado River, likely would be shocked by its modern-day taming, and by the complex, hardly equitable distribution formula that greens 1.7 million acres of desert and quenches 25 million residents in seven western states. But he might be all the more surprised by the water crisis lapping at the southeastern U.S. After all, nature graces the South with an average of 50 inches of rain a year, more than double the amount Powell deemed enough to grow—with no irrigation—any crop that could take the heat. The South is also blessed with some of the largest aquifers in the country: The Southeastern Coastal Plain Aquifer flows for 122,000 square miles under Mississippi, Alabama, South Carolina, and Georgia. In Florida, it meets up with one of the most productive aquifers in the world, the Floridan, which serves a steady flow of groundwater to major metro areas from Savannah to Orlando and beyond.[11]

During Powell's time, the South was also soggy home to more than half the nation's wetlands. In those days, they were considered dismal swamps. Congress gladly deeded them to the states to drain for development in the Swamp Lands Acts of 1849, 1850, and 1860. Since then, the region has lost more wetlands than any other, with most converted to agricultural crops in the Lower Mississippi River Valley, eastern North Carolina, and the Florida Everglades.[12]

Powell lived before invention of the diesel-powered water pump. He likely wouldn't have imagined 300 million people living in the United States. And he surely wouldn't

Previous page, A drought at Lake Lanier, a reservoir that provides drinking water for Atlanta, reveals a tree that is usually submerged. *This page,* A sinkhole, 320 feet across and 90 feet deep opened up in Winter Park, Florida in 1981. It was later converted into an urban lake.

WE CONTINUED TO LIVE AS IF WATER WERE LIMITLESS RIGHT UP TO THE MOMENT WHEN IT NEARLY RAN OUT.

have dreamed that the water-logged South could drain, dredge, ditch, dam, and pump its way to water scarcity and conflict. But that's just what we did.

In the 19th century, we worked to drain the swamplands, most vigorously in Louisiana and Florida, where respectively seven million and nine million acres of wetlands are now cities and farms. The Everglades drainage project turned into a disaster for not just the environment, but people, too: The great swamp was South Florida's freshwater reserve.

In the early 20th century, we set out to control rivers, from the grand social work of the Tennessee Valley Authority to the everyday dams of the Chattahoochee. In the post-war growth heydays, we pumped the prodigious aquifers, ignoring multiple signs that warned of groundwater's limits: Saltwater intrusion into freshwater wells from Miami up the Eastern seaboard; scourges of sinkholes like the one that swallowed a Central Florida Porsche dealership in 1981.

The growth-and-greed decades, when Florida, Georgia, and the Carolinas began to rival the West in population gains and housing starts, were blind to those and many other signs. Water litigation boiled across the South: Virginia took Maryland to court over the historic Potomac that borders the states. South Carolina's attorney general went straight to the U.S. Supreme Court to try to stop North Carolina from draining millions of gallons from the Catawba River that both states rely on. At the same time hydro-hypocrite North Carolina was trying to poke its straw into the shared Catawba in the southeast corner of the state, it was working to block Virginia Beach from doing the same with the shared Roanoke River on the northeast side.

Through it all, Southerners continued to live as if water were limitless. St. Petersburg, Florida, sucked up so much groundwater from neighboring counties that large lakes turned to dust and tall trees sank to eye-level. In Arkansas, rice farmers pumped their Alluvial Aquifer to depletion. In Atlanta, the real estate industry killed a measure requiring water-wasting toilets be replaced with efficient ones upon sale of an existing home.

We continued to live as if water were limitless right up to the moment when it nearly ran out. That moment came in fall 2007, a year and a half into the worst drought to settle on the southeast U.S. since record-keeping began in 1895. Lake Lanier, by then the primary freshwater source for more than 5 million people, dipped to a 90-day reserve. So did North Carolina's Falls Lake, which supplies Raleigh.

At the headwaters of the Everglades, Lake Okeechobee, back-up water supply for another 5 million people in southeast Florida, plummeted to its lowest level ever—so low that wildfires burned for miles across the dry lake bed.

"It was bleak," says Raleigh planning director Mitchell Silver. "It was the urgent topic of conversation."

It was the urgent topic of prayer as well. Georgia Governor Sonny Perdue, a Baptist, led a public prayer service on the steps of the gold-domed state capitol "to very reverently and respectfully pray up a storm." He quoted Psalm 65, which praises God for water abundance:

You visit the earth and water it, you greatly enrich it;
the river of God is full of water;
you provide their grain, for so you have prepared it.
You water its ridges abundantly, you settle its furrows;
you make it soft with showers, you bless its growth.[15]

The next fall, Tropical Storm Fay shepherded a flock of storms that soaked the Southeast. And Georgia's politicians, who had long derided water planning as something out of the Communist Manifesto, began to repent. In spring 2010, Perdue signed the Water Stewardship Act, which vaulted Georgia over any other southeastern state on conservation, with water-efficient building requirements and a daytime irrigation ban.

The missteps of warring over water, profligate pumping, and edifice over ecosystems had clear lessons: Fighting aggravates water scarcity, putting each side in the combatant mindset of figuring how to get more and more water rather than working together to use less. Water is best stored in nature—aquifers, rivers, and wetlands. Finally, the bigger the infrastructure project, the bigger the unintended consequences for future generations. Case in point: the ongoing Everglades restoration project, a federal-state fix of the Army Corps' 1948 plumbing job on the once-vast wetland. The feds estimate that repairing the Glades will take 30 years and $11 billion, though more recent state estimates put the price tag as high as $30 billion.[16]

For a while, it looked as if the South would heed the lessons; as if the big drought had scared us into a new era of water consciousness. In 2009, U.S. District Court Judge Paul Magnuson ruled that Lake Lanier was never authorized to quench Atlanta. He gave Alabama, Florida, and Georgia three years to come up with a water-sharing plan for the Hooch and have Congress okay it. Otherwise, he'd cut Atlanta off the reservoir. Magnuson's 97-page ruling ended with one of the most sensible statements uttered in the twenty-year legal battle and perhaps in the history of the region's water management:

Too often, state, local, and even national government
actors do not consider the long-term consequences
of their decisions. Local governments allow unchecked
growth because it increases tax revenue, but these
same governments do not sufficiently plan for the resources
such unchecked growth will require. Nor do
individual citizens consider frequently enough their
consumption of our scarce resources, absent a crisis …
Only by cooperating, planning, and conserving
can we avoid the situations
that gave rise to this litigation.[17]

Governor Perdue did not concur. In a step backward to interminable legal battles, he ordered Georgia's lawyers to appeal Magnuson's "game-changing" ruling.[18] He and the governors of Florida and Alabama continued to work toward a sharing agreement. But for the most part, the South returned to its old water order. Rain inspired Raleigh and other cities to lift irrigation restrictions, freeing citizens to once again soak lawns and hose down driveways. Legislatures used the recession as an excuse—to both spend more on "shovel-ready" water-infrastructure projects, and *not* spend more on water-conservation programs.

Perhaps the most disturbing trend in the South post-drought is the regional disconnect between groundwater and surface water. Those who've plundered their aquifers are now eyeing rivers to make up the difference. In southwest Florida, developers who over-pumped the region's aquifer to the point of crisis next turned to the Peace River to supply new growth. Today, scientists are watching the aptly named Peace go completely dry in places it never did before.[19] In Arkansas, the rice farmers who emptied the Alluvial Aquifer are shifting to a major diversion of the White River to flood their fields.[20] In the Orlando area, utilities that over-pumped their part of the Floridan Aquifer got the go-ahead from water managers to begin tapping the north-flowing St. Johns River for future supply.

All are old and tired solutions for a region young and vibrant enough to avoid the devastating mistakes of the arid West, where almost every river is so over-allocated there isn't enough for all legal users, much less fish and wildlife, during times of drought.

It bears repeating that Major Powell was a scientist, in his time probably the most knowledgeable in the nation about water supply. Powell thought the eastern half of the country would never have to fight over water—that we would never even need irrigation. So here's the question to ask ourselves now: What assumptions are we making today that will seem equally far-fetched in fifty or a hundred years?

If Perdue hopes to find the answer in the Bible, he and his gubernatorial brethren might turn to Psalm 46:

> *There is a river, the streams whereof shall*
> *make glad the city of God ... God is in the midst of her,*
> *she shall not be moved, God shall help her ...*[21]

Gov. Sonny Perdue and his wife Mary, along with various religious and political leaders, participate in a "pray for rain" vigil during Georgia's drought in 2007.

HOT SPOTS

There's no doubt that we're facing a water crisis of global proportion, but this is also a crisis that changes shape. In some regions, people are driven from their homes and farms by drought, while in other areas, residents are fleeing floodwaters. In some regions, there is enough water, but it's too polluted to drink or there is enough water only for the wealthy and well connected. The fault may rest with government corruption, global warming, mismanagement, resource exploitation or corporate greed. The crisis looks different if you live in Detroit or Atlanta or Las Vegas. It looks different in South Africa or India or Ecuador.

  Essentially our water woes are composed of "hot spots" around the globe—areas that are particularly hard hit by various manifestations of this crisis. On the following pages, you'll see a sampling of what our water crisis looks like in some of these places. Truly capturing the magnitude of this crisis is too big for any one book, but here is a start.

KALA DERA, INDIA One of Coca-Cola's bottling plants in India is in the farming community of Kala Dera in the desert state of Rajasthan. Kala Dera is a water-stressed area, and the Indian government designated the area's groundwater "over-exploited" in 1998. Yet, Coca-Cola built a new plant there in 2000. In the next nine years after Coca-Cola started its bottling operations, groundwater levels fell over 72 feet. The sharp drop in water levels has meant no successful crops for thousands of Kala Dera's farmers and severe shortages in drinking water for the community. A study paid for by Coca-Cola recommended the company shut down the plant or relocate it. So far, Coca-Cola has chosen to ignore the study, and continues to mine for water in the desert.

PHOTOGRAPH BY LYNSEY ADDARIO

HOT SPOTS

SACRAMENTO-SAN JOAQUIN DELTA, CALIFORNIA Northern California has far more water than the population-dense and thirsty southern part of the state. To meet that imbalance, the state has created a vast plumbing network where water from the north is pumped to the south after it passes through the Delta, which supports a vital ecosystem, threatened species, and a farming community. But drought and increasing demand has sent California into shortage and put the Delta in crisis. Some legislators are hoping to solve the problem by building more big infrastructure, but others are instead pushing for new water management ideas that will more equitably share water among California's environment, fishermen and women, farmers, and everyone else who call the state home.
PHOTOGRAPH BY ROBERT DAWSON

HOT SPOTS

NIGER DELTA, NIGERIA The Niger Delta has been hailed as one of the world's 10 most important wetland and coastal marine ecosystems. But since the discovery of oil there in 1956, the region's environment has been devastated and its 31 million residents live in desperate conditions. The government has raked in $600 billion in revenue, but this does not help the average Nigerian caught in the crossfire of the government's military, militant groups, and multinational oil giants warring over black gold. The result has been over 300 oil spills a year, and more than 7,000 since 1960. The amount of oil spilled each year is equal to the size of the Exxon Valdez spill. Toxins and industrial waste have contaminated water sources, leaving people to bathe, drink, grow food, and cook with polluted water and eat fish tainted by chemicals.
PHOTOGRAPH BY ED KASHI/VII

HOT SPOTS

ARAL SEA, CENTRAL ASIA Once the fourth-largest freshwater lake in the world, the Aral Sea, which straddles Uzbekistan and Kazakhstan, has seen its volume shrunk by over 75 percent. Beginning in the 1960s, the Soviet Union diverted millions of gallons of water for irrigation projects to grow rice and cotton. The sea's once vibrant fishing economy has been decimated by the lack of fresh water flowing into the lake and the increase of salt and mineral concentrations. The local communities face water pollution, dust storms, and public health problems. An estimated 75 million tons of toxic dust from pesticides and salts from the area are spread across Central Asia each year. The once thriving seaside fishing village of Muynak is now a desert town more than 60 miles from the sea.

PHOTOGRAPH BY DIETER TELEMANS

HOT SPOTS

UPPER DELAWARE RIVER, U.S. In 2010 American Rivers named the Upper Delaware River the most endangered river in the U.S. The source of drinking water for 17 million people in New York, New Jersey, and Pennsylvania, the river has come under threat from a practice of the natural gas industry called hydraulic fracturing, or "fracking." The watershed sits above a geologic formation known as the Marcellus Shale that contains natural gas reserves. In the next 20 years, energy companies are hoping to drill tens of thousands of wells to extract oil using fracking, which involves shooting a slurry of water and toxic chemicals into the wells in order to release the gas. The process has already resulted in both surface and groundwater pollution. In Pennsylvania alone, gas companies have been responsible for 1,500 environmental violations in just two years.
PHOTOGRAPH BY J HENRY FAIR

APPALACHIA, U.S. The southern Appalachian Mountains have never been touched by the glacial fingers from the last ice age and consequently, the region is one of the country's most biodiverse. This ecological richness has long been under threat from coal mining, but since the 1970s when mountaintop removal coal mining began, things have become dire. The practice allows coal companies to clear all the vegetation off of mountaintops, then blast the rock away with millions of pounds of explosives. The debris is then pushed into valleys, destroying important habitat and ruining thousands of miles of streams. Sludge dams, giant lagoon impoundments of mining waste, often leak into wells and streams, further contaminating drinking water. Appalachia's waterways have been decimated by a practice that provides only 5 percent of the country's coal production.
PHOTOGRAPH BY PAUL CORBIT BROWN

Conflicts

Some experts think the next wars will be about water, not oil.
Certainly, water shortages are causing problems in many parts of the world.

Here's a look at problem areas where water
is playing a prominent role:

Klamath River Oregon/California

The Klamath River Basin has been an
icon for water conflict since 2001 when,
during a major drought, the federal government shut off
farmers' water supplies to ensure that there was enough
water in the Klamath River for endangered salmon and
sucker. Fishermen and Native American tribal members
experienced their own pain the next year when low water
flows in the river resulted in a massive salmon die-off.

Years spent trying to find common ground between the
Klamath Basin's stakeholders — irrigators, fishermen, and
the Native American community — came to a head in
2010 when the groups announced a deal with electric
utility PacifiCorp to remove four dams on the river in a
collaborative effort to solve the region's water woes.

U.S.-Mexico Border

California/Mexico: The "All-American Canal," which runs along
the U.S.-Mexico border and carries water from the Colorado River
to the massive farms in Southern California's Imperial Valley,
also supplies water to Mexico through accidental seepage. U.S.
plans to line the dirt canal may eliminate drinking water for at
least 500 families in two Mexican towns and dry out 14,000
farms in the Mexicali Valley.

Ecuador

Ecuador's Constitution was the first to establish the human right to
water as well as grant rights to nature. It dictates that the management
of water remain public and within the community, but increasingly
in the country, control of water is being put in the hands of a few
and even privatized. Indigenous groups have organized massive
actions to protest a proposed water law that would further allow
private companies control of precious water resources.

Bolivia

Oscar Olivera Foronda, a plucky shoe factory worker, touched off
a wave of protests in 2000 that got Bolivia to cancel its private
water contract with Bechtel.

Israel and the Palestinian territories

The Palestinian enclave in the Gaza Strip has a paltry per capita water availability of 37 gallons per day if and when the Israelis, who use the water upstream for agriculture, agree to release it.

The first modern water war started when Syria triggered the 1967 Arab-Israeli Six Day War by trying to divert the Jordan River away from Israel. The Israelis ended up getting control of the Jordan River, Golan Heights, and West Bank aquifer.

The recently built security fence around the West Bank has isolated many Palestinian villages from the wells they rely on for drinking and irrigation water. Israel controls 90% of the freshwater supply in the region, including the large groundwater aquifer under the West Bank and the Jordan River. Israel recognized Palestinians' right to West Bank water in the 1995 Oslo Accords, but Palestinians say their use is limited to insufficent amounts or altogether prohibited. Israelis are divided on whether they can give up more of their share of the water from the aquifer. Any future peace settlement should include agreements on water as well as land.

China and Tibet

Tensions could mount in coming years as China controls the Tibetan plateau, the source of major rivers that provide water for China, India, Pakistan, Nepal, Bhutan, Bangladesh, Myanmar, Thailand, Vietnam, Laos and Cambodia. Incredibly, the countries affected contain 85% of the people in Asia and nearly half the population of the entire globe.

Not only does China wield formidable power with its hand on the tap for so many people, but increasingly the rivers originating in the plateau are threatened by receding glaciers from climate change, as well as record levels of water pollution from industrial activities including deforestation, mining, and manufacturing.

India and Pakistan

The next war between India and Pakistan could be triggered by their long-running dispute over the Chenab River, a tributary of the Indus River and the lifeblood of Pakistan farming, which runs through India-controlled Kashmir. India is building a dam at Baglihar.

Darfur

Genocidal warfare has roots in conflict over water and chronic water scarcity.

Egypt, Ethiopia, Sudan

Egypt gets 96% of its water from the Nile, 85% of which flows from Ethiopian highlands. Ethiopia has studied the feasibility of building dams upstream for a freshwater source for the exploding population and to make and sell electricity. With the Nile Basin population expected to nearly double in 25 years, the scramble for water will become more intense.

Ethiopians are blaming Egyptians for wasting too much water in Lake Nasser where 40% of it evaporates. But the Egyptians are not budging on demands for most of the water and the World Bank is withholding funds to prevent dam construction.

Turkey, Iraq and Syria

The two rivers that begin in Turkey—the Tigris and Euphrates—nourished the first civilization in human history. But in the last 30 years, with the implementation of Turkey's ambitious Southeastern Anatolia Project, these two lifelines are being harnessed, effectively threatening Iraq and Syria downstream through a sort of "water politics."

Internal conflict is also heating up as minority groups and poor agricultural communities are threatened by flooding and relocation due to the dams. Lack of water has forced the relocation of entire populations and nations are descending toward conflict over water allocation and accessibility.

The Ataturk Dam on the Euphrates River stores enough water to allow farmers to irrigate cotton. The water-intensive crop is subsidized by a $32 billion project that will eventually result in 22 dams and 19 electrical power stations on the Euphrates and Tigris rivers.

A pier juts out into Shasta Lake, the largest reservoir in California. The lake was formed by damming the McCloud, Pit, and Sacramento Rivers.

Thinking Outside the Bottle

KELLE LOUAILLIER

*"It struck me ... that all you had to do is take the water out of the ground
and then sell it for more than the price of wine, milk, or for that matter, oil."*
—GUSTAVE LEVEN, *past chairman of Perrier (now owned by Nestlé)* [1]

Bart Sipriano lived on his own land, a modest ranch at the end of a dead-end road in East Texas. City water pipes didn't make their way out that far, but Sipriano had his own source—a 100-year-old well that provided all the water he and his wife needed for drinking,

cleaning, and cooking. At least that's how it used to be.

Four days after Nestlé began its pumping operation for an Ozarka-brand bottled water plant next door, Sipriano awoke to an unwelcome surprise: nothing but a drip when he turned on the faucet. Later, peering down his well shaft, he found that his well had been sucked dry.

"I'd been here twenty years, and I never had any problems until Ozarka came out here," he told a *Dallas Observer* reporter.

Sipriano sued Nestlé to restore his well, but the Texas State Supreme Court ruled in the corporation's favor, thanks in part to Texas' industry-friendly water laws. [2]

Sipriano is one of the thousands whose livelihood has been upset by the bottled water industry that has targeted rural communities' spring water, profited from municipal tap water, and launched ad campaigns that have undermined people's trust in public water systems.

Few could have foreseen the rapid growth of this boutique industry into a $100 billion international juggernaut. [3] Thirty years ago the boom was nothing more than a glint in a marketing representative's eye, but now the industry is a growing threat to public control over humanity's most vital resource.

As in much of the industrialized world, strong public water systems have been a cornerstone of national prosperity in the U.S. and Canada. These systems have generally been managed by local governments that are accountable to the public through the democratic process. This has helped assure access to safe and healthy drinking water. [4]

It was unthinkable just three decades ago that a person would pay a $1.50 or more for what they could have free at a water fountain or for virtually nothing at the tap. Drinking water was a public trust and a basic human right.

But today the bottled water industry is a $15 billion business in the United States alone [5] and its growth has come at a significant environmental and social cost. A poll conducted in the early 2000s found that three out of four people in the U.S. were drinking bottled water, and one out of five people were drinking only bottled water. [6]

The growth of the market has come at the expense of communities from California to Texas to Maine. [7] It has also come at a great expense to the public's confidence in municipal water supplies, which continue to be highly reliable and more regulated than bottled water.

As the bottled water industry has grown, the political will to adequately fund public water systems has diminished. The gap between what these systems need and the capital available to them is more than $22 billion and growing [8]—a huge, but not impossible problem.

Perhaps the biggest challenge to public water systems

has been the fact that municipalities are now spending millions in taxpayer dollars on contracts with bottled water corporations for a resource they already provide in a more economically and environmentally friendly manner.[9]

The industry has achieved great inroads, but it hasn't been easy.

Jeff Caso, a former senior vice president with Nestlé, was quoted in *Ad Age* in 2003 as saying, "We sell water ... so we have to be clever."[10]

In reality, the industry needs to be not just clever, but well endowed. It has taken tens of millions of dollars in flashy advertising to open up the market.[11] And to create this market the industry's largest players, Nestlé, Coke, and Pepsi have needed to somehow imply their product is better than what you can get from the tap.

So far, their ad money has paid off. A 2007 survey in Philadelphia found that 20 percent of residents refuse to drink tap water, even though there doesn't appear to be any problem with the water itself. The Water Department has had no health-based violations in at least 10 years.[12] In a

mately caused one in three consumers to drop the bottle and turn back to the tap.[14]

For the first time in more than a decade, the U.S. bottled water market posted a decline in sales in 2008. This unprecedented drop in sales was followed by a further decline in 2009, when according to the Beverage Marketing Corporation, U.S. bottled water sales fell 2.7 percent (by volume).[15]

This is thanks in large part to a coalition of public officials, restaurants, faith communities, student groups, and national organizations that came together to "think outside the bottle" in an effort to preserve our common values about water for the benefit of generations to come and to protect the environment.

Each year, about 38 billion plastic water bottles end up in U.S. landfills (it takes more than 700 years for plastic to decompose). The amount of oil used annually to produce plastic water bottles for U.S. consumers could fuel more than one million cars for a year. And this doesn't include the impact on local aquifers from water mining and the en-

IT TAKES MORE THAN 700 YEARS FOR PLASTIC TO DECOMPOSE.

U.S. Conference of Mayors taste test the water even ranked 12th among 93 cities.[13]

Attitudes like those in Philadelphia may be common but the tide is turning. Global corporations have underestimated the lengths communities will go to in order to keep their water in the public trust. They also haven't banked on a huge public outcry in response to the truths about bottled water.

Education and action at the grassroots level have spawned award-winning films like the viral animated short, *The Story of Bottled Water*, as well as popular books like *Bottlemania*. It has also compelled a range of governmental action, changes in corporate practice, and ulti-

vironmental impacts from trucking millions of gallons.

But even as public pressure grows, bottled water industry executives are pushing back. In an effort to ensure business growth they are engineering new niche markets such as infused water and vigorously attaching their products to environmental and social causes in "bluewashing" campaigns that are as transparent as their product.[16]

And most importantly, in order to keep the profits rolling in, they need access to as much cheap water as possible. They have two tactics: target rural communities to mine their spring water and use public water systems. Nestlé has perfected the first tactic.

Nestlé Targets Rural Communities

In the decade since Nestlé moved next door to Bart Sipriano, the multinational has built or proposed spring sites or bottling plants in dozens more rural communities across North America, making the corporation the largest water bottler on the continent.[17]

While Nestlé is the biggest player in the industry, it is by no means alone. Hundreds of corporations, large and small, are moving to control water formerly held in the public trust.

Why the current rush to profit from water?

For one, water is being given to these corporations practically free, allowing for quick returns and enormous profit margins. The giveaway is the fault of a host of problems, from outdated lawmaking (that could not have foreseen the commodification of water) to good old-fashioned backroom politicking.

Nowhere is this more apparent than in the recent struggle between the citizens of the tiny town of McCloud, California and multinational giant Nestlé.

The economically rebounding former logging town is nestled in the foothills of the Cascades in the shadow of Mount Shasta. The poet Joaquin Miller once described the peak that marks McCloud's place on the map as, "Lonely as God, and white as a winter moon."

What better image to decorate the label of a water bottle? That's what Danone, Coke, and other bottlers must have thought when they set up shop there.

Three plants have been built around Mount Shasta since 1990, but it was not until 2003 that Nestlé's designs on the McCloud watershed began to take shape. At a public meeting that year, the board governing McCloud's water ser-

---

WATER LEADER   WORKING TO KEEP THE FLOW

Jim Olson, Public Trust Attorney

IN 2001, JIM OLSON BECAME LEGAL COUNCIL for Michigan Citizens for Water Conservation (MCWC) in the case of *MCWC v. Nestlé*. The case launched the first high-profile battle against bottled water withdrawals in the U.S., and Olson's arguments outlined the risks of groundwater mining years before many recognized a global water crisis was at hand. Today Olson has transformed the court battle into a public education and legislative campaign to protect the water of the Great Lakes Basin. As chair of the Flow for Water coalition, Olson has advocated for state and federal laws establishing "public trust" as a legal principle for protecting lakes, streams, and groundwater from exploitation and diversion.

FIVE MYTHS ABOUT BOTTLED WATER

1) Myth **Bottling plants are beneficial for communities.**

REALITY Groundwater levels have dropped by as much as 40 feet in Mehdiganj, India, home to a Coca-Cola bottling facility.

In Gandhre, India, Coke has drawn water for its factory operations that could have otherwise served 75,000 villagers a day.

2) Myth **Bottled water tastes better.**

REALITY A November 2007 poll by CBS News in Chicago found that two-thirds of the participants preferred tap to the bottled brand names or couldn't tell which was which.

3) Myth **Bottled water is inexpensive.**

REALITY Bottled water costs hundreds or thousands of times more than tap water.

4) Myth **Bottled water is cleaner and safer than tap water.**

REALITY The Food and Drug Administration regulates only 30 to 40 percent of bottled water sold across state lines.

Plastic bottles can leach chemicals into the water.

A 2008 survey by Environmental Working Group found that a range of pollutants from fertilizer residue to industrial solvents continue to appear in popular bottled water brands.

5) Myth **Bottled water doesn't negatively impact the environment.**

REALITY U.S. plastic bottle production requires more than 17 million barrels of oil, enough to fuel 1 million cars.

Each year, about 38 billion plastic water bottles end up in U.S. landfills.

vices approved a 50-year deal under which the corporation agreed to pay the city between $300,000 and $400,000 a year to house a million-square-foot bottling facility.

A sweet deal for a town on the mend, right?[18]

Locals didn't think so. The contract had been negotiated behind closed doors with the local water utility and made available to the public just days before the meetings. Requests for longer public review and debate were denied.[19]

What's more, it was revealed that the agreement had the corporation paying just 1/64 of a cent per gallon which it would then resell at an average price of more than $1 per gallon. The agreement was set to lock these bargain prices in for the next 50 years, with an automatic 50-year extension[20]—essentially a century-long deal.

All of a sudden the math wasn't adding up for residents. They knew the plan meant a significant impact on health, safety, and local traffic flow, with an estimated 200-300 diesel trucks servicing the plant per day, for one.[21]

Judging from the experiences of nearby communities, they also could not count on the plant to provide needed jobs. While Nestlé promised 240 new jobs, locals knew better. Other area plants had hired far fewer laborers and had tended to draw their employees from elsewhere.[22]

Of most concern was that Nestlé had not even bothered to perform a required environmental review. Citizen groups, like the McCloud Watershed Council, raised a series of worries about potential habitat destruction, surface water decline, and depletion of groundwater wells.[23]

Locals began bracing for the inevitability of this outcome, believing their politicians had been manipulated and rushed into approving an unfavorable contract before the public had the chance to weigh in.

Nestlé's public relations shop conceded to the *Sacramento News and Review* that the corporation had already put $1.5 million into sealing the deal, with an undisclosed chunk of that going to PR and lobbying.[24]

"People need to wake up and see the contract doesn't give them anything," said Sid Johnson, a ranch caretaker and McCloud resident. "We've got a foreign corporation coming in to buy our water supply for peanuts."[25]

Residents weren't going to let the initial backroom deal ride, however. One local group, Concerned McCloud Citizens, took the corporation to court causing the Siskiyou County Superior Court to rule the contract null and void. But despite losing legal challenges and the ongoing public indignation, Nestlé continued to push its plans forward. Only after six years, scrutiny by the California Attorney General, and damning national media exposure did Nestlé finally relent, fixing its sights downstream instead.

In search of a new site for a bottling plant, in late 2009 Nestlé secured access to a facility at the Flourin Fruitridge Industrial Park in Sacramento and was granted status as an industrial user of the city's municipal water. Such zoning not only allowed Nestlé to circumvent all environmental impact assessments, public review, and permitting hurdles (obstacles that had impeded its designs on McCloud's water), it also effectively granted Nestlé unlimited access to the city's water—at the "industrial" rate for water use—approximately $0.71 for 748 gallons.

Per the terms of its initial contract with the city, Nestlé expressed intentions to extract an average of 320,000 gallons of water a day for which it would pay roughly $304 to

UP TO 40 PERCENT OF BOTTLED WATER, INCLUDING AQUAFINA AND DASANI, COMES FROM THE SAME SOURCE AS TAP WATER.

bottle and sell under the name Nestlé Pure Life. Retail price for 320,000 gallons of Nestlé Pure Life ... $453,587![26]

If the demand for bottled water continues to grow at the current rate, Nestlé and others will likely need to find many more water sources like McCloud in the coming decades. And if history is any indication they will look first to regions that are struggling economically and are politically vulnerable.

As is the case with so many extractive industries, the bulk of the profits will be made elsewhere, while local communities are left to deal with the externalized costs.

Coke and Pepsi Take on the Tap

In the early 1980s, Pepsi developed a clever marketing device to challenge Coke's share of the soft drink market—a blind taste test called the Pepsi Challenge.[27]

Twenty years later the top two leaders of the soft drink market are still squaring off—this time over their bottled water brands Dasani (Coke) and Aquafina (Pepsi).

Just as each is working to corner the growing market, consumers are poking holes in the advertising used to make these brands the most popular bottled water.

Stealing a page from the Pepsi Challenge, people across the country have been setting up card tables, dixie cups, and blindfolds to perform their own Tap Water Challenges. Passersby are asked to take a sip of Dasani, Aquafina, and tap water and see if they can taste the difference.

What is most surprising about the results is that for the amount each corporation spends talking about enhanced taste and special filtering, the majority of test participants can't tell the difference. Straw polls conducted by news organizations have found similar results. In a November 2007 poll by CBS News in Chicago, two-thirds of the participants preferred tap to the bottled brand names or couldn't tell which was which.[28]

One reason for this might be that up to 40 percent of bottled water, including Aquafina and Dasani, comes from the same source as tap water[29]—the same source these corporations have cast doubts upon in order to build a market for their brands.

In a 2007 poll conducted by the University of Arkansas, researchers found that young people were overwhelmingly choosing bottled water over tap water because they felt it was somehow cleaner.[30] To figure out where such an impression is formed one need look no further than bottled water labels depicting snow-capped peaks and claims of purity and state-of-the-art purification.

This kind of marketing casts no direct aspersions on public water, but there is an indictment by implication. Why would consumers pay $1.50 for a product when they could have virtually the same thing for next to nothing? What does the emphasis on "state-of-the-art purification" imply about the adequacy of tap water treatment? Why have these corporations been so reluctant to tell consumers their product is from city water systems?

Consumer groups have demanded that Pepsi and Coke fully disclose the health and safety of their products time and again. Both corporations have refused.

Why?

Much of the answer may lie in how differently bottled and tap water are regulated. Both are evaluated using similar standards, but tap water is tested far more frequently and has more independent oversight by state and federal environmental authorities (the Environmental Protection Agency and the Department of Environmental Protection). Lacking adequate capacity to regulate bottled water through the Food and Drug Administration, the government relies on bottled water corporations to police themselves,[31] which in some cases has resulted in bottled water contaminations that were concealed for weeks before the public was warned.[32]

Most importantly, public water systems are required to make health and safety information available to the public. Bottled water corporations are not, though you'd think it'd be in their interests to do so.

Consumers have reason to be concerned. In 2004 Coke was forced to recall more than half a million Dasani bottles in the United Kingdom after finding samples that contained higher than permitted levels of the chemical bromate. As it turns out, Coke's "state-of-the-art" purification systems can in fact cause this chemical to form.

A more recent 2008 survey by Environmental Working Group confirmed that a range of pollutants from fertilizer residue to industrial solvents continue to appear in popular bottled water brands. Peter Gleick wrote in his book *Bottled & Sold: The Story Behind Our Obsession With Bottled Water*, about a well-known benzene contamination in Perrier. But what most consumers don't know, he added, is that, "In addition to benzene, bottles have been found to contain mold, sodium hydroxide, kerosene, styrene, algae, yeast, tetrahydrofuran, sand, fecal coliforms and other forms of bacteria, elevated chlorine, 'filth,' glass particles, sanitizer, and, in my very favorite example, crickets."

This raises an even bigger question: Who are we allowing to control this essential resource and why?

In India, Coke has made immense profits at a tremendous human cost as a result of pumping groundwater to make everything from soda to Dasani.

Not far from the holiest of Hindu cities, along the Ganges River, is the village of Mehdiganj. And though water is the daily object of worship along this great Indian river, in this nearby village it is a source of despair.[33]

Mehdiganj's latest neighbor is one of Coke's more than 60 bottling facilities in India[34] and villagers are convinced the plant is pulling water needed for irrigation, causing crops to suffer and wells to run dry.

"Water levels are down everywhere," Nandlal Master, a local school teacher told the *Atlanta Journal Constitution*. "We want Coke to go away."[35]

Coke dismisses community concerns, even as groundwater levels surrounding Mehdiganj have receded, in some cases by as much as 40 feet.[36] Coke's regional spokespeople point to agriculture and weather cycles as the problem for India's water woes. Coke has also effectively used the prospect of jobs and investment to pit those in desperate

need of a paycheck against those who have seen their livelihoods dry up. (Unemployment in Mehdiganj is as high as 65 percent.) [37]

But while Coke is finger-pointing and using economic misfortune to make its case for privatizing local water resources, communities like Mehdiganj are paying a dire long-term price.

Elsewhere in India, in Gandhre village, Coke has drawn water for its factory operations that could have otherwise served 75,000 villagers a day.[38] In Plachimada, Coke has extracted hundreds of thousands of gallons of clean water through electric pumps, resulting in the desiccation of hundreds of wells. As a result, residents are forced to travel great distances to access water in a country already strapped for water.[39]

When the news in the international press got ugly about Coke's practices, the bluewashing began. In February 2005, Coke's vice president for environment and water resources gave remarks at the Global Water Futures Workshop at Sandia National Laboratory touting the corporation's new water conservation efforts.[40]

Then in June 2007, Coke entered a partnership with the World Wildlife Fund, to the tune of $20 million, to fund watershed protection programs in seven global watersheds.[41] Such a partnership has allowed Coke to project a green public image while avoiding its obligation to directly address the problems it has created.

But no amount of public relations can change reality. The United Nations estimates that two-thirds of the world population, five billion people, will lack access to enough clean drinking water by 2025.[42]

Coke and its competitors sometimes argue that bottled water is the one source of clean, safe, and reliable drinking water for many communities in the developing world, where the global crisis is most rife.

But wouldn't it be a better investment to build local public water systems that can stand the test of time than to ask locals to buy bottled water?

Mayors Lead the Bottled Water Backlash

In 2003, California Assembly Member Ellen Corbett (D-San Leandro) introduced a bill in the state legislature requiring bottled water to meet some of the same labeling and water quality standards as tap water.[43]

PHOTOGRAPH BY JIM WEST

The bill garnered little media attention and invited the ire of a Nestlé subsidiary and a host of surrogates for major bottlers, namely the International Bottled Water Association (which now employs a former spokesperson for Big Tobacco as its vice president of communications).[44] The bill never made it to the governor's desk.

But by 2007, the public climate had shifted considerably. Assembly Member Corbett's bill was signed into law by California's Republican governor, Arnold Schwarzenegger. [45]

Earlier in the year, California also began a domino effect among national mayors. San Francisco's Gavin Newsom became one of the first prominent mayors to cancel his city's bottled water contracts.

"All of this waste and pollution is generated by a product that by objective standards is often inferior to the quality of San Francisco's pristine tap water," Newsom wrote in a two-page executive order.[46]

In raw economic terms, San Francisco was in a position to save the $500,000 a year it was spending on bottled water contracts. But Newsom didn't stop there. Partnering with the progressive mayors of Salt Lake City and Minneapolis, he took the bottled water fight to the U.S. Conference of Mayors—a forum where bottlers like Coke are on the Business Council as dues-paying members[47]—and won.

Mayor Rocky Anderson (Salt Lake City), R.T. Rybak (Minneapolis), and Newsom got a resolution passed, calling for renewed investment and support for public water systems.[48] The resolution also called for the U.S. Conference of Mayors to look at the impact of plastic water bottles on the municipal waste stream.[49] The following year, the conference resolved to phase out city spending on bottled water.

The industry found itself fighting to address the new political will to challenge the bottled water industry. As more and more cities canceled contracts and got behind the spirit of the mayors' resolution, the bottled water industry began testing out some new talking points. On radio talk shows, industry associations began claiming that they too supported public water systems and that bottled water wasn't meant to supplant the tap, but to give consumers choice.

That sounded pretty nice, until reporters started doing some digging about how the industry's claims stacked up against its track record.

Major bottlers were differentiating their water from the tap by advertising state-of-the-art filtration. At the same time the industry's trade associations were lobbying against legislation that required water bottlers to disclose safety and health information on their bottled water.[50] So how was the consumer to know all the benefits of this state-of-the-art filtration?

The trade groups representing major bottlers also came up with a scheme to respond to the three mayors' concerns about plastic water bottle waste. They began trumpeting their dedication to recycling programs, but the same trade associations were working across North America to oppose "bottle bills" that would support bottle-recycling programs.[51] These bottle bills would have placed a small deposit on plastic bottles in order to help deal with the more than four billion pounds of plastic bottles that usually wind up in landfills.[52]

"The trade groups must have assumed that the media, legislators, and advocates wouldn't attempt to crack their shell game," said Leslie Samuelrich, spokesperson for Corporate Accountability International's Think Outside the Bottle campaign.

The players behind the industry's public relations machine were the American Beverage Association (Coke and Pepsi's voice in the media and halls of government) and the International Bottled Water Association (which does Nestlé's dirty work).

Undaunted by these powerful industry trade groups, mayors sensed the groundswell of public support to look at the bottled water problem. They knew that standing up to this lobby would present challenges, but that doing so would allow them to stand out as advocates for people nationwide.

As one city after another cut its contracts, states began getting into the act. Illinois took action first, then Virginia.[53] And in May 2009, New York Governor David Paterson issued the furthest reaching executive order to date, explaining, "Taxpayers have spent billions of dollars to ensure that we have clean drinking water supplies. If we are going to make such significant investments, we should reap the benefits and use that water."

And the victories haven't been limited to the U.S. In December 2008, the city of Toronto became the largest city in the world to ban the purchase and sale of bottled water on city premises and to make a serious commitment to improve access to public drinking water in city facilities.

Think Outside the Bottle

From outward appearances these official actions may have appeared to come from the top down. But the fact is, for years grassroots organizations have fought for accountability from the bottled water industry.

"We were early on concerned with what these corporations were doing to transform an essential public resource, and basic human right, into a commodity," said Samuelrich. "And frankly, in the beginning, reporters and lawmakers did not show much interest."

But then groups across the continent that were challenging Nestlé's abuses in their communities began sharing stories and resources, and Coke's abuses in India gained the attention of activists the world over.

Corporate Accountability International, the Polaris Institute, and its allies, members, and student volunteers began talking to people about the bottled water farce at campuses and community forums across the country. The groups' environmental and religious allies began outreach at churches, synagogues, and in living rooms armed with tools such as "Inside the Bottle: An Exposé of the Bottled Water Industry," a report by the Polaris Institute that provided an overview of the ten key problems with bottled water.

As the grassroots campaign blanketed the U.S and Canada, lead groups took their demands straight to the corporations.

After just over a year of grassroots pressure and months of dialogue, Pepsi came around. In July 2007, Pepsi an-nounced that its Aquafina brand would spell out "public water source" on its labels. The news appeared on every major television network and most every major paper. In 2008, Nestlé followed suit.

These victories speak to the power of grassroots action and education. But the victory will require a long-term commitment by thousands of dedicated individuals. The U.S. Congress has even echoed public concern and called on the continent's largest bottlers to disclose the source of their bottled water and recent quality tests. Still, bottlers like Coke (Dasani) stubbornly refuses to answer to its consumer—even to the potential detriment of its brand image.[54] (On Earth Day 2010, Corporate Accountability International launched OpenTappiness.org to challenge Coke to stop holding out on source labeling.)

North American public education and action campaigns such as Corporate Accountability International's "Think Outside the Bottle," Polaris Institute's "Inside the Bottle," and Food and Water Watch's "Take Back the Tap" are gaining momentum. Individuals are visiting the campaigns' Web sites and taking the pledge to opt for tap over bottled water by the thousands.

These same individuals are also asking their cities to follow suit. Student groups are persuading their campuses to cancel contracts. National organizations are pressuring trade associations to come clean and to stop interfering in policy in the public interest.

Taking water "back" from the bottlers will be no small task. But in the same way water has begun to be parceled out among bottlers large and small, it can be reclaimed by individuals and officials from city hall to the state house. People can begin by taking a personal pledge to opt for tap over bottled water. They can encourage others to do the same and set in motion local organizing plans to get their cities to cancel bottled water contracts, rebuild confidence in public water systems, and invest the resources needed to ensure our water systems will remain under public control and will continue to serve and strengthen our communities now and for future generations.

FACT Americans throw away 38 million plastic water bottles a year.

THE
VALUE OF WATER

An Art Exhibition 2011-2012
Cathedral of St. John the Divine, New York City

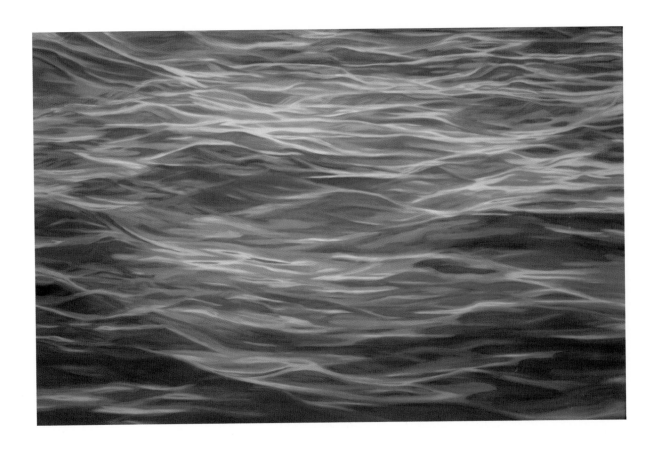

FREDERICKA FOSTER
Baywater IV, 2009
Oil on canvas, 42" x 64"

The Burden of Thirst

TINA ROSENBERG

Aylito Binayo's feet know the mountain.
Even at four in the morning she can run down the rocks to the river by starlight alone and climb the steep mountain back up to her village with 50 pounds of water on her back. She has made

this journey three times a day for nearly all her 25 years. So has every other woman in her village of Foro, in the Konso district of southwestern Ethiopia. Binayo dropped out of school when she was eight years old, in part because she had to help her mother fetch water from the Toiro River. The water is dirty and unsafe to drink; every year that the ongoing drought continues, the once mighty river grows more exhausted. But it is the only water Foro has ever had.

The task of fetching water defines life for Binayo. She must also help her husband grow cassava and beans in their fields, gather grass for their goats, dry grain and take it to the mill for grinding into flour, cook meals, keep the family compound clean, and take care of her three small sons. None of these jobs is as important or as consuming as the eight hours or so she spends each day fetching water.

In wealthy parts of the world, people turn on a faucet and out pours abundant, clean water. Yet nearly 900 million people in the world have no access to clean water, and 2.5 billion people have no safe way to dispose of human waste—many defecate in open fields or near the same rivers they drink from. Dirty water and lack of a toilet and proper hygiene kill 3.3 million people around the world annually, most of them children under age five. Here in southern Ethiopia, and in northern Kenya, a lack of rain over the past few years has made even dirty water elusive.

Where clean water is scarcest, fetching it is almost always women's work. In Konso a man hauls water only during the few weeks following the birth of a baby. Very young boys fetch water, but only up to the age of seven or eight. The rule is enforced fiercely—by men and women. "If the boys are older, people gossip that the woman is lazy," Binayo says. The reputation of a woman in Konso, she says, rests on hard work: "If I sit and stay at home and do nothing, nobody likes me. But if I run up and down to get water, they say I'm a clever woman and work hard."

In much of the developing world, lack of water is at the center of a vicious circle of inequality. Some women in Foro come down to the river five times a day—with one or two of the trips devoted to getting water to make a beer-style home brew for their husbands. When I first came to Foro, some 60 men were sitting in the shade of a metal-roofed building, drinking and talking. It was midmorning. Women, Binayo says, "never get five seconds to sit down and rest."

On a hot late afternoon I go with her to the river, carrying an empty jerry can. The trail is steep and in places slippery. We scramble down large rocks alongside cacti and thornbushes. After 50 minutes we reach the river—or what is a river at certain times of the year. Now it is a series of black, muddy pools, some barely puddles. The banks and rocks are littered with the excrement of donkeys and cows. There are about 40 people at the river, enough so that Binayo decides the wait might be shorter upstream. The wait is especially long early in the morning, so Binayo usually makes her first trip before it is light, leaving her son Kumacho, a serious-faced little boy who looks even younger than his four years, in charge of his younger brothers.

We walk another 10 minutes upstream, and Binayo claims a perch next to a good pool, one fed not only by a dirty puddle just above but also a cleaner stream to the side. Children are jumping on the banks, squishing mud through their feet and stirring up the water. "Please don't jump," Binayo admonishes them. "It makes the water dirtier." A donkey steps in to drink from the puddle feeding Binayo's pool. When the donkey leaves, the women at the puddle scoop out some water to clear it, sending the dirty water down to Binayo, who scolds them.

After half an hour it is her turn. She takes her first jerry can and her yellow plastic scoop. Just as she puts her scoop in the water, she looks up to see another donkey plunk its hoof into the pool feeding hers. She grimaces. But she cannot wait any longer. She does not have the luxury of time.

An hour after we arrive at the river, she has filled two jerry cans—one for her to carry back up, one for me to carry for her. She ties a leather strap around my can and puts it on my back. I am grateful for the smooth leather—Binayo herself uses a coarse rope. Still, the straps cut into my shoulders. The plastic can is full to the top, and the 50-pound load bounces off my spine as I walk. With difficulty, I make it halfway up. But where the trail turns steepest I can go no farther. Sheepishly, I trade cans with a girl who looks to be about eight, carrying a jerry can half the size of mine. She struggles with the heavier can, and about 10 minutes from the top it is too much for her. Binayo takes the heavy jerry can from the girl and puts it on her own back, on top of the one she is carrying. She shoots us both a look of disgust and continues up the mountain, now with nearly 12 gallons of water—100 pounds—on her back.

"When we are born, we know that we will have a hard life," Binayo says, sitting outside a hut in her compound, in front of the cassava she is drying on a goatskin, holding Kumacho, who wears no pants. "It is the culture of Konso from a long time before us." She has never questioned this life, never expected anything different. But soon, for the first time, things are going to change.

When you spend hours hauling water long distances, you measure every drop. The average American uses 100 gallons of water just at home every day; Aylito Binayo makes do with two and a half gallons. Persuading people to use their water for washing is far more difficult when that water is carried up a mountain. And yet sanitation and hygiene matter—proper hand washing alone can cut diarrheal diseases by some 45 percent. Binayo washes her hands with water "maybe once a day," she says. She washes clothes once a year. "We don't even have enough water for drinking—how can we wash our clothes?" she says. She washes her own body only occasionally. A 2007 survey found that not a single Konso household had water with soap or ash (a decent cleanser) near their latrines to wash their hands. Binayo's family recently dug a latrine but cannot afford to buy soap.

Much of the cash they do have is used for $4 to $8 visits to the village health clinic to cure the boys of diarrhea caused by bacteria and parasites they regularly get from the lack of proper hygiene and sanitation and from drinking untreated river water. At the clinic, nurse Israel Estiphanos said that in normal times 70 percent of his patients suffer waterborne diseases—and now the area was in the midst of a particularly severe outbreak. Next to the clinic a white tent had arisen for these patients. By my next visit, Estiphanos was attending to his patients wearing high rubber boots.

Sixteen miles away in Konso's capital, at the district health center almost half the 500 patients treated daily were sick with waterborne diseases. Yet the health center

BRINGING CLEAN WATER CLOSE TO PEOPLE'S HOMES IS KEY TO REVERSING THE CYCLE OF MISERY.

Feliciano dos Santos, Sanitation Solutions

FELICIANO DOS SANTOS USES MUSIC TO HELP teach the principles of sanitation in remote villages of his home country Mozambique, where more than half the population live in extreme poverty. His work is guided by the belief that water and sanitation problems must be solved before other development projects can be successful. His organization, Estamos, promotes a low-cost composting toilet, EcoSans, which converts human waste into nutrient-rich fertilizer.

itself lacked clean water. On the walls of the staff rooms were posters listing the principles of infection control. But for four months a year, the water feeding their taps would run out, said Birhane Borale, the head nurse, so the government would truck in river water. "We use water then only to give to patients to drink or swallow medicine," he said. "We have HIV patients and hepatitis B patients. They are bleeding, and these diseases are easily transmittable—we need water to disinfect. But we can clean rooms only once a month."

Even medical personnel weren't in the habit of washing hands between patients, as working taps existed at only a few points in the building—most of the examining rooms had taps, but they were not connected. Tsega Hagos, a nurse, said she had gotten spattered with blood taking out a patient's IV. But even though there was water that day, she had not washed her hands afterward. "I just put on a different glove," she said. "I wash my hands when I get home after work."

Bringing clean water close to people's homes is key to reversing the cycle of misery. Communities where clean water becomes accessible and plentiful are transformed. All the hours previously spent hauling water can be used to grow more food, raise more animals, or even start income-producing businesses. Families no longer drink microbe soup, so they spend less time sick or caring for loved ones

stricken with waterborne diseases. Most important, freedom from water slavery means girls can go to school and choose a better life. The need to fetch water for the family, or to take care of younger siblings while their mother goes, is the main reason very few women in Konso have attended school. Binayo is one of only a handful of women I met who even knows how old she is.

Access to water is not solely a rural problem. All over the developing world, many urban slum dwellers spend much of the day waiting in line at a pump. But the challenges of bringing water to remote villages like those in Konso are overwhelming. Binayo's village of Foro sits atop a mountain. Many villages in the tropics were built high in the hills, where it is cooler and less malarious, and easier to see the enemy coming. But Konso's mountaintop villages do not have easy access to water. Drought and deforestation keep pushing the water table lower—in some parts of Konso it is more than 400 feet below ground. The best that can be done in some villages is to put in a well near the river. The water is no closer, but at least it is reliable, easier to extract, and more likely to be clean.

Yet in many poor nations, vast numbers of villages where wells are feasible do not have them. Boring deep holes requires geological know-how and expensive heavy machinery. Water in many countries, as in Ethiopia, is the responsibility of each district, and these local governments have

Displaced Somali girls and women dig with cups
and dishes in the sand of a dry riverbed in search of
drinking water near their camp.

little expertise or money. "People who live in slums and rural areas with no access to drinking water are the same people who don't have access to politicians," says Paul Faeth, president of Washington, D.C.-based Global Water Challenge, a consortium of 24 nongovernmental groups. So the effort to make clean water accessible falls largely to charity groups, with mixed success.

The villages of Konso are littered with the ghosts of water projects past. In Konsos around the developing world, the biggest problem with water schemes is that about half of them fall into disrepair soon after the groups that built them move on. Sometimes technology is used that can't be repaired locally, or spare parts are available only in the capital. But other reasons are achingly trivial: The villagers can't raise money for a $3 part or don't trust anyone to make the purchase with their pooled funds. The 2007 survey of Konso found that only nine projects out of 35 built were functioning.

Today a U.K.-based international nonprofit organization called WaterAid, one of the world's largest water-and-sanitation charities, is tackling the job of bringing water to the forgotten villages of Konso. At the time of my visit,

WATER IS OFTEN MOST EXPENSIVE TO PROVIDE FOR THOSE WHO CAN LEAST AFFORD IT—PEOPLE IN THE REMOTE, DROUGHT-STRICKEN VILLAGES OF THE WORLD.

WaterAid had repaired five projects and set up committees in those villages to manage them, and it was working to revive three others. At the health center in Konso's capital, it was installing gutters on the sloped roofs of the buildings to conduct rainwater to a covered tank. The water is now being treated and used in the health center.

WaterAid is also working in villages like Foro, where no one has ever successfully brought water. Their approach combines technologies proven to last—such as building a sand dam to capture and filter rainwater that would otherwise drain away—with new ideas like installing toilets that also generate methane gas for a new communal kitchen. But the real innovation is that WaterAid treats technology as only part of the solution. Involving the local community in designing, building, and maintaining new water projects is considered just as important. Before beginning any project, WaterAid asks the community to form a WASH (water, sanitation, hygiene) committee of seven people—four of whom must be women. The committee works with WaterAid to plan projects and involve the village in construction. Then it maintains and runs the project.

The people of Konso, who grow their crops on terraces they have painstakingly dug into the sides of mountains, are famous for hard work, and they are an asset—one of Konso's few—in the quest for water. In the village of Orbesho, residents even built a road themselves so that drilling machinery could come in. Last summer their pump, installed by the river, was being motorized to push its water to a newly built reservoir on top of a nearby mountain. From there, gravity would pipe it down to villages on the other side of the mountain. Residents of those villages had contributed a few cents apiece to help fund the project, made concrete, and collected stones for the structures, and now they were digging trenches to lay pipes.

From a distance they looked like a riotously colored snake: 200 people, mostly women in rainbow-striped peplum skirts and red or green T-shirts, forming a wavy line up the side of the mountain from the pump to the reservoir. Some men were helping lay fat pipes in the trench. The scene was almost festive with the taste of progress. Hundreds of people had come every day for four days to spend their mornings digging. The trench was about half finished, and each day the snake moved farther up the mountain.

If installing a water pump is technically challenging, encouraging hygiene is a challenge of a different kind. Wako Lemeta is one of two hygiene promoters WaterAid has trained in Foro. Lemeta, rather shy and pokerfaced, stops by Binayo's house and asks her husband, Guyo Jalto, if he can check their jerry cans. Jalto leads him to the hut where they are stored, and Lemeta uncovers one and sniffs. He nods approvingly; the family is using WaterGuard, a capful of which purifies a jerry can of drinking water. The government began to hand out WaterGuard at the beginning of the recent outbreak of disease. Lemeta also checks if the family has a latrine and talks to villagers about the advantages of boiling drinking water, washing hands, and bathing twice a week.

Many people have embraced the new practices. Surveys say latrine use has risen from 6 to 25 percent in the area

Health

The World Health Organization estimates that a combination of unsafe water, inadequate sanitation and poor hygiene kills 200 people an hour.

200 Every hour, every day, every year.

←——— 3' long worm grows inside the leg ———→

GUINEA WORM DISEASE
Caused by drinking water containing a water flea that harbors the larvae of a parasitic worm. The larvae pass through the intestinal wall and mature inside the body. After about a year the worm, now 3 feet long, bursts through an inflamed blister, often in the leg, exposing its head. It must be carefully wound out of the body onto a small stick.

The number of people who die from these diseases **every day** is the equivalent of eleven jumbo jets crashing every day, with no survivors.

WATERBORNE DISEASES

4,800 people die every day from diseases associated with lack of access to safe drinking water, inadequate sanitation, and poor hygiene.

RIVER BLINDNESS
(Onchocerciasis) affects more than 20 million people in Central and South America and Africa. It is transmitted by small flies that breed in water.

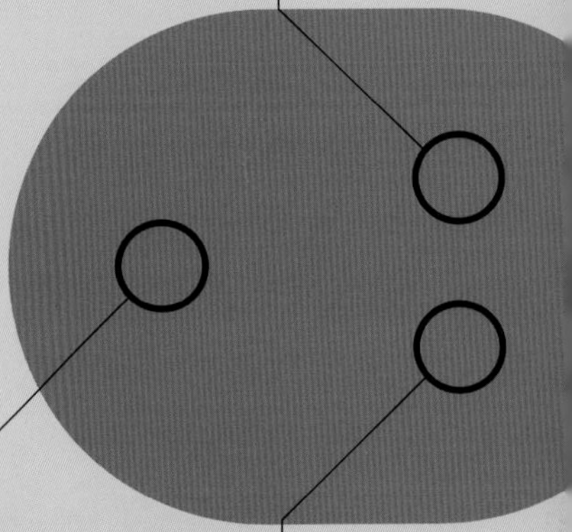

DIARRHEA
In 1998, 308,000 people died from war in Africa, but more than 2 million died from diarrheal diseases.

In the past 10 years, diarrhea has killed more children than all the people lost to armed conflict since World War II.

1.8 million children die each year from this disease alone.

In China, India and Indonesia, twice as many people die from diarrheal diseases as die from HIV/AIDS.

BILHARZIASIS
(Schistomiasis) affects more than 200 million people worldwide, mostly in the tropics. It is acquired by swimming in infected lakes and rivers. Tiny flukes penetrate a bather's skin and cause bleeding in the intestinal walls or bladder, and may affect other organs such as the liver.

TRACHOMA
An infectious disease spread by direct physical contact between people, and by flies. Lack of water for washing eventually leads to blindness. Trachoma affects three times as many women as men.

DENGUE
A mosquito-borne infection estimated to affect 50 million people a year. It's sometimes called breakbone fever as it results in severe bone and muscle pain. No vaccine is currently available. A potentially fatal complication of dengue is DHF (dengue hemorrhagic fever).

TYPHOID FEVER
The source of infection is the feces of a diseased person. It is commonly spread by contamination of drinking water by sewage, or by flies that carry bacteria from feces to food. If untreated, fatal complications may develop. An estimated 17 million people are infected every year.

CHOLERA
Infection is caused by drinking water that is contaminated by a bacterium. The World Health Organization reported 5,000 deaths in 2000, 87% of them in Africa.

GRAPHIC BY NIGEL HOLMES

FACT In 1999 Bolivia granted a multinational consortium 40-year rights to provide water and sanitation services to the city of Cochabamba.

PHOTOGRAPH BY ALDO CARDOSO

since WaterAid began work in December 2007. But it is a struggle. "When I tell them to use soap," Lemeta explains, "they usually tell me, 'Give me the money to buy it.'"

Similar barriers must be overcome to keep a program going after the aid group leaves. WaterAid and other successful groups, such as Water.org, CARE, and A Glimmer of Hope, believe that charging user fees—usually a penny per jerry can or less—is key to sustaining a project. The village WASH committee holds the proceeds to pay for spare parts and repairs. But villagers think of water as a gift from God. Should we next pay to breathe air?

Water and money have long been an uneasy mixture. Notoriously, in 1999 Bolivia granted a multinational consortium 40-year rights to provide water and sanitation services to the city of Cochabamba. The ensuing protests over high prices eventually drove out the company and brought global attention to the problems of water privatization. Multinational companies brought in to run public water systems for profit have little incentive to hook up faraway rural households or price water so it is affordable to the poor.

Yet someone has to pay for water. Although water springs from the earth, pipes and pumps, alas, do not. This is why even public utilities charge users for water. And water is often most expensive to provide for those who can least afford it—people in the remote, sparsely populated, drought-stricken villages of the world.

"The key question is, who decides?" says Global Water Challenge's Faeth. "In Cochabamba nobody was talking to the very poorest. The process was not open to the public." A pump in a rural village, he says, is a different story. "At the local level there is a more direct connection between the people implementing the program and the people getting access to water."

The Konso villagers own and control their pumps. Elect-ed committees set fees, which cover maintenance. No one seeks to recoup the installation costs or to make a profit. Villagers told me that, after a few weeks, they realized paying a penny per jerry can is actually cheap, far less than what they were paying through the hours spent hauling water—and the time, money, and lives lost to disease.

How would Aylito Binayo's life be different if she never had to go to the river for water again? Deep in a gorge far from Foro, there is a well. It is 400 feet deep. During my visit it was nothing much to look at—above ground it was only a concrete box with a jerry can inverted over it for protection, surrounded by a pyramid of bramble bushes. But here's what was to happen by March: A motorized pump would push the water up the mountain to a reservoir. Then gravity would carry it back down to taps in local villages—including Foro. The village would have two community taps and a shower house for bathing. If all went well, Aylito Binayo would have a faucet with safe water just a three-minute stroll from her front door.

When I ask her to imagine this easier life, she closes her eyes and reels off a long list of chores. She will go the fields to help her husband, collect grass for the goats, make food for her family, clean the compound. She will be with her sons, instead of leaving a grave little four-year-old in charge of his younger brothers for hours on end. "I don't know whether to believe it will work. We are on top of a mountain, and the water is down below," she says. "But if it works, I will be so happy, so very happy."

I ask her about her hopes for her family, and her answer is heartbreaking in its modesty: to get through the new hunger brought on by the drought, to get through this new wave of disease—to scramble back to the meager life she had known before. She doesn't dream. She has never dared think that someday life could change for the better—that there could arrive a metal spigot, with dignity gushing out of the end.

In 2000 the people of Cochabamba, Bolivia fought back after privatization of their water services led to rate hikes and cut-offs.

Industrial Agriculture's Big Thirst

WENONAH HAUTER

You know things are bad when reservoirs are converted into cornfields. On a 2008 trip from Beijing, I searched in vain for a glimpse of the Miyun reservoir that once provided drinking water for Beijing's 17 million residents. Instead of lapping waves,

there was an ocean of corn. The water was gone.

This sight may become more common as water-intensive agriculture practices collide with water scarcity. Agriculture is the single largest user of water worldwide, dwarfing everything else. Drinking, cooking, and washing by six billion people combined with all industrial water consumption pale in comparison to watering crops and livestock. Global agriculture uses nearly two quadrillion gallons of rainwater and irrigation water annually—enough to cover the entire United States with two feet of water.[1]

Obviously, crops and animals need water to thrive and sustain a hungry and growing population, but intensive agricultural practices exert more stress on watersheds than rainfed cultivation of ecologically appropriate crops. Even irrigation can sustainably maintain fields during periods of drought. But the worldwide expansion of industrial-scale cultivation of water-intensive crops and feedlots on more marginal land magnifies the pressure on already overstretched water resources. In America, recent high crop prices spurred increased corn cultivation in more arid regions of the high plains and the Rockies. In Central Asia, irrigation of cotton has almost completely eliminated the Aral Sea, once the fourth largest freshwater lake in the world.

The scale of water withdrawal from rivers, reservoirs, and groundwater for agriculture taxes available water resources. In the developing world, 85 percent of water withdrawals go toward agriculture; rich countries funnel 40 percent of water to agriculture.[2]

Industrial agriculture's use of water is a cycle of overuse, waste, and pollution. Unfortunately, most of us are a part of that cycle, too. What we eat and how we grow our food is key to our global water crisis. Your hamburger, cup of coffee, and cotton shirt have a water footprint that is determined by the industrial agriculture model. But we have the power to change this model, if we can harness the political will of a new generation of consumers, farmers, and activists.

Agribusiness's Big Thirst

Farmers are not solely responsible for the tremendous pressure industrialized agriculture puts on water systems. The handful of giant agribusinesses and food processing companies that dominate the food chain keep farm prices low, which only pushes farmers to produce more. Most farmers resort to water-intensive and chemical-dependent practices to sell enough farm products to make a living.

In the United States and around the world, only a few companies sell the seeds, buy the harvests, slaughter the livestock, and turn farm products into the food consumers buy. Farms that are far away from wealthy metropolitan areas are especially dependent on agribusiness buyers. The four largest firms in the United States slaughter 84 percent of the cattle, crush 80 percent of the soybeans, and process

Tomato crops being grown in a center-pivot irrigation circle near Al Faw in an area of the Arabian desert known as the Empty Quarter, which is the world's largest sand sea and one of the hottest places on earth.

FACT It takes more than 150 gallons a day to maintain a cow
on mega-dairies and about 20 gallons for beef cattle
on industrial feedlots.

66 percent of the hogs.[3] Even in recent years, when prices were higher, the few companies that sold seeds, fertilizers, and fuel could jack up their prices, so higher production costs gobbled most of the gains from increased farm prices. Two corn seed firms (Monsanto and DuPont's Pioneer Hi-Bred) control about 60 percent of the seed market and 80 percent of U.S. corn is grown from Monsanto-patented seed traits.[4] In 2009 and 2010, the leading corn seed companies raised prices between 20 and 40 percent.[5]

What This Means for Irrigation

Irrigation has been used for thousands of years to increase agricultural productivity and provide a safeguard against drought. But in the past fifty years, mechanical irrigation pumps and sprinklers brought more marginal land into cultivation. Irrigated cultivation is the single largest consumer of global water resources—amounting to 660 trillion to 1 quadrillion gallons annually.[6] Increased water extraction has overtapped watersheds, and poorly designed irrigation systems can make fields so waterlogged or salt-laden that soil fertility is completely compromised.[7]

A recent U.S. Department of Agriculture survey reported the United States applied 30 trillion gallons of irrigation water to 55 million acres of cropland in 2008.[8] As crop prices rose between 2003 and 2008, farmers irrigated 2.4 million more acres of cropland and installed 31,000 more wells.[9] Even wealthy countries have been slow to adopt more efficient irrigation techniques despite leaks and losses from wasteful irrigation systems.[10] Only about 4 percent of U.S. irrigated cropland uses more efficient drip or precision irrigation systems.[11]

In the developing world, irrigated farmland doubled to about 500 million acres between the 1960s and 2000.[12] Most irrigated cultivation in the developing world uses two to three times more water than crops require, which wastes between half and 80 percent of irrigation water through leaks, runoff, and evaporation.[13]

The rising pressure on water systems from increasing irrigation has strained groundwater and river resources.

Today, many aquifers are pumped for irrigation beyond their recharge capacity in parts of the United States, China, India, and North Africa.[14] China's water withdrawals are 25 percent higher than the recharge rate and parts of Northern India pump 50 percent more water than the aquifers can refill.[15]

The rush to biofuels provides a cautionary example of how changes in agriculture markets can wreak havoc on water supplies. In recent years, the pursuit of biofuel sources encouraged industrial agriculture to guzzle even more water. As gasoline prices skyrocketed during 2007 and 2008, investment in new ethanol plants drove up demand for corn, resulting in more cultivation, more irrigation, and more chemical fertilizer and pesticide application. The increased demand for corn brought more acres of corn into production—including 2.2 million new acres of irrigated corn, a 22 percent increase between 2003 and 2008.[16] Adding further pressure to the water table, it takes about four gallons of water to produce each gallon of ethanol—or an estimated 52 billion gallons of water in 2010.[17] Much of the water used to irrigate corn and refine ethanol is drawn from the ever-threatened Ogallala aquifer, which runs beneath eight western U.S. states and provides nearly a third of all U.S. irrigation water.[18] Ninety-seven percent of the Ogallala water withdrawal is used for agriculture and some sections of the aquifer have drained over 150 feet since the 1950s.[19] Since the refineries draw from the same overtapped aquifers as the corn farms, these plants can compete with rural communities for scarce water resources.

Factory Farm Faucets

Industrial scale livestock operations crammed with thousands of hogs, tens of thousands of cattle or even hundreds of thousands of chickens consume torrents of water. In the United States, livestock operations withdraw more than two billion gallons of water every day.[20] Small and medium-sized livestock farms are disappearing under pressure from these factory farms and giant meatpackers and processors. As recently as 1992, a quarter million

U.S. farmers raised hogs. In just over a decade, the number plummeted 70 percent by 2004.[21] Despite the declining number of farms, the number of hogs stayed the same, as the remaining farms got much larger. In 1992, less than a third of hogs were raised on farms with more than 2,000 animals, but by 2007, 95 percent of hogs were raised on these giant operations.[22]

These crowded, hot animals need a lot of water, not only to drink but also to flush their waste out of the buildings where they are confined. Each factory farm-raised hog drinks about five gallons of water daily.[23] It takes more than 150 gallons a day to maintain a cow on mega-dairies and about 20 gallons for beef cattle on industrial feedlots, including water for drinking as well as hosing down the dairies and feedlots.[24] Now, thirsty factory farms have expanded into Central Europe, the former Soviet Union, Brazil, Mexico, India, China, and the Philippines, as well as dry areas of the U.S., such as New Mexico. Today, industrial livestock facilities produce about two-thirds of the world's poultry meat and eggs and more than half the world's pork.[25] This shift to factory farming has taken its toll on water resources.

Toxic Pollutants

While water dedicated to irrigate crops and slake livestock depletes water resources, pollution from industrialized farms degrades downstream water supplies and aquifers. Fertilizers, pesticides, and manure from factory farms constitute the leading pollution source for America's impaired rivers and lakes, and a major cause of water impairment for the country's estuaries.[26]

WATER LEADER   WORKING TO KEEP THE FLOW

KickStart, Appropriate Technology

KickStart customers

KICKSTART WAS FOUNDED IN KENYA IN JULY 1991 by Nick Moon and Martin Fisher as an international social enterprise with the goal of lifting people out of poverty. The organization's focus on micro-irrigation has led them to design small, human-powered pumps that are sold in local retail shops. These low-cost pumps enable subsistence farmers to become "farmerpreneurs" by harvesting and selling high value crops throughout the year. They increase their farm incomes by as much as ten-fold and make enough to properly feed and educate their children, and pay for health care. To date over 100,000 small-scale farmers in Africa are using these pumps to lift their families out of poverty.
For more information visit *kickstart.org*.

Over the last 50 years, the use of synthetic fertilizer in the United States has nearly tripled, rising from 7.5 million tons in 1960 to 22.9 million tons in 2007.[27] These fertilizers are often over-applied. A Cornell University study found that most farmers apply twice as much nitrogen fertilizers than the crops need, which lets excess nitrogen enter the water supply.[28] When nitrogen fertilizer leaches into groundwater, it forms nitrate.[29] Too much nitrate in drinking water has been linked to adverse human health effects, including methemoglobinemia ("blue-baby syndrome") which can be fatal.[30] Chronic exposure to drinking water contaminated with nitrates also has been linked to cancer, thyroid disease, and diabetes.[31]

Fertilizer runoff can saturate coastal waters with nutrients that generate oxygen-depleting algae blooms that create "dead zones" where most aquatic life cannot survive.[32] Farms in the Corn Belt were the main source of the pollution that created the growing dead zone in the Gulf of Mexico.[33] These oxygen-depleted estuaries have also become increasingly common worldwide.

The industrial agriculture model also deploys a toxic cocktail of pesticides and herbicides that can contaminate surface and groundwater. The use of herbicides, pesticides, fungicides, and other chemical applications in the United States more than doubled since the 1960s, rising from 215 million pounds in 1964 to 494 million pounds in 2004.[34] One in fifteen urban streams had pesticide levels that exceeded at least one human health benchmark between 1992 and 2001, according to the U.S. Geological Survey.[35] The survey found that half of rural streams and three-quarters of urban streams had pesticide levels that were above key water quality criteria for aquatic life—and a quarter of rural streams and half of urban streams ex-ceeded aquatic life benchmarks for DDT, which has been banned for nearly 40 years.[36]

It's a global problem, too. International trade in pesticides has doubled over the past 25 years, with global imports rising 97 percent from 1990 to 2006.[37] Many developing countries produce fruits and vegetables for export to wealthy consumers, and these crops represent more than one-fourth of global pesticide applications.[38] The adoption of agrochemical farming in the developing world can have significant public health impacts. Pesticides poison an estimated 25 million farmworkers in the developing world each year.[39] A 2008 study in India found that farming communities with higher pesticide use had significantly higher cancer rates, and that the pesticides likely contributed to these higher levels of disease.[40]

It's not just the inputs that are toxic. Commercial confined livestock and poultry operations produce an estimated 500 million tons of manure each year, three times more than the entire U.S. population.[41] Taxpayer-financed USDA programs spent $179 million between 2003 and 2007 to cover manure management costs for industrial dairies and hog operations alone.[42] The Union of Concerned Scientists has estimated that it would cost $4 billion just to fully mitigate the soil damage caused by large-scale hog and dairy operations.[43] The manure is usually over-applied to fields—contributing to the nutrient loads that runoff to surface water and lead to coastal dead zones—or stored in lagoons that can leak or burst, degrading watersheds and contaminating groundwater.

Globalized Food Trade Taps Rural Water Supplies

Global trade in agricultural products—and the freshwater it takes to produce these commodities and food products—can exert even more pressure on watersheds. The water withdrawals used to cultivate the global agriculture trade is known as "virtual water." Even mundane things contain a tremendous amount of virtual water used to grow and process crops into consumer goods. For example, an 8-ounce cup of coffee contains 37 gallons of virtual water and a pair of leather shoes represents 2,000 gallons of water.[44] One seventh of worldwide agricultural water consumption goes toward exports.[45] Global virtual water trade

in crops and livestock represents more than 300 trillion gallons of water annually.[46]

When irrigated corn grown with water drawn from the overstretched Ogallala aquifer is exported, the communities that rely on that water see it shipped out of their community. The same is true with products we import. The fruits and vegetables grown in arid areas of Mexico and Africa for American and European consumers compound the water scarcity of these communities.

The agriculture trade in virtual water merely offshores the environmental costs of industrial agricultural production. The exporting nation depletes water resources and discharges agriculture pollutants to produce the food it ships overseas. For example, the international meat trade involves exporting corn and soybeans to factory farms that in turn ship the meat to overseas consumers. According to the Royal Swedish Academy of Sciences this process can "substantially alter the magnitude and the pattern of global resource use and result in rising pressure on environmental resources in producing regions to sustain feed and meat use in consuming regions."[47]

Exporting Unsustainable Agriculture to the Developing World

Today, big agribusiness is using the 2008 global food crisis to justify an expansion of industrialized agriculture in the developing world. Although the crisis was brought about by skyrocketing prices, not lack of production, the seed, agrochemical, and grain trading companies are calling for a second "Green Revolution." The initial Green Revolution introduced large-scale, agrochemical-dependent farming techniques to much of Asia and Latin America in the 1950s and 1960s in order to stave off famine. It also effectively delivered the developing world's agricultural production into the hands of a few multinational corporations.

The program, driven by philanthropists, development agencies, and international financial institutions like the World Bank, brought high-yield conventional crops to the developing world. But the Green Revolution also trans-

Impact

At home, the average American uses between 100 and 175 gallons of water a day. That is less than 25 years ago, but it does not include the amount of water used to feed and clothe us.

This page shows how many gallons of water are needed to produce some **meal-sized portions:**

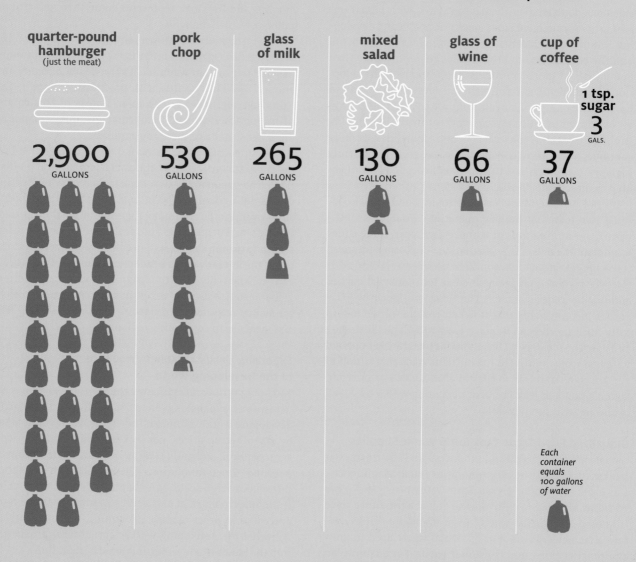

quarter-pound hamburger (just the meat)	pork chop	glass of milk	mixed salad	glass of wine	cup of coffee
2,900 GALLONS	530 GALLONS	265 GALLONS	130 GALLONS	66 GALLONS	37 GALLONS

1 tsp. sugar
3 GALS.

Each container equals 100 gallons of water

And this is how many gallons of water are needed to produce quantities of some **everyday foods:**

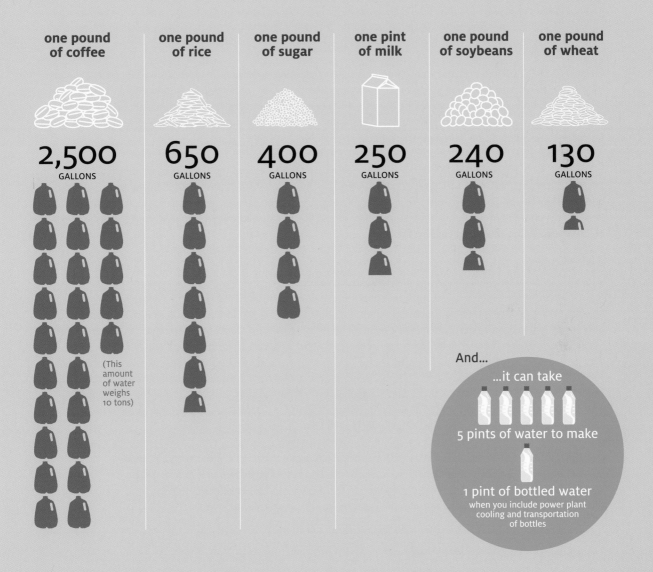

one pound of coffee	one pound of rice	one pound of sugar	one pint of milk	one pound of soybeans	one pound of wheat
2,500 GALLONS	**650** GALLONS	**400** GALLONS	**250** GALLONS	**240** GALLONS	**130** GALLONS

(This amount of water weighs 10 tons)

And...

...it can take

5 pints of water to make

1 pint of bottled water
when you include power plant cooling and transportation of bottles

Rebalance the agricultural market. The U.S. government should begin to enforce antitrust laws put in place in the early 1900s to protect farmers, workers, and all citizens against the monopolistic and oligopolistic power and vagaries of corporations. With the power of the government behind them, farmers should be on an even footing with agribusiness in terms of access to an open, transparent crop and livestock market.

Buy local to save water. Consumers should use their food purchases to address the water crisis. As much as possible, they should buy food products grown organically and locally (or regionally). This will help to prevent not only water pollution but also trading water, via food, from one region, state, or country to the next. Eating low on the food chain—less meat and dairy products—saves water. The amount of water used to produce animal products far exceeds the amount used for growing vegetables and grains.

Rethink U.S. agriculture policy. We need to completely revamp the farm policy in the United States to stress supply management and a conservation reserve, and we should enact policies that rebalance commodity prices so they exceed production cost. Farm policy should encourage and reward local and sustainable agriculture. In short, national and international agriculture policy should put farmers, consumers, and the environment first— before the economic interests of agribusiness.

Change the policies of the international finance institutions. The World Bank, the International Monetary Fund, and other international aid agencies have used their immense power and resources to promote export-oriented industrialized agriculture in the developing world. The high-yield varieties of crops they encourage countries to grow require imported irrigation pumps, diesel, fertilizers, and pesticides. This not only wastes water but also results in massive pollution. It is time for a new model of development that puts feeding people first and relies on traditional agriculture practices that are appropriate for the local ecology.

Rethink international trade policy. International free trade agreements promote an unsustainable, export-oriented agricultural model that benefits agribusinesses while farmers, consumers, and the environment lose out. U.S. trade negotiators should abandon efforts to conclude the Doha Round agreement at the WTO, which would dramatically accelerate the devastating effects of industrialized agriculture.

Support the concept of food sovereignty. A global network of social organizations representing small farmers, fishermen, indigenous people, and agricultural trade unions have been leading international discussions to lay out an agenda that would address agriculture's role in causing the world water crisis and provide food security for people around the world.

formed these countries' diverse food production systems into single-crop monocultures (chiefly rice, corn, and wheat) that relied on high-cost seeds, agrochemicals, and intensive water use and irrigation. Even Nobel Laureate Norman Borlaug, the godfather of the Green Revolution, noted that the rapid rise of ill-planned irrigation schemes to accommodate the new crops in Asia often led to water-logged or salty fields, which reduced productivity.[48]

After the 2008 food crisis, a new generation of philan-thropists led by the Bill and Melinda Gates Foundation and the U.S. Agency for International Development are pushing to renew investment in industrial agriculture in the developing world. Many donors and agribusinesses also are pressing for the adoption of genetically modified crops as a promised remedy for global hunger and climate change. So far, there have been little or no productivity gains from genetically modified seeds that are widely used in the United States and no drought-tolerant seeds have been developed.[49] All of the biotechnology solutions rely on high-cost seeds and heavy agrochemical applications, and in the United States much of the GM corn and soybeans are heavily irrigated. Nonetheless, proponents continue to focus on the prospect of a biotechnology breakthrough instead of investing in proven farming techniques and policies that are suited to local conditions.

Agribusiness-driven solutions of globalization and a renewed global push for industrial agriculture cannot resolve the food system's pressure on soil, water, and the environment. A truly sustainable solution will not come from the corporate interests that got us into this mess. A new food, farm, and environmental social movement fo-cused on sustainability and equity must challenge the corporate-controlled food chain.

A growing body of strong scientific evidence is demon-strating that sustainable agriculture can feed the planet, fight climate change, and reduce the water footprint of industrial agriculture. In 2009, a World Bank-sponsored scientific review found that industrial agriculture had so degraded soil fertility and water resources that the global food and farming system needed a transformational over-haul. The director of this peer-reviewed International As-sessment of Agricultural Knowledge, Science, and Tech-nology concluded, "Business as usual is not an option."[50] A 2008 UN study found that low-impact agriculture could increase yields and improve food security and farmer in-comes while reducing environmental degradation.[51] A 2007 University of Michigan study concluded "organic agricul-ture has the potential to contribute quite substantially to the global food supply, while reducing the detrimental en-vironmental impacts of conventional agriculture."[52]

Many families are embracing organic agriculture and local foods as part of an alternative to industrial farming. Increasing numbers of people are looking to understand where their food comes from and are turning away from the corporate food giants and toward farmer's markets, ur-ban agriculture programs, and direct marketing arrange-ments with independent farmers. Many are even trying their hand at growing their own food. The U.S. Department of Agriculture found a 200 percent increase in farmer's markets from 1994 to 2009 and the National Gardening As-sociation estimated that 1 million new food gardens were being planted in 2010. Local food is becoming a hot topic, with an organic garden at the White House and even a real-ity "Food Revolution" show on network TV.

We need to build on this momentum. The growing awareness of food and farming has focused attention on the corporate control of America's kitchens. But we cannot shop our way out of business as usual; big policy changes are needed as well to break up agribusiness monopolies and support small and medium-sized family farms. If we are to feed future generations, our long-term goal must be to create a food system based on sustainable, diversified family farms that are providing food locally and region-ally. If we remain on the current path, industrialized ag-riculture will drain the planet's freshwater resources and leave only agrochemical pollutants in its place. The choice is ours, but we must do the work that is necessary to realize this vision for the future.

Beyond Public vs. Private

JEFF CONANT

The city of Detroit, Michigan has become a symbol. Straddling two of the Great Lakes in one of the most water-rich regions of the United States—indeed, of the world—the city has been beset by a plague of water service shutoffs: As many as 47,000

Detroit residents have reportedly had water services shut off in the last decade. A city that is famously "post-industrial," Detroit has become synonymous with factory closures, "white-flight," urban decay, poverty, and the devastation of an American Dream which, especially for low-income people and people of color, has always been just that: a dream.

But with its strong heritage of working-class struggle and community organizing, Detroit has also come to represent something positive: a sense of dignity and renewal. This dignity is nowhere more evident than in the campaign for access to clean water—a fight that is also taking place across the U.S. from Appalachian mining communities to California mountain towns to Native American reservations.

After years of disastrous water service in Detroit, in April 2009 a number of local organizations came together to form what they call the People's Water Board, whose intention, in the words of Sierra Club organizer Melissa Damaschke, is "to shadow the Municipal Board of Water Commissioners to hold them accountable for decisions they make with regard to water."

In a city with one of the largest public water utilities in the nation, why should an ad-hoc board of citizens need to shadow its officials and hold them accountable? "During the late nineties, people came into our office with problems with utilities like lights and gas," said Marian Kramer, an organizer with the Michigan Welfare Rights Organization (MWRO). "We found out that some of them had had their water shut off. If they are the head of the household, not

having water lays the foundation for having children taken away. So a family's water was off, but parents were keeping it a secret. Between 2001 and 2002, we found out that some 40,700 people were without water."

In the ensuing years, the numbers continued to grow. With unemployment soaring and water rates rising, Detroit's growing jobless population simply could not pay their water bills. With social service agencies mandated to safeguard children at risk of living without basic services, the resulting water shutoffs were not merely leaving people thirsty; they were devastating homes and breaking up families.

"And then there's the whole privatization issue," says Priscilla Dziubek, an organizer with the East Michigan Environmental Action Council. "We're losing city jobs to private contracts. While they haven't signed a water contract with a private corporation, they've piecemealed it out."

The Failure of the Public Sector to Protect and Serve

In the United States, with a strong history of public water, it may be hard to fathom so many people living without such a basic service. Across the country, 86 percent of us still get our drinking water from a public utility. In the U.S., as in Europe, public water services helped to create the political stability and financial equity necessary for modern development. Indeed, government investments in water and sanitation services in the late 19th and early 20th centuries eliminated waterborne diseases such as cholera, typhoid, and intestinal parasites, making public funding for water the very basis of public health. But if most water utilities in the U.S. are still under public control, it is because people have fought to protect them.

While the failure of Detroit's Water and Sewerage Department is an extreme case, it is indicative of the general trend; a public utility capable of leaving 47,000 homes without water access has clearly ceased to serve the public. Part of the blame falls to federal spending priorities. Proceeding from congressional appropriations, the State Revolving Fund for water (SRF) gives states seed money for low-interest loans to municipalities, which then use those funds to maintain their systems. SRF appropriations have dropped by more than half over the last decade, from $1.6 billion in 1995 to $688 million in 2007.[1]

It is easy to suppose that if there were funds for water —a fully funded federal or state trust, for example, to provide for both upkeep of water infrastructure and support for those who've been failed by other forms of public support (from the education system to the legal system), then families in Detroit wouldn't be losing their children for lack of basic services.

Detroit is far from the only community in the U.S. that lacks adequate water service. For low-income communities and communities of color, both urban and rural, water service can be spotty regardless of whether it is private or public. The federal Safe Drinking Water Act (SDWA) requires all drinking water to meet health standards set by the Environmental Protection Agency (EPA); yet, the EPA reports that over the last five years, more than 49 million people have been served water with concentrations of contaminants exceeding health limits.[2]

A 1984 survey by the EPA found that water consumed in low-income households had significantly higher levels of disease-causing bacteria.[3] Since then, despite the rise of the environmental justice movement, there appear to have been few studies that looked at water contamination specifically in relation to race and class. But related data confirms that the trend still is prevalent: Today the EPA estimates that 40 million people are exposed to lead poisoning each year, with up to 20 percent of cases traceable to drinking water. Low-income children and African American and Latino children consistently have higher rates of lead in their blood than higher income people and those of Anglo descent.

A 2004 study showed that African Americans are more than twice as likely, and Hispanics more than three times as likely as non-Hispanic whites, to live in homes with incomplete plumbing.[4] Similarly, 11.7 percent of Native Americans on reservations and 30 percent of Alaska Natives lack plumbing. In the rural subdivisions known as *colonias* that spring up along the 2,000-mile border between the U.S. and Mexico, about one quarter of residences lack treated water and 44 percent lack any form of sewage whatsoever.[5]

It is precisely this failure of public water that has encouraged the private sector to move in. But study after study, as well as protest after protest, shows that privatization only makes matters worse.

Uprising in Detroit: The People's Water Board Works to Take Back Control

In the outlying neighborhood of Highland Park, ground zero of Detroit's water woes, an emergency financial manager had been appointed by the governor to get the city out of a financial crisis. With the authority to override the elected city council members and the mayor, her remedy was to downsize departments, replace local workers with corporate consultants, and increase revenue from the water department by raising rates and enforcing collection. The Detroit Water and Sewerage Department (DWSD) introduced an aggressive plan of utilities debt collection: those who couldn't pay the hike in water prices had their water turned off. In order to keep residents from turning their water back on, DWSD workers cemented the valves shut.

Dziubek of the East Michigan Environmental Action Council had worked previously with another group, the

FACT One in six Detroiters is jobless. In some neighborhoods unemployment is at 50 percent.

Sweetwater Alliance, to fight Nestlé on water bottling. "When we started hearing from MWRO about the water shutoffs," she says, "to us it was the same issue: water affordability, the right to water."

While much of the globe is facing water scarcity due to rising populations and ever-increasing consumption patterns, this is not Detroit's issue. The city's water agency supplied 20 percent less water in 2009 than it had six years before, essentially due to a steep decline in both population and industrial activity. The city's population has dropped from nearly two million in 1950 to around 850,000 today;

each year more than 10,000 residents flee in search of greener pastures. One in six Detroiters is jobless; and in some neighborhoods as many as half the people who live there are unemployed.

Yet, while poverty grows and water use decreases due to depopulation, the rates charged for water have been increasing; in 2008 the average water bill increased by almost $55, and in 2009 the average bill came to $83 a year, with another increase predicted for the coming year.

In response to the water shutoffs, the Michigan Welfare Rights Organization began a direct action campaign

STUDY AFTER STUDY, AS WELL AS PROTEST AFTER PROTEST, SHOWS THAT PRIVATIZATION ONLY MAKES MATTERS WORSE.

against DWSD, developing a water affordability plan to ensure that no one would have to pay more than $40 a year for water. With growing popular support, MWRO pushed for a moratorium on water shutoffs. But by 2006, the number of homes without water had risen to 45,000. In 2007, DWSD finally adopted a Water Affordability Plan, but where the original plan was to support upwards of 45,000 people, the plan implemented served only 1,100. With an increasing number of bills going into arrears, the city began adding unpaid bills to property tax bills, increasing the possibility that residents could lose both their children and their homes.

Shutoffs are only part of the problem; pollution is another. According to the Sierra Club Legal Defense Fund, over 23 billion gallons of raw sewage was dumped into the Great Lakes in 2006; the chief culprit, among many, was the Detroit Wastewater Treatment Facility. The high cost of upgrading and expanding the aging sewage system causes DWSD to pass the buck on to its customers in the form of rate increases. But Detroit's water shutoffs are not merely a consequence of the need for improved maintenance, compounded by urban flight. Contrary to reason, citizen water conservation efforts also lead to rate increases: the less water DWSD sends through its pipes, the more it costs.

Such disastrous policies are not just management failures; they are the consequence of political and economic decisions. The DWSD's policy of charging more for less may be traceable to the department's need to pay off its massive $5.4 billion debt. Some 43 percent of the city's water revenue does not go to improve or maintain service, but to keep the DWSD's doors open.

While it's a public agency, DWSD has virtually no public accountability. In June 2010, with the city's water problems still unresolved, a U.S. District Court Judge appointed a group of Detroit's top business leaders, including executives from GM and Ford, to study the possibility of refinancing the department's debt; one of the chief options they are looking at is the outright sale of the city's water department to a private company.

In an age when corporations have succeeded in defining the priorities of an entire global culture, there are no definitive victories in protecting rights and resources. But a significant landmark was achieved in 2010 when citizens of Detroit instituted the People's Water Board. Made up of a wide range of groups including MWRO, the Detroit Black Food Security Network, and the water workers' union AFSME local 207, PWB's first public move was demanding that the minutes and agendas from Water Board meetings be published on the Internet and made available at the Detroit Public Library. They won this small demand, but have yet to make further headway. "We've asked for a moratorium on water shutoffs and gotten really nowhere with that," Dziubek says.

Members of the People's Water Board demonstrate before every meeting of the official Water Board; they force commissioners to cross their picket line, and then they enter the meetings and give public comments. Just as importantly, they're organizing and educating citizens. "We're building the coalition," Dziubek says. "The larger the coalition, the more pressure we'll be able to put on both the mayor and the water board. With more people every day losing the ability to pay their water bills, our numbers are growing."

PHOTOGRAPHS LEFT, JIM WEST; RIGHT, GEORGE WALDMAN

Left, Demonstrators picket the Detroit Water Department protesting thousands of water shut-offs at the homes of poor families. *Right*, Activists protest the selling of water bottled from the Great Lakes Basin.

Once Water Is Privatized, No End of Speculation Follows

In the 1990s the words "water privatization" entered the political vocabulary to signify what appeared to be an emerging threat. "What next?" people asked when they learned that multinational corporations were buying up water systems and reaping unheard-of profits. "They'll bottle and sell the air?"

And yet, seen in the larger, historical and global perspective, the privatization of public wealth, whether through outright ownership or more insidious forms of undermining the public good, was nothing new; since the early days of the industrial revolution, the enclosure of the commons has been a reigning tendency worldwide. Still, a visceral response to the first wave of water privatization

was appropriate to the profoundly emotional affront of selling off one of our most basic resources, and many campaigns that rose up to challenge privatization were, to a significant extent, successful. Yet, despite widespread outcry, the last few years have seen the impacts of resource privatization, and the attendant failure of the public sector to protect much of anything, grow even more extreme.

Under most service privatization arrangements, multinational corporations take control of water distribution networks, sewerage systems and treatment plants, controlling access, and passing profits to their shareholders. A current trend involves not outright ownership, but a leasing arrangement where a company makes a one-time, upfront payment to the city in return for control of the water system over a set period, often up

IT'S NOT MERELY WHO OWNS THE WATER, BUT...

to 99 years. Over the life of the lease, the company regains its investment—and the profit it owes its shareholders—through water bills. Many cities, like Detroit, have partial forms of privatization, where public agencies, divorced from meaningful government or citizen oversight, subcontract virtually all of their departments to private companies.

Privatization of municipal services is and will continue to be an issue of serious concern, especially as cash-strapped towns, cities, and municipalities are pressured to sell or lease public services in order to stay afloat. One current trend reveals the water-rich and cash-poor cities of the rust belt Midwest, like Milwaukee, Chicago, Cleveland, and Detroit, to be fertile ground for this strategy.

But outright privatization is not the only game in town for would-be water barons. With "blue gold" at a premium, the market is limited only by the imagination and the human capacity for greed; once water becomes a commodity, no end of speculation follows.

In New Mexico in 2007, a previously unknown private finance venture called Augustin Plains Ranch LLC filed an application with the state engineer to drill 37 deep wells and annually pump up to 54,000 acre-feet of water. Augustin proposed to use the water for everything from farming to recreation, even including in its application the magnanimous possibility that it would pipe water from near the headwaters of the Gila River across the state to the Rio Grande "to reduce the current stress on the water supply" of the river.[6]

To the north, a water speculator with the unlikely name of Aaron Million is laying similar plans, to pipe billions of gallons of river water from wild Wyoming to the suburban sprawl of Colorado. At an estimated cost of $3 billion, Million wants to build a 10-foot-diameter pipeline running 560 miles east from Wyoming to Denver and Colorado Springs. It would carry 80 billion gallons a year—more than Denver's public water utility currently supplies.[7]

The well-worn phrase "water is the new oil" is nowhere more deeply embraced than down south in Texas where T.

Boone Pickens, "a modern-day John D. Rockefeller," owns more water than any other individual in the U.S. His plans are well underway to sell some 65 billion gallons a year to Dallas, over 250 miles and 11 counties away from where he pumps it out of the ground. Even in the free market heartland of Texas, Pickens has come to embody capitalism unleashed. "There are people who will buy the water when they need it," he says. "And the people who have the water want to sell it. That's the blood, guts, and feathers of the thing."[8]

Alongside privatization of municipal services and what water justice advocates in the global south call "the privatization of territories and bioregions," are other forms of enclosure such as privatization of entire waterways through the construction of dams and irrigation; privatization by contamination from mining, oil extraction, manufacturing, energy generation, and agribusiness; privatization by water bottling, with water drawn from public or communally held groundwater sources, bottled and sold for between 1,000 and 10,000 times the cost of production; and privatization due to the monopoly of technology, when the same industries and multinational corporations that have caused water contamination and scarcity turn around and profit through sales of drills, pumps, desalination, purification and filtration plants, and other technologies that are handsomely presented as the primary avenues of escape from the water crisis.

Looking at privatization through such a broad lens reveals that the battle over public versus private misses a key factor, one that is perhaps more important in determining water access: It's not merely who owns the water, but who has the right to pollute and exploit it.

If water justice means stewarding water in ways that ensure everyone has access, it does not merely entail keeping water in public hands; it means challenging the structural causes of inequity by building public accountability and people's empowerment, through community participation.

Extractive Industries' Assault on Water

Increasingly, private corporations are rendering ground and surface waters unusable with the regulatory blessing of public agencies. Nowhere is the failure of public water policy more evident than in the staggering abuses of the coal industry. Coal mining is one of the greatest contributors to global warming and is a massive source of water abuse and pollution. According to the Union of Concerned Scientists, in order to create steam to turn its turbines, a typical 500-megawatt coal-fired power plant draws about 2.2 billion gallons of water a year—enough to support a city of 250,000 people.

In Appalachia, the practice known as mountaintop removal mining exemplifies the drastic abuse of extractive industries and the failure of government to regulate them. Mountaintop removal mining involves clear-cutting native forests, blasting away mountaintops to expose coal seams, and then dumping the waste into deep mountain valleys. The solid waste is used as "valley fill," often burying streams, and the slurry, a toxic cocktail of wash-water rich in carcinogenic chemicals and heavy metals, is stored in massive coal slurry impoundments often in the headwaters of a watershed, and subject to frequent spills.

Another region whose water resources have been devastated by coal extraction is Black Mesa, straddling the Navajo and Hopi Nations in Arizona. Water that collects in the ancient Black Mesa aquifer slowly percolates from the northwest corner of the Navajo reservation into a set of shallow, subterranean basins near the Hopi reservation in the south, discharging after many years into a host of gentle washes and springs. Many Hopi and Navajo rely on the aquifer for drinking, irrigation, and religious purposes —the springs it feeds are sacred to the Hopi people. But the largest user by far is the Peabody Western Coal Company, which mixes the water with coal to form slurry and shoots it hundreds of miles by pipeline to a power station in Nevada. Once the slurry reaches the power plant, the coal is extracted and the water used to cool the plant's generators.

Since Peabody began tapping the aquifer 30 years ago, draining more than a billion gallons of water from the reservoir each year, water levels in some Black Mesa wells have dropped by more than 100 feet, many springs have slackened to less than half their original volume, and washes used by local farmers have declined or dried up altogether. And, studies show, as the water pressure changes, contaminated water from another aquifer leaches in.

When Peabody negotiated its initial arrangement with the Hopi and Navajo in the mid-1960s, the Department of the Interior included an escape clause that could be triggered if the company's pumping adversely affected the aquifer and its users. Yet despite clear negative impacts, the government has never exercised its authority to pull Peabody's lease. Native lands have a distinct relationship with U.S. federal law and as tribal "assets" are legally held in trust by the government. This responsibility obligates the federal government to protect tribal interests—especially when the government exercises control over natural resources on tribal lands, as it does on Black Mesa. Yet, in countless well-documented cases, the government has betrayed its already dubious trust responsibility. Throughout native territories, ground and surface waters convey the toxic residue of resource extraction and

...WHO HAS THE RIGHT TO POLLUTE AND EXPLOIT IT.

Maria Lambert of Prenter Hollow, West Virignia, showing the water that regularly comes through her faucet since a mountain top removal mining operation began nearby. Behind her are the jugs of water she has to carry daily in order to have clean water for cooking and drinking.

FACT A typical 500-megawatt coal-fired power plant draws about 2.2 billion gallons of water a year, which is enough to support a city of 250,000 people.

PHOTOGRAPH BY PAUL CORBIT BROWN

governmental neglect, and tribal governments are poorly equipped to prevent such abuses.

In April 2010, as part of a long-running campaign, the Black Mesa Water Coalition forced the government to withdraw Peabody's permit to operate at Black Mesa. Wahleah Johns, co-director of the group, called the ruling "an important step toward restorative justice for indigenous communities," and "precedent-setting for all other communities that struggle with environmental protection." However, she said, "We cannot ignore that irreversible damage from coal mining continues."

Enei Begaye, also of the Black Mesa Water Coalition, says, "Winning water justice is not just about keeping the companies out. To win means to rebuild and revitalize our community. That means providing a way for our people to live that doesn't require us to sell the water."

Improve Regulations or Expand Rights?

Most campaigns to protect and improve water access in the U.S., like most environmental struggles, are "site fights" with the goal of enacting or improving government regulations or denying permits for specific harmful activities. The struggle to keep water in public hands is, in large part, about ensuring that it is protected by public entities, such as the EPA. Yet, under a system of laws bent, over the course of centuries, to the will of corporations, public entities, from the town council to the federal government, have little sway in protecting the rights of people.

From the very beginning, the U.S. Constitution was written to protect the rights of the owning class and its corporations. After the Civil War, the Fourteenth Amendment gave equal protection and the right to due process to African American men; a business-minded judiciary seized the moment to extend these rights to corporate persons as well. When the Supreme Court held that corporations have First Amendment rights to free speech and, in a later case, said that free speech includes spending money on political campaigns, corporate power was further consolidated.

Through the legal doctrine of "precedent"—the principle that a court's interpretation of law is based on previously upheld decisions—corporations have by now gained complete protection under the Constitution, making them, in most cases, exempt from both community decision-making and local and state law. Struggles for "the human right to water" are reduced to pleas for safe drinking water, despite the complex web of social, cultural, and ecological relations that are inherent to water issues.

Communities across the country have begun asking the question, "With corporations running the public agenda, what does a real water justice victory look like?" Beginning in Pennsylvania's coal country and expanding to small towns and municipalities nationwide, citizen activists have launched a movement, not to bring corporate profiteers under the law, but to change the law so that such activities are not regulated, but prohibited.

In March 2009, after a six-year battle to prevent Nestlé Waters from sucking their aquifers dry, citizens of Shapleigh, Maine, passed an ordinance that gives citizens the right to local self-governance, gives rights to ecosystems, and denies corporations the rights of personhood. The ordinance puts groundwater resources in a common trust to be used for the benefit of Shapleigh residents. Like the hundred-or-so similar ordinances that have been passed nationwide, this one has yet to be challenged. A statement from the community of Shapleigh puts it bluntly: "We are tired of Nestlé behaving as if they are a colonial power with a right to our water resources. We decided that we will behave as if we have the power."

In the next state over, an Anti-Corporate Water Withdrawal Ordinance that passed in 2006 in Barnstead, New Hampshire prohibits corporations from owning, withdrawing or hauling water from the community, and eliminates corporate constitutional privileges. Across the country, in the rural hamlet of Mt. Shasta, California, where the mountain's majestic volcanic peak rises to

14,000 feet above the headwaters of the Sacramento, McCloud, and Pit Rivers, townspeople are gearing up to vote on a similar rights-based ordinance to prevent PG&E, the state's private energy monopoly, from seeding the clouds with silver-iodide to increase rainfall to fill its hydroelectric reservoirs. Speaking at a city council meeting, Mt. Shasta resident John Roshak said, "This is a chance for our community to stand with those communities in Appalachia facing mountaintop removal, with those in the Gulf facing the loss of their fisheries to the BP oil spill, and with all communities seeing their environments massacred by corporate personhood."

While popular movements in the United States bear significant differences from their counterparts in the global south, one commonality is that victories for water justice are predicated not on state intervention, but more broadly, on community oversight and control. In countries where public agencies, historically, are either corrupt (as in many Latin American countries following centuries of colonization and decades of dictatorship) or ineffective in the face of corporate power, Latin American water activists do not necessarily believe, as many progressives in the U.S. do, that "public equals good."

With this concern always in mind, members of the InterAmerican Network for the Defense and Protection of the Right to Water (Red VIDA in its Spanish acronym) demand that water services be not merely public, but also "transparent," "participatory," and "community-driven." To

this end, several agencies in Latin America have established citizen oversight boards to ensure community control. This is precisely what the people of Detroit have done, against all odds, in establishing their People's Water Board.

One form of transparent, participatory, and community-driven public water management initiated and promoted by the Red VIDA, is called Public Utility Partnerships (affectionately known as PUPs). A form of institutional cooperation, collaboration, and consultation between successful public utilities and other utilities in need of financial and technical support, PUPs emerged in Latin America in response to privatization, as citizens groups demanded a voice in utility reforms. Many PUPs combine cross-border partnerships between public agencies with directly democratic forms of citizen oversight. According to a 2009 report by Public Services International and Transnational Institute, over 130 such partnerships exist in 70 countries;[9] in the short time they've existed, PUPs have become remarkably successful by forging open, democratic and dynamic relationships between committed public sector workers and communities.[10]

While such mutual-aid driven structures appear rare in the U.S., they have a long history. In the late 1960s and early 1970s, many states established citizen utility boards, also referred to as residential utility consumer action groups. These voluntary organizations were (and are) funded through membership dues to pay a small staff of organizers, lawyers and advocates to represent the needs of utility customers. Another participatory model is embodied by many municipal utility districts, where a

public utility is governed by an elected board of directors on a one-person, one-vote system, ensuring that all areas of the city have representation equal to their population. A third model is the utility cooperative, where consumers of the utility have the sole right to elect its governing body; more than 100 million people in the U.S. belong to utility co-ops today.[11]

Rights-based organizing and public-community partnerships represent emerging efforts at building grassroots democracy; but democratizing water governance requires democratizing our society, and building participatory, water-conscious strategies for urban planning, agriculture, energy, consumption, and waste. As Enei Begaye says, "To really win the battle to protect our water, the lifeblood of Mother Earth, we need to rebuild our communities in a just way. We can do our part to become locally sustainable, but there will always be pressure to sell off pieces of this and pieces of that, as long as communities outside the reservation don't reduce their consumption."

To truly protect ground and surface waters and to put control of basic services into the hands of citizens, ordinary people need to care enough, to be empowered to govern, and to have access to both money and political power; also required is strong regulatory oversight, the withdrawal of corporate permits, (and of corporate charters when necessary), and a restitution of human and natural rights over and above the fictitious rights of corporations.

As Priscilla Dziubek of Detroit said, "Water is life; it should be a higher priority." This doesn't just mean asking the government to do a better job of protecting our water. It means redesigning our communities with water justice as a first priority. Because our water is not merely public, the way a bus line or a highway or even a library is; and it is certainly neither private, nor property. As the Navajo of Black Mesa and the mountain people of Appalachia and the urban folks of Detroit have shown through their deep commitment and the dignity of their struggles, our water is our very home.

"WATER IS LIFE; IT SHOULD BE A HIGHER PRIORITY."

THE
VALUE OF WATER

An Art Exhibition 2011-2012
CATHEDRAL OF ST. JOHN THE DIVINE, NEW YORK CITY

SAMANTHA SCHERER
Floodplains is a series of postcard-sized watercolors depicting
moments captured during recent flood events

ix, 2008
Watercolor on paper, 4" x 6"

xix, 2008
Watercolor on paper, 5" x 7"

xvii, 2008
Watercolor on paper, 4" x 6"

A young woman in Hubei Province in China looks toward the Three Gorges, the world's largest dam.

A Short History of Dams

JACQUES LESLIE

By every standard, China's Three Gorges Dam is monumental.
It is not just the world's largest dam, but by some measures the
world's largest manmade structure, and the reservoir behind
it is the world's largest manmade creation.

The dam does not aspire to elegance; it juts rigidly across a bend in the Yangtze River like a provocation, an advertisement for the use of brute force to subdue nature. It is both a technological astonishment and an ecological debacle.

Yet it was threatening to become an international embarrassment even before it became fully operational in 2008. The dam has already broken records for its width (nearly one and a half miles across), reservoir size (nearly 400 miles long), hydropower capacity (a prodigious 18,200 megawatts), cost (between $25 billion and $40 billion), displaced people (at least 1.6 million), and flooded communities (13 cities, 140 towns, 1,350 villages).

Three Gorges is no anomaly, for dams are the ultimate expression of the majestic, deluded spirit of the fading Industrial Age. They were constructed on a seductive, impossible premise—conquering nature—and for a few generations at least, seemed to live up to expectations. Dam builders oozed with civic pride, and a grateful public regarded dams as beneficent providers of electricity, irrigated water, and flood control. Now, however, the Age of Consequences has arrived, and it is becoming increasingly clear that dams' benefits are temporary, while the damage they inflict on societies and landscapes approaches permanence.

Take the environmental impacts: Though the Three Gorges reservoir has not quite reached its projected full capacity because of drought, the dam is already causing massive damage. First, the reservoir is turning into a cesspool. Hundreds of factories, mines, and waste dumps were inundated as the reservoir filled; now their effluents are combining with untreated sewage that continues to

be dumped into the Yangtze River to create a festering mire. Polluted river water surrounds upstream ports, and sewage is backing up into tributaries, causing toxic algae blooms. One city alone, Chongqing, releases almost a billion tons of untreated wastewater into the Three Gorges reservoir each year.

The rising reservoir has also set off landslides in the notoriously unstable cliffs that border it. In March 2007, a group of hydraulic engineers and environmentalists reported that more than 4,700 landslides had already taken place and warned that their continuing threat requires preventive actions or evacuation of an additional 1,000 localities. Eight months later, the government acknowledged that it must relocate as many as two million or more people threatened by landslides. Some of those people will be resettled for the second time as a result of the dam's construction.

The creation of the vast reservoir has even changed the local climate, increasing rainfall and fog and lowering temperatures.

The problems extend all the way down the Yangtze to its mouth and beyond. The Chinese freshwater dolphin has probably gone extinct as a result of the dam's construction, and many other fish species have declined dramatically. Saltwater has moved up the river as the flow of fresh water has declined, and tidal wetlands near the mouth are quickly deteriorating because the naturally silty river brings them less than half the amount of sediment it did before the dam's construction. Within two months after the reservoir began to fill, scientists detected a massive

DAMS ARE THE ULTIMATE EXPRESSION OF THE MAJESTIC,

decline in the plankton that forms the bottom of the food chain in the East China Sea. By one projection, fish catches in the East China Sea, one of the world's biggest fisheries, will decline by a million tons a year as a result.

Compare these adverse consequences against the dam's presumed benefits. China has suffered grievously from floods, most recently in 1998, when a Yangtze flood killed 3,000 people and left 14 million people homeless, and Three Gorges is intended to provide the antidote in the form of flood control. Yet even in this respect it is likely to disappoint, for the reservoir's flood control capacity is only a twentieth of the annual flow of the Yangtze's upper reaches and thus will have little hope of warding off a huge spate.

To maximize the dam's flood control potential, officials would have to keep the reservoir's water level low during the flood season, which would cut into hydropower production, the dam's other major benefit. At its peak, Three Gorges will meet nearly a ninth of China's electricity needs, but its production will gradually decline as the reservoir fills with sediment.

No matter what, Three Gorges' impact will be vast. And the same is true for dams across the globe. The world's biggest manmade structures, they exist on more than 60 percent of the world's 200-plus major river systems, and their reservoirs collectively blot out a terrain larger than California. They have shifted so much weight that geophysicists believe they've slightly altered the speed of the earth's rotation, the tilt of its axis, and the shape of its gravitational field.

Dams are so plentiful that merely counting them accurately has proved impossible. It is believed that the world possesses between 50,000 and 54,000 large dams, but even the higher figure may underestimate China's contribution, currently pegged at the already-astounding number of 22,000. For smaller dams, the numbers descend into guesswork. In the United States, an inventory managed by the Army Corps of Engineers places the total of significant dams at 79,777, while the sum of dams compiled by individual states—with varying criteria for included dams, ranging in height minimums from 20 to 35 feet—amounts to more than 99,000.

From the inception of the modern dam era, ushered in by Hoover Dam in 1935, advocates viewed dams as passkeys to the modern world. Energy from Hoover, Grand Coulee, and other early hydroelectric dams transformed the American West, enabling the growth of such cities as Los Angeles, San Diego, and Phoenix, and facilitating the Allied victory in World War II by powering the factories that built American warplanes and ships. Even now, dams' turbines generate a fifth of the world's electricity supply, and the water they store makes possible as much as a sixth of the earth's food production.

It took decades before the realization set in that this bounty was accompanied by a vast array of unintended consequences. Only then did the wisdom of environmentalist Aldo Leopold, writing presciently in 1933, gain trac-

DELUDED SPIRIT OF THE FADING INDUSTRIAL AGE.

Yosemite's Hetch Hetchy Valley before and after dam construction. *Left*, Painting by Albert Bierstadt, mid 19th century; *middle*, panorama 21st century; and *right*, O'Shaughnessy Dam, 2006.

tion: "We build storage reservoirs or power dams to store water, and mortgage our irrigated valleys and our industries to pay for them, but every year they store a little less water and a little more mud. Reclamation, which should be for all time, thus becomes in part the source of a merely temporary prosperity."

The prosperity has long been evident, but so, increasingly, is its transience, for dams have lifetimes as surely as any natural thing. On average, the sediment trapped in reservoirs reduces their storage capacity by 1 percent a year, and has filled more than half the capacity of some reservoirs within a decade. In China, where most soil erodes easily, the reservoirs fill up at a rate of 2.3 percent a year. One dam on the silty Yellow River, the Yangouxia, lost almost a third of its storage capacity even before it began operating.

The breadth of damage that dams inflict is stunning. A study of a single dam in the tiny southern African country of Lesotho identified 20,000 environmental consequences as a result of altering its river's flow. Dams fragment the riverine ecosystem, isolating upstream and downstream animal populations, and, by preventing all but the largest floods, cut off the river from its floodplain. As a result, animals victimized by dams include not just the river's native fish, but a broad range that relies on a watered floodplain as far from the river as several miles.

Reservoirs change river temperatures dramatically. Deep reservoir water is usually colder in summer and warmer in winter than river water, while surface reservoir water is warmer throughout the year. For 240 miles below Glen Canyon Dam on the Colorado, the water is too cold for native fish to reproduce.

A reservoir traps not just sediment but nutrients. Algae thrive on the nutrients, and end up consuming the reservoir's oxygen. The water turns acidic, which makes it more erosive. It emerges from the dam "hungry," more energetic after shedding its sediment load, ready to capture new sediment from the riverbed and bank. As it scours the downstream river, the bed deepens, losing its gravel habitats for spawning fish and the tiny invertebrates they feed on.

"A dammed river," Wallace Stegner wrote, "is not only stoppered like a bathtub, but it is turned on and off like a tap." Instead of varying with snowmelt and rainfall, its flow is regulated to meet the requirements of power generation and human recreation. Most fluctuations reflect electricity demand: the river level changes hour by hour, and is lower on Sundays and holidays. These quick shifts intensify erosion, eventually washing away riverbank trees, shrubs, and grasses as well as riverine nesting areas. Riverside creatures lose needed food and shelter.

In many areas, water piped from reservoirs slowly poisons the land with salt. Salinity has affected a fifth of the world's agricultural land; each year it forces farmers to abandon a million hectares and becomes a factor on an additional 2 million hectares. Even using high-quality water,

The Flaming Gorge Dam near Dutch John, Utah rises 502 feet high and impounds the Green River, forming a reservoir that stretches 91 miles.

Untitled, Flaming Gorge,
near Dutch John, UT, 2007,
39 x 55 inch.

Downstream impacts
disrupts water and sediment flow; reduces biodiversity; causes suffering in communities from poor water quality, lower crop production and decreased fish populations.

Dam
blocks fish migration; disrupts water and sediment flow; poses safety hazard as structures age.

Reservoir
displaces communities; floods and fragments ecosystems; increases water-born diseases; triggers earthquakes.

Rotting Vegetation
releases greenhouse gases contributing to global warming; degrades water quality.

a farmer applying the unremarkable sum of 10,000 tons of water a year to a single hectare strews two to five tons of salt across that plot. It's precisely the process by which ancient Mesopotamia turned into the barren desert of contemporary southern Iraq. Salt problems are severe in China, India, Pakistan, Central Asia, the Colorado River basin, and California's San Joaquin Valley.

The changes in the water's composition are registered all the way to the river's mouth and beyond. Without its customary allotment of sediment, the coastline is subject to erosion. By one estimate, dams have reduced by four-fifths the sediment reaching the Southern California coast, causing once wide beaches to disappear and cliffs to fall into the ocean.

Estuaries, where riverine fresh water mixes with ocean salt water, are crucial in the development of plankton, which support a huge abundance of marine life. Deprived of large portions of fresh water and nutrients, the estuaries decline, and with them the fisheries.

Migrating fish such as salmon and steelhead trout find their paths obstructed, both as juveniles swimming downstream to mature and as adults going upstream to spawn. For this reason, the Columbia River, where 2 million fish returned annually to spawn just before the dam era began, hosted half that number at the turn of the 21st century. Now most remaining stocks in the upper Columbia are in danger of extinction. Only by multiplying all these effects by the number of the world's river basins studded with dams can their full environmental impact be appreciated.

Who Benefits?
The most obvious beneficiaries of dams are politicians, bureaucrats, and builders, all of whom reap benefit from the dams' huge price tags. Think of the towering political leaders of the 20th century—Roosevelt, Stalin, Mao, Nehru. They all loved dams. Dams provide jobs and generous portions of money to constituents, some of whom don't mind donating a portion back to the politicians. Bureaucrats like dams because that's where the action is: the expense of dams ensures power to its overseers. The constituents include dam builders, road builders, engineers, electricians, carpenters, cooks, plus every sort of professional that boomtowns attract, from developers to prostitutes.

Dams' attraction to farmers is obvious. Supported by funding from central governments and international agencies, farmers rarely pay more than 20 percent of the real cost of irrigated water. The subsidies distort the farmers' economic outlook: instead of planting crops that match the hydrology of their fields, they take advantage of abundant cheap water to plant crops that guzzle water, even if the crops bring a low return.

Who Loses?
The biggest losers are people displaced by dams. They're usually minorities, often uneducated and powerless, and

therefore hard to count or sometimes even notice, particularly by a government's ruling elite.

In India, 40 percent of people displaced by dams are tribal people, who represent only 6 percent of the country's population. Generations of indigenous people often have inhabited the same land, which is desirable to them precisely because a river runs through it. If the government bothers to relocate them, it's usually to inferior land, where they're resented by settled residents. Rates of illness and death usually increase after relocation.

The World Commission on Dams, which conducted the most thorough study ever done of dams' social and environmental impacts, concluded in November 2000 that dams have displaced between 40 million and 80 million people. As startling as that sum is, it omits a larger group, the floodplain residents living downstream from dams whose livelihoods are jeopardized by the sudden loss of fish, plants, herbs, or nutrient-bearing floods that enrich their fields—their number is in the low hundreds of millions.

On top of all this, dams are dangerous. The weight of reservoir water often triggers earthquakes—the most powerful one, a magnitude 6.3 tremor in western India in 1967, killed about 180 people, injured 1,500, and leveled a village, leaving thousands of inhabitants homeless.

Occasionally, too, dams fall down—Chinese dams are notorious for collapsing. Thousands were built with little or no engineering expertise in mass campaigns during the Great Leap Forward and Cultural Revolution, and became known for their "bean curd construction." Chinese anti-dam activists have reported that by 1981, some 3,200 dams—3.7 percent of all Chinese dams—collapsed.

The most lethal episode occurred in August 1975, when

Mehta Patkar, Fighting Big Dams

MEHTA PAKTAR, ONE OF INDIA'S MOST renowned social activists, spent decades spearheading Narmada Bachao Andolan (Save the Narmada Movement), an organization fighting for the rights of indigenous people struggling to save their communities and their livelihoods from the creation of large dams on India's Narmada River. Her work has expanded to form the National Alliance of People's Movements, which seeks an alternative to globalization. Patkar has organized massive rallies and hunger strikes, and endured jail time and police brutality. Her work has earned her the Right Livelihood Award and a Goldman Environmental Prize, as well as a commissioner appointment on the World Commission on Dams.

a typhoon triggered the failure of as many as 62 dams in Henan, inundating a vast swath of densely populated villages for up to two weeks. Chinese authorities successfully suppressed news coverage of the catastrophe until two decades later, when the New York–based Human Rights Watch published an account. It estimated that 85,000 people were drowned, and another 145,000 people died in the ensuing famine and epidemics.

But dam collapses are not just a Chinese phenomenon. In 1963, accelerating seismic activity that was probably caused by the filling of the reservoir behind what was then the world's fourth-highest dam, the 856-feet-tall Vaiont in the Italian Alps, unloosed a huge landslide into the reservoir. That produced a monstrous wave that towered over the dam by 360 feet and reached the downstream town of Langarone in two minutes, drowning 2,600 people.

Dams' massiveness and lethality make them tempting military targets, a prospect that has grown more foreboding in an era of skyscraper assaults and suicide bombings. Yet in the world's most bomb-plagued country, Iraq, explosives may not even be necessary to bring down the nation's biggest dam, called the Mosul. The U.S. Army Corps of Engineers labeled it "the most dangerous dam in the world" in September 2006.

The United States has its own dam safety problems. In 2009, the American Society of Civil Engineers awarded the United States' dam infrastructure a "D," a grade that is still justified a year later. For starters, the nation's dam stock is rapidly aging. Most dams need major repairs between 25 and 50 years after they're built, and the average U.S. dam is more than 51 years old; some were built more than a century ago. As dams age, their danger increases. This is not just a matter of advancing decrepitude, but "hazard creep"— the tendency of developers to build directly downstream from dams, in the path of floods that would follow dam failures. The result is that even though Americans now build few dams, more and more dams threaten humans with loss of life.

Chiefly for this reason, the number of U.S. dams iden-tified in one estimate as capable of causing death and needing rehabilitation more than doubled between 1999 and 2006, from more than 500 to nearly 1,400. The civil engineers' report placed the number of unsafe dams much higher, at more than 4,000.

Unlike, say, waterways and sanitation facilities, a majority of dams—about 56 percent of inventoried dams in the United States—are privately owned, which is one reason dams are among the country's most dangerous pieces of infrastructure. Many private owners can't afford the cost of repairing aging dams; some owners go so far as to resist paying by tying up official repair demands in court or, in one instance, by campaigning to weaken state dam safety laws.

Climate change will make dams more dangerous, as increases in precipitation volume undermine the flood assumptions that underlie dam designs. Consider that in October 2005 and May 2006, two strong but hardly cataclysmic New England rainstorms caused the overtopping or breaching of more than 400 dams in three states; a much fiercer storm would compromise far more dams, exacerbating flooding and potentially endangering thousands of people.

Who Foots the Bill?
The many controversies dams have generated have reduced the World Bank, once the world's leading dam financier, to a virtual bystander in international dam construction. At the peak of its efforts, from 1970 to 1985, it supported an average of 26 dams a year. But as awareness of dam's social and environmental impacts grew, resistance to the projects spread, to such an extent that the bank supported only four dams a year over the following decade.

Midway through the 1990s, choking on its frustration, the bank reluctantly embraced a proposal by dam opponents to create an independent commission that would assess dams' performance and set down rules for future construction. The bank hoped that if anti-dam groups were represented on the commission, they would have no grounds for protest after agreeing to reasonable rules for

Inhabitants of Wushan, Chongqing are among the millions who have been displaced by dam construction in China.

AMERICAN SOCIETY OF CIVIL ENGINEERS AWARDED THE UNITED STATES' DAM INFRASTRUCTURE A "D" GRADE.

building dams. The bank made one provision— that the commission assess not just the bank's dams but all large dams—in an apparent attempt to divert attention from the bank's many problem-ridden dams.

The bank then joined forces with the World Conservation Union (IUCN), a Geneva-based quasi-official nonprofit, to create what became known as the World Commission on Dams. To ensure balance, its 12 commissioners were drawn equally from three categories —"pro-dam," "mixed," and "anti-dam."

Dam stakeholders were skeptical that such a diverse group could reach consensus, but as time went on, the commissioners developed rapport, and found a way to work toward a common objective. As late as September 1999, 14 months before the commission issued its final report, World Bank senior water adviser John Briscoe lauded its "absolutely extraordinary process" and declared, "We have every confidence" that it will deliver "very good advice." Bank officials even spoke confidently of using the World Commission on Dams' approach to launch another commission on oil, gas, and mining.

As it turned out, the commission's advice was notably sharp-edged. It said large dams showed a "marked tendency" toward schedule delays and cost overrun; that irrigation dams typically produced neither the expected volume of water nor recovered their costs; that environmental impacts were "more negative than positive" and in many cases "led to irreversible loss of species and ecosystems"; and that their construction had "led to the impoverishment and suffering of millions."

The commission even challenged the conventional assumption that dams provide "clean" energy; on the contrary, it said, dam reservoirs, particularly shallow tropical ones, emit greenhouse gases released by vegetation rotting in reservoirs and carbon inflows from watersheds. In hopes of heading off future tragedies before they occur, the commission listed 26 recommendations to guide future dam construction. Some, such as examining cheaper and less destructive options before deciding on a dam,

PHOTOGRAPH BY PIERRE MONTAVON/STRATES/PANOS

THE ALTERNATIVE TO DAMS

The World Commission on Dams found major problems with water-supply and irrigation dams. Seventy percent of water-supply dams did not meet their targets, and half of large-scale irrigation projects underperformed. The WCD report included numerous suggestions for alternatives to dams for water supply, including the following:

Irrigation & Agriculture Sector

● Improve performance and productivity of existing systems

● Use alternative supply-side measures that incorporate rain-fed, local, small-scale, and traditional water management and harvesting systems, including groundwater recharge methods

Source: World Commission on Dams

Water Supply Sector

● Revitalize existing sources

● Introduce appropriate pricing strategies

● Encourage fair and sustainable water marketing and tranfers, recycling, and reuse

● Employ local strategies such as rainwater harvesting

Above, A Living Machine® at Guilford County schools in North Carolina uses a series of wetland installations to naturally cleanse the school's wastewater. That water then goes right back into use irrigating three athletic fields and re-charging their aquifer.

were commonsensical, while others, such as obtaining the consent of affected indigenous people, were matters of social justice.

The bank responded by turning its back on its own creation, taking 13 months to issue a response rejecting the commission's recommendations, and instead touting the far less restrictive policies it already had in place.

But if the bank expected that it would resume its central role in dam building, it was mistaken. On the one hand, the World Commission on Dams report has not suffered the fate of most commission reports, fading quickly into oblivion. A decade since its unveiling, few institutions have embraced all the report's recommendations, but it has become a standard, a compilation of best practices against which less rigorous approaches are measured. Unheeded but not forgotten, it hovers over dam projects as an admonition to dam builders in the name of human decency and environmental sanity.

At the same time, China's government-owned Exim Bank has supplanted the World Bank as the world's leading financier of international dams. For the world's remaining undammed rivers, this is a foreboding development. Whereas the World Bank adhered to modest social and environmental standards, Chinese projects embrace no standards at all. China's dam projects seem straightforwardly designed to provide a form of recompense for the natural resources that China imports from the host countries. In addition, some of the projects provide hydropower for Chinese overseas investments in mines, factories, and oil exploration.

International Rivers, a Berkeley, California-based nonprofit that monitors trends in dam construction, has counted 47 recent dam projects in Africa and Asia with Chinese involvement, and more are planned. Many have provided support for outcast regimes in such countries as Burma and Sudan.

PHOTOGRAPH BY WORRELL WATER TECHNOLOGIES

INVESTING IN REPAIRS IS LESS GLAMOROUS THAN DAM BUILDING, BUT IT IS FAR MORE COST-EFFECTIVE.

What's the Alternative?

Most of the desirable alternatives to dams involve cheaper, lower-tech, decentralized approaches that respect natural processes instead of trying to conquer them. The cheapest may be the most widely overlooked: conservation.

To a degree, water conservation can be achieved with honest pricing, for if, say, California farmers were charged the true delivery cost of the water that irrigates their fields, they'd quickly stop growing water-guzzling crops. Instead, Arnold Schwarzenegger, the self-proclaimed environmentalist governor, has proposed the construction of two new dams to meet water demand in coming decades, and a coalition of California leaders is promoting bonds to finance them. Yet according to a study by the respected Pacific Institute, California could meet water demand through 2025 while cutting water use by 20 percent simply by adopting sensible conservation measures; among them replacing lawns with low-water gardens and requiring home appliances to meet water-efficiency standards.

Throughout the world, municipal water systems are notorious for poor maintenance; in the world's largest cities, water lost to leaks ranges from 40 to 60 percent. Investing in repairs is less glamorous than dam building, but it is far more cost-effective. Even without price reforms, agriculture, which uses 70 percent of water devoted to human uses worldwide, is a fertile realm for conservation; for instance, the replacement of flood irrigation by drip systems can double water efficiency.

As water has grown scarce, many cultures have been surprised to discover the benefits of reviving traditional water harvesting techniques. In the Indian state of Rajasthan, the building of communal ponds has recharged depleted aquifers and revived dried-up streams; in the Middle East, officials are discovering that ancient self-regulating aqueducts called *qanats* can be reliable sources of water.

In the energy sector, conservation also makes sense—by one estimate, it could cut U.S. consumption by as much as 50 percent, reducing the need for reliance on hydropower.

In addition, in some countries, electricity lost between power stations and customers' meters amounts to 40 percent or higher. Where conservation and effective maintenance don't deliver sufficient savings, new energy technologies—including solar, wind, wave and tidal, geothermal, and fuel cells—all show potential and would benefit from more investment in research.

Alternate technologies are a key to one of the most promising dam-related developments in the world; the likely demolition of four dams on the Klamath River, which flows from South-central Oregon to the northern California coast. Less than a decade ago, the Klamath was considered the country's most contentious basin, as farmers and ranchers faced off against native tribes and commercial fishermen over the river's oversubscribed and algae-ridden water, while the population of salmon and other native fish plummeted.

After years of simmering animosity, the groups agreed in 2005 to try to negotiate a settlement, and emerged five years later with a comprehensive deal supported by most of the basin's major stakeholders, including PacifiCorp, the utility that owns the dams. Under the agreement, a limited amount of river water would be guaranteed to the farmers and ranchers while the river receives enough water for salmon restoration. The dams would not be dismantled until 2020, providing the utility another decade of revenue that would help defray the cost of removal. Two of the dams would be the tallest dams taken down anywhere in the world. If the agreement passes its last hurdles, including passage of federal legislation and a California bond measure, the Klamath's reputation for strife may be turned on its head, as the basin becomes known as a dam removal pioneer.

It's an indication of how far we've been misled by dams' transient promises that compared with the Yangtze and its monumental Three Gorges, the Klamath River and its four obsolescent dams are far more likely to show the way to a livable future.

SAVING OUR MOST CRITICAL RESOURCE

Making Water a Human Right

MAUDE BARLOW

The global water justice movement has been demanding a change in international law to settle once and for all the question of who controls water. Great progress has been made. It must be commonly understood that water is not a commercial good,

although of course it has an economic dimension, but rather a human right and a public trust. It is imperative to have a binding law to codify that states have the obligation to deliver sufficient, safe, accessible, and affordable water to their citizens as a public service. While "water for all, everywhere, and always" may appear to be self-evident, the fact is that the powers moving in to take corporate control of water have resisted this notion fiercely. So have many governments, either because, in the case of rich governments, their corporations benefit from the commodification of water, or in the case of poor governments, because they fear they would not be able to honor this commitment.

Groups around the world have been mobilizing in their communities and countries for constitutional recognition of the right to water within their borders and at the United Nations for a full treaty that recognizes the right to water internationally. (The terms covenant, treaty, and convention are used interchangeably at the U.N.)

Rosmarie Bar of Switzerland's Alliance Sud explains that behind the call for a binding convention are questions of principle. Is access to water a human right or just a need? Is water a common good like air or a commodity like Coca-Cola? Who is being given the right or the power to turn the tap on or off—people, governments or the invisible hand of the market? Who sets the price for a poor

district in Manila or La Paz—the locally elected water board or the CEO of Suez? The global water crisis cries out for good governance, says Bar, and good governance needs binding, legal bases that rest on universally applicable human rights. A U.N. covenant would set the framework for water as a social and cultural asset, not an economic commodity. As well, it would establish the indispensable legal groundwork for a just system of distribution. It would serve as a common, coherent body of rules for all nations, rich and poor, and clarify that it is the role of the state to provide clean, affordable water to all of its citizens. Such a covenant would also safeguard already accepted human rights and environmental principles in other treaties and conventions.

Michigan lawyer Jim Olson, who has been deeply involved in the fight against Nestlé, says the point must be "repeated and repeated" that privatization of water is simply incompatible with the nature of water as a commons, and therefore, with fundamental human rights. "Water is always moving unless there is human intervention. Intervention is the right to use, not own and privatize to the exclusion of others who enjoy equal access to use water. It is important to distinguish between sovereign ownership and control of water, enjoyed by states or nations through which water flows or moves, and private ownership. Sovereign state ownership is not the same and has to do with control and use of water for the public welfare, health and safety, not for private profit."

If on the other hand, says Olson, the state sides with the World Bank and negotiates private rights to its water with corporations, that state has violated the rights of its citizens, who would have redress under the principle of human rights if the covenant is well crafted.

A human rights convention or covenant imposes three obligations on states: the Obligation to Respect, whereby the state must refrain from any action or policy that interferes with the enjoyment of the human right; the Obligation to Protect, whereby the state is obliged to prevent third parties from interfering with the enjoyment of the human right; and the Obligation to Fulfill, whereby the state is required to adopt any additional measures directed toward the realization of that right. The Obligation to Protect would oblige governments to adopt measures restraining corporations from denying equal access to water (in

itself an incentive for water companies to leave) as well as polluting water sources or unsustainably extracting water resources.

At a practical level, a right-to-water covenant would give citizens a tool to hold their governments accountable in their domestic courts and the court of public opinion, and for seeking international redress. Says the World Conservation Union, "Human rights are formulated in terms of individuals, not in terms of rights and obligations of states vis-à-vis other states as international law provisions generally do. Thus by making water a human right, it could not be taken away from the people. Through a rights-based approach, victims of water pollution and people deprived of necessary water for meeting their basic needs are pro-

IT MUST BE COMMONLY UNDERSTOOD THAT WATER IS NOT A COMMERCIAL GOOD.

vided with access to remedies. In contrast to other systems of international law, the human rights system affords access to individuals and NGOs."

The union also states that a right-to-water covenant would make both state obligations and violations more visible to citizens. Within a year of ratification, states would be expected to put in place a plan of action, with targets, policies, indicators, and time frames to achieve the realization of this right. As well, states would have to amend domestic law to comply with the new rights. In some cases, this will include constitutional amendments. Some form of monitoring of the new rights would also be established and the needs of marginalized groups such as women and indigenous peoples would be particularly addressed.

A covenant would also include specific principles to ensure civil society involvement to convert the U.N. convention into national law and national action plans. This would give citizens an additional constitutional tool in their fight for water. As stated in a 2003 manifesto on the right to water by Friends of the Earth Paraguay, "An inseparable part of the right is control and sovereignty of local communities over their natural heritage and therefore over the management of their sources of water and over the use of the territories producing this water, the watersheds, and aquifer recharge areas."

A right-to-water covenant would also set principles and priorities for water use in a world destroying its water heritage. The covenant we envisage would include language to protect water rights for the Earth and other species, and would address the urgent need for reclamation of polluted waters and an end to practices that destroy the world's water sources. As Friends of the Earth Paraguay put it, "The very mention of this supposed conflict, water for human use versus water for nature, reflects a lack of consciousness of the essential fact that the very existence of water depends on the sustainable management and conservation of ecosystems."

Success at the United Nations

Water was not included in the 1947 United Nations Universal Declaration of Human Rights because at that time water was not perceived to have a human rights dimension. The fact that water has not been an enforceable human right has allowed decision-making over water policy to shift from the U.N. and governments toward institutions and organizations that favor the private water companies and the commodification of water such as the World Bank, the World Water Council, and the World Trade Organization.

However, for more than a decade, calls have been made at various levels of the United Nations for a right-to-water convention and finally that call has been heard. Civil society groups argued that because the operations of the water companies had gone global and were being backed by global financial institutions, nation-state instruments to deal with water rights were no longer sufficient to protect citizens. International laws were needed, we argued, to control the global reach of the water barons. We also noted that at the 1990 Rio Earth Summit, the key areas of water, climate change, biodiversity, and desertification were all targeted for action.

This lobbying started to pay off and the right to water was recognized in a number of important international U.N. resolutions and declarations. These include the 2000 General Assembly Resolution on the Right to Development, the 2004 Committee on Human Rights resolution on toxic wastes, and the May 2005 statement by the 116-member Non-Aligned Movement on the right to water for all. Most important is General Comment Number 15, adopted in 2002 by the U.N. Committee on Economic, Social, and Cultural Rights, which recognized that the right to water is

Everybody needs water as much as they need air or food. So what happens when a corporation steps in and turns public water into private profit? It can spell disaster in a poor community or a place where clean water is scarce. Ten years ago, Bolivians made headlines when protests by Cochabamba's people overturned a private water contract that made water rates catastrophically expensive. Since then, people around the world have

1) Uruguay Bans Privatization

Since 2004, water activists around the world have celebrated "Blue October," marking a citizen-led movement that succeeded in reforming the Uruguayan constitution to ban water privatization.

In 2000, the Uruguayan government signed an agreement with the International Monetary Fund to privatize the nation's water and sanitation systems. A broad coalition of environmental organizations, trade unions, artists, community activists, politicians, and progressive academics formed to fight the agreement. The coalition led a four-year campaign to change the Uruguayan constitution to recognize public water as a human right and ban the privatization of water services. The coalition's petition drive gathered the signatures of 10 percent of the population and put the measure on the ballot. In October 2004, the constitutional measure passed with 60 percent of the vote, and the water system returned to public ownership.

2) Kerala Shuts Down Coke Plant

Plummeting groundwater levels and growing pollution caused by a large Coca-Cola plant in Plachimada, a village in a remote part of Kerala, India, led to crop failure and illness. In 2002, the women of Plachimada began a vigil in front of the plant gates. For over four years they maintained a constant presence there to fight one of the most powerful companies on the planet.

As a result of their dedicated activism, the state government forced the factory to close in 2004 and two years later imposed a broader statewide ban on the use of groundwater in soft-drink production. The government of Kerala is now seeking compensation for the community's agricultural and health losses. Coke denies any responsibility for pollution or overuse, and continues to pursue reopening the plant.

been fighting to keep water public. From Canadian towns banning wasteful bottled water to cities across France reclaiming privatized water systems, there's a growing global movement of citizens taking back their water. Here are some key wins.

3) Soweto Activists Take Prepaid Water Meters to Court

Soweto was the center of resistance to South Africa's apartheid regime. Apartheid is gone, but for ordinary Sowetans, the daily struggle continues, this time over water. The South African government's push for water privatization includes installation of prepaid water meters—which make water unavailable to the neediest people and are a documented factor in cholera outbreaks.

The Phiri 5, a group of Sowetan activists, took the government to court, claiming that their rights had been violated when prepaid water meters were forced upon only the poorest citizens. The Johannesburg High Court ruled in their favor in April 2008, but that decision was overturned on appeal in October 2009. Nonetheless, the courage of these five Sowetans has raised awareness worldwide of the dangers of prepaid water meters.

These are no longer isolated acts of resistance. For more than a decade, a global water justice movement has played an active role in creating international support for local struggles. By sharing stories through the Internet, the traditional media, and global conferences, water justice activists strengthen grassroots campaigns by connecting them to a global water struggle. People around the world are taking inspiration from these and many other examples of the power citizens wield when they act together to protect the right to water and preserve water as a commons.

– *Maude Barlow, Anil Naidoo,*
and Meera Karunananthan

Source: *Yes!* Magazine

FACT In 2010 the U.N. passed a resolution
on the right to drinking water;
122 countries voted in favor of it
and 41 abstained, including the U.S.,
Canada, Australia, and the U.K.

a prerequisite for realizing all other human rights and "indispensable for leading a life in dignity." (A General Comment is an authoritative interpretation of a human rights treaty or convention by an independent committee of experts that has a mandate to provide states with an interpretation of the treaty or convention. In this case, the interpretation applies to the International Covenant on Economic, Social, and Cultural Rights.) General Comment Number 15 is therefore an authoritative interpretation that water is a right and an important milestone on the road to a full binding U.N. convention.

But as John Scanlon, Angela Cassar, and Noemi Nemes of the World Conservation Union point out in their 2004 legal briefing paper "Water as a Human Right," General Comment Number 15 is an interpretation, not a binding treaty or convention. To clearly bind the right to water in international law, a binding covenant is needed. So the pressure for a full covenant intensified. In early 2004, Danuta Sacher of Germany's Bread for the World and Ashfaq Khalfan of the Right to Water program at the U.N. Center on Housing Rights and Evictions called a summit, and a new international network called Friends of the Right to Water was born. The network set out to mobilize other water justice groups and national governments to join the campaign to strengthen the rights established in General Comment Number 15 and put in place the mechanisms to ensure implementation of the right to water through a covenant.

In November 2006, responding to a call from several countries, the newly formed U.N. Human Rights Council requested the Office of the High Commissioner for Human Rights to conduct a detailed study on the scope and content of the relevant human rights obligations related to access to water under international human rights instruments, and to include recommendations for future action. While the request does not specifically refer to a covenant, many see this process as having the potential to lead to one. In April 2007, Anil Naidoo of the Council of Canadians' Blue Planet Project, another founding member of Friends

of the Right to Water, organized to present a letter of endorsement calling for a right-to-water covenant to U.N. Commissioner Madam Louise Arbour, signed by 176 groups from all over the world.

All this hard work paid off when, on July 28, 2010 the United Nations General Assembly voted overwhelmingly, for the first time, to adopt a resolution recognizing the human right to drinking water and sanitation. One hundred and twenty-two countries voted in favor of the resolution, none opposed, and 41 abstained. The General Assembly also voted to call for member states to provide financial resources and technology to help realize this right in poorer countries.

This was an incredible feat because the growing demand for water has rendered it a potentially valuable global commodity, and a strong set of adversaries came together to oppose any language of rights at the U.N. These forces included the World Bank, which was promoting a program of water privatization in the developing world; the big water utility companies benefiting from this program; and the aid agencies of some big northern countries whose governments had bought into a market model of development. Canada led the opposition to any progress on the right to water at the U.N., even weakening the mandate of the independent expert appointed by the Human Rights Council two years ago to study and report on the situation.

Fed up with the delay and obfuscation, a number of countries from the global South (led by Bolivia, whose glaciers are melting due to climate change) decided to put a clear up or down vote to the General Assembly and force every country in the world to say where it stands on this most basic of rights. To its shame, Canada was one of the countries, along with the United States, Britain, Australia, and New Zealand, that led the opposition to the resolution. Some tried to get the sponsoring countries to dilute the

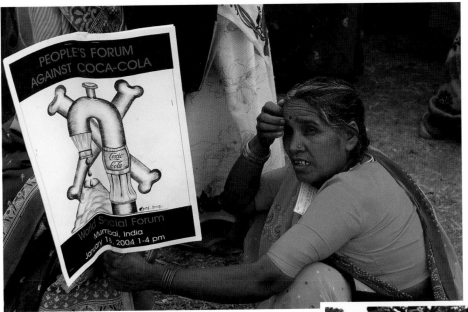

Top, A woman protests at the World Social Forum in Mumbai, India in 2004 against Coca-Cola's use of groundwater for bottling; *middle*, employees of the water district in Davao City, Philippines say no to efforts that will lead to water privatization; and *bottom*, dirty water is thrown in a U.K. action against the use of the country's aid budget to privatize water in African nations.

resolution by removing sanitation or adding the words "access to" water and sanitation, which would have meant that governments only had to provide access to these services, not the services themselves, to those without means. Others, including Canada, proposed a "consensus" resolution that would have just restated the status quo and the need to wait for the report of the independent expert. When it was clear they could not get the support for their alternatives, the big five simply abstained.

This vote marked a historic landmark in the fight for water justice in several ways. Countries representing 5.4 billion people—the vast majority of the population on Earth—voted in favor of the human right to water and sanitation. The language of the resolution itself set the gold standard for all future deliberations on the right to water. While a resolution is not binding, it does nevertheless demonstrate the intent of the General Assembly, and when the time comes for a more binding declaration or convention, the clear and unequivocal wording of this resolution will serve as the template.

Finally, it was important because there was a clear split in the powerful countries of the global North. Many broke with the naysayers and voted for the resolution, including Germany, Spain, and France. Most emerging powerhouse countries, including China, India, Russia and Brazil, also voted in favor. This demonstrates a global shift in influence away from the once-dominant Anglo powers and their model of development.

When Pablo Solon, Bolivian ambassador to the UN, stood up to introduce the resolution, he referred to a new report on diarrhea showing that every 3.5 seconds, a child dies in the global South from dirty water. Then he held up his fingers and counted—1, 2, 3. As he paused, the great hall went dead quiet. Then, the General Assembly voted.

Grassroots Take the Lead

Clearly, the stage has been set for another form of contest. Having been successful in forcing the United Nations to deal with the right to water, the global water justice movement must now work hard to make sure it is the right kind of instrument.

Many are working hard within their countries to assert the right to water for all through domestic legislative changes. On October 31, 2004, the citizens of Uruguay became the first in the world to vote for the right to water. Led by Adriana Marquisio and Maria Selva Ortiz of the National Commission for the Defence of Water and Life, and Alberto Villarreal of Friends of the Earth Uruguay, the groups first had to obtain almost 300,000 signatures on a plebiscite (which they delivered to Parliament as a "human river"), in order to get a referendum placed on the ballot of the national election, calling for a constitutional amendment on the right to water. They won the vote by an almost two-thirds majority, an extraordinary feat considering the fear-mongering that opponents mounted.

The language of the amendment is very important. Not only is water now a fundamental human right in Uruguay, but also social considerations must now take precedence over economic considerations when the government makes water policy. As well, the constitution now reflects that "the public service of water supply for human consumption will be served exclusively and directly by state legal persons" that is to say, not by corporations.

Several other countries have also passed right-to-water legislation. When apartheid was defeated in South Africa, Nelson Mandela created a new constitution that defined water as a human right. However, the amendment was silent on the issue of delivery and soon after, the World Bank convinced the new government to privatize many of its water services. Several other developing countries such as Ecuador, Ethiopia, and Kenya also have references in their constitutions that describe water as a human right, but they, too, do not specify the need for public delivery. The Belgium Parliament passed a resolution in April 2005 seeking a constitutional amendment to recognize water as a human right, and in September 2006, the French Senate adopted an amendment to its water bill saying that each person has the right to access to clean

RECLAIMING WATER AS A COMMONS FOR THE EARTH AND ALL PEOPLE.

water. But neither country makes reference to delivery.

The only other country besides Uruguay to specify in its constitution that water must be publicly delivered is the Netherlands, which passed a law in 2003 restricting the delivery of drinking water to utilities that are entirely public. But the Netherlands did not affirm the right to water in this amendment. Only the Uruguayan constitutional amendment guarantees both the right to water and the need to deliver it publicly, and is therefore a model for other countries. Suez was forced to leave the country as a direct result of this amendment.

Other exciting initiatives are underway. In August 2006, the Indian Supreme Court ruled that protection of natural lakes and ponds is akin to honoring the right to life—the most fundamental right of all, according to the court. Activists in Nepal are arguing that the right to health guaranteed in the country's constitution must include the right to water. The Coalition in Defense of Public Water in Ecuador is celebrating its victory over the privatization of its water by demanding that the government take the next step and amend the constitution to recognize the right to water. The Coalition Against Water Privatization in South Africa is challenging the practice of water metering on the basis that it violates the human rights of Soweto's citizens. President Evo Morales of Bolivia has called for a "South American convention for human rights and access for all living beings to water" that would reject the market model imposed in trade agreements. At least a dozen countries have reacted positively to this call. Civil society groups are hard at work in many other countries to introduce constitutional amendments similar to that of Uruguay. Ecofondo, a network of 60 groups in Colombia, has launched a plebiscite toward a constitutional amendment similar to the Uruguayan amendment and they have gathered two million signatures. Dozens of groups in Mexico have joined COMDA, the Coalition of Mexican Organizations for the Right to Water, in a national campaign for a Uruguayantype constitutional guarantee to the right to water.

A large network of human rights, development, faith-based, labor, and environmental groups in Canada has formed Canadian Friends of the Right to Water, led by the Blue Planet Project, to get the Canadian government to change its opposition to a U.N. covenant on the right to water. A network in the United States led by Food and Water Watch is calling for both a national water trust to ensure safekeeping of the nation's water assets and a change of government policy on the right to water. Riccardo Petrella has led a movement in Italy to recognize the right to water, which has great support among politicians at every level. Momentum is growing everywhere for a right whose time has come.

This, then, is the task: nothing less than reclaiming water as a commons for the Earth and all people that must be wisely and sustainably shared and managed if we are to survive. This will not happen unless we are prepared to reject the basic tenets of market-based globalization. The current imperatives of competition, unlimited growth, and private ownership when it comes to water must be replaced by new imperatives—those of cooperation, sustainability, and public stewardship. As Bolivia's Evo Morales explained in his October 2006 proposal to the heads of states of South America, "Our goal needs to be to forge a real integration to 'live well.' We say 'live well,' because we do not aspire to live better than others. We do not believe in the line of progress and unlimited development at the cost of others and nature. 'Live well' is to think not only in terms of income per capita but cultural identity, community, harmony between ourselves and with Mother Earth."

There are lessons to be learned from water, nature's gift to humanity, which can teach us how to live in harmony with the earth and in peace with one another. In Africa, they say, "We don't go to water ponds merely to capture water, but because friends and dreams are there to meet us."

Saving Our Water Infrastructure

ELIZABETH ROYTE

After writing a book about bottled and tap water in the United States, I started a blog called "Bad Water," about the different ways that failing infrastructure might effect drinking water quality. I wrote about water mains that ruptured, treatment plants that

couldn't handle their inflow, and fissured water tanks—in short, the various events that trigger boil-water notices and potentially turn tap-water drinkers into dedicated bottled-water buyers.

I knew that the vast majority of Americans have good drinking water, and that most people can drink from their community water supplies without worry. But the systems that deliver water aren't infallible in the best of times, and now, after decades of ignoring our infrastructure, pipes are fracturing with greater frequency. Scared by boil water alerts, many are tempted to give up on tap altogether. But relying on bottled water makes little sense in the long run: it costs too much, and the environmental toll—of pumping water, trucking it to bottling plants, filtering it, delivering bottles to stores, and sending trucks around to collect the empties—is way too high.

My blog was a straightforward exercise in data collection: I wanted to see how often and where these disruptions occur. I learned that pipes break in places that experience sudden temperature swings (no surprise), and that smaller water systems sometimes have more trouble than larger systems, which have more revenue to maintain their assets. Still, that doesn't mean big cities don't suffer. In January 2009, Washington, D.C. saw 112 water main breaks; Warren, Michigan, had 107 in one particularly cold month. Warmer places aren't immune to crackups, either.

A municipal water pipe belonging to Augusta Water Works. The American Society of Civil Engineers gave the country's water infrastructure a grade of D-.

In the summer and fall of 2009, Los Angeles experienced 101 water main breaks after the city imposed outdoor watering restrictions, which caused pressure in the pipes to fluctuate wildly.

Every day, water systems across the country leak more than 7 billion gallons of water—enough to supply more than 70 million people a day. When I discovered that the U.S. has 240,000 watermain breaks a year, and that only one in four leaks reaches the earth's surface, I took my blog off the Internet, overwhelmed by the futility of staying abreast.

Our Aging Infrastructure

Pipes break because they're old—up to 100 years old in some places—and because the earth around them—waterlogged or frozen—shifts. In 2009, the American Society of Civil Engineers gave the nation's drinking water and wastewater infrastructure a grade of D-. Tom Curtis, deputy executive director of the American Water Works Association (AWWA), which represents water utilities, thinks the engineers are being dramatic. "The system isn't collapsing," he says. "But we are at a turning point." He grades our water infrastructure a C.

Either way, it's bad news. Broken or leaky pipes waste water that's been expensively pumped and treated. They lower water pressure, which can allow contaminants, like disease-causing bacteria, fertilizer, pesticides, and sediment—which can block the efficacy of chlorine—from the surrounding area into drinking water. Old pipes can also become tuberculated—clogged with deposits of iron, manganese, or other metals. Tubercles can drastically reduce water pressure—a hazard to firefighting—and, should they break off, compromise water quality.

Population growth, increasing urbanization, and climate change will further strain our water systems. Bigger, more intense storms can rupture pipes, overwhelm treatment plants with sheer volume, and flush pollutants from land surfaces into water. Drought presents another set of problems: Utilities may have to change the depth of their intake pipes when reservoirs drop; they may need to build aeration systems to combat low-oxygen conditions; or if they rely on groundwater, they may have to deepen their wells. In coastal areas, some utilities facing saltwater intrusion—from overpumping or rising sea levels—have been forced to pressurize aquifers with fresh water or to abandon wells entirely.

To repair our drinking water and wastewater infrastructure, let alone respond to climate change and possibly remove low levels of contaminants that are currently unregulated, will cost $335 billion above current spending over the next twenty years, according to the Environmental Protection Agency (EPA). The AWWA puts the bill at $300 billion over thirty years. Using either set of figures, says Curtis, "utilities are already spending about seventy percent of what is needed." Experts agree that finding the extra $10 to $17 billion a year shouldn't be an impossible task—it's only a matter of determining which of several proposed funding mechanisms will get us there. At that point, agreement grinds to a halt.

How to Find the Money

Forty years ago, the majority of water funding came straight from the feds. After passing the Clean Water Act and the Safe Drinking Water Act in the 1970s, Congress made water infrastructure grants to municipalities covering up to 75 percent of a facility's capital costs (the rest of the money came from bonding and ratepayers). In the '80s and '90s, Congress established two State Revolving Fund (SRF) programs that made low-interest loans to utilities—

usually in smaller, rural areas—for wastewater and drinking water infrastructure. But during the Reagan and then Bush administrations, allocations for the revolving funds dwindled.

"Philosophically, they didn't believe in federal funding for local systems," Rebecca West, immediate past president of the Water Environment Federation (WEF), says. "Most communities stepped up and did what they needed." Some raised water rates; some sold or leased their water systems to private companies that promised salvation; and some deferred repairs until grants came through. But in the meantime, more pipes broke and the cost of repairs rose.

Ideas for funding the nation's infrastructure fit into three basic categories: establishing a federal clean-water trust fund; establishing a federal water infrastructure bank; and raising just about everyone's water rates, a strategy known as "full cost pricing." (Most water districts don't charge the full amount for constructing and maintaining systems. In larger cities, this could raise rates by a few dollars a month; systems with fewer ratepayers would end up charging more.) The WEF and the AWWA, which represent and receive funding from private water companies in addition to public suppliers, favor the latter approach, which theoretically provides enough money for utilities to actually do their jobs. The EPA, too, supports full-cost pricing, not the least because it signals water's value and is hoped to encourage conservation.

But raising water rates has a political problem: it makes ratepayers howl, and it dissuades them from re-electing officials who propose such hikes. This, despite the fact that Americans pay among the lowest water rates in the developed world, and far less than they pay for such nonessential services as cable TV and cell phones.

There are, of course, those who truly cannot afford higher water bills, and that category is growing as unemployment rises. But under full-cost pricing, David Zetland, a natural resources economist, says, "No one will be denied water. Every household will get some water for free" or at very lost cost. (Ten dollars a quarter of a year,

An empty pool next to the Salton Sea, a saline lake located below sea level in the desert of Southern California.

say, for 3,000 gallons a month—sufficient for drinking, washing, and bathing.) The next block of water will cost significantly more, and the next block even more. "If you want to fill a swimming pool—what we call lifestyle water—you'll bear the cost of that," Zetland says.

There are other ways to address equity issues, including community, state, or federal assistance programs, government-financed "water stamps," and programs in which customers opt to round up their bills—from $38.40 to $39, say—in order to help those in need.

Others remain wary of full-cost pricing. "It's a great way for private water companies to profit off the back of rate-payers," Mitch Jones, water policy analyst for the consumer group Food and Water Watch, says. "Water is different from other needs, like electricity. You cannot live without it." Jones worries, too, about the practicality of metering all water use, which would be a requisite for full-cost accounting. "It sounds easy, but it could be very intrusive."

Trust Fund or Water Bank?

In 2009, Congressman Earl Blumenauer, D-Oregon, introduced the Water Protection and Reinvestment Act (WPRA), a bipartisan bill that would establish a trust fund for drinking water and sewage treatment projects. The fund would raise $10 billion a year through taxes (levied at the manufacturer level) on water-based beverages, flushable

PHOTOGRAPH BY ROBERT DAWSON

Who has safe water?

% of the population with access to improved drinking water (2000)

- more than 90%
- 76% to 90%
- 51% to 75%
- 1% to 50%
- no data available

Haiti

Mauritania
Burkina Faso
Guinea
Chad
Equatorial Guinea
Angola
Dem. Rep. of Congo

Oman
Eritrea
Ethiopia
Rwanda
Madagascar

Afghanistan

Laos
Cambodia

Papua New Guinea

1.1 billion people do not have access to safe drinking water. That's about a sixth of the world's population.

The average distance that women in Africa and Asia walk to collect water is **3.7 miles** daily. Sometimes the water source is just an open pool, used by animals.

If we do not change our ways, by the year 2025 as much as **two-thirds of the world** will be living with water scarcity or total water deprivation.

Dangers in the U.S.

West Nile encephalitis and West Nile meningitis are forms of severe disease that affect a person's nervous system. The disease is spread by mosquitoes, which breed in water.

This map shows cases of West Nile Virus infection in humans reported by the Centers for Disease Control, 2006.

■ more than 400	■ 201 to 400	■ 101 to 200	■ 11 to 100	■ 1 to 10	☐ no cases

(Idaho: 996 cases, 21 deaths)

There were 4,269 cases with 177 fatalities. 34% of the cases were West Nile meningitis or encephalitis; most of the rest were West Nile Fever, a milder disease.

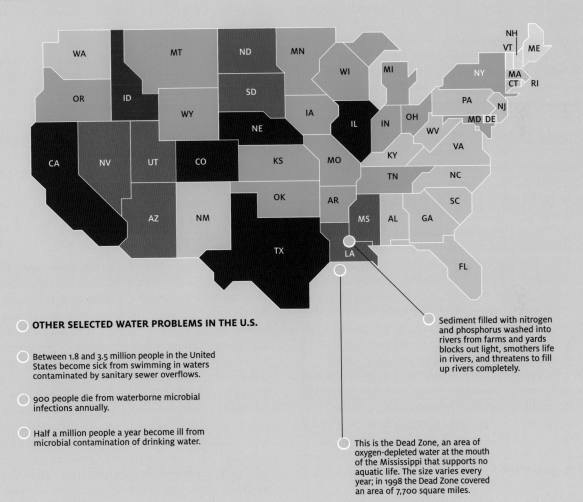

○ **OTHER SELECTED WATER PROBLEMS IN THE U.S.**

○ Between 1.8 and 3.5 million people in the United States become sick from swimming in waters contaminated by sanitary sewer overflows.

○ 900 people die from waterborne microbial infections annually.

○ Half a million people a year become ill from microbial contamination of drinking water.

Sediment filled with nitrogen and phosphorus washed into rivers from farms and yards blocks out light, smothers life in rivers, and threatens to fill up rivers completely.

This is the Dead Zone, an area of oxygen-depleted water at the mouth of the Mississippi that supports no aquatic life. The size varies every year; in 1998 the Dead Zone covered an area of 7,700 square miles.

GRAPHIC BY NIGEL HOLMES

products, pharmaceuticals, and corporate profits. The funds would be distributed as grants and loans through the State Revolving Fund mechanism.

WPRA has the support of many environmental groups, in addition to groups that represent contractors and civil engineers, and a majority of the public (according to a 2005 survey conducted by pollster Frank Luntz, 86 percent of Americans would favor Congressional legislation to create a long-term, sustainable, and reliable trust fund for clean and safe water infrastructure). The bill lacks industry support, unsurprisingly, and Food and Water Watch, which supports the idea of a trust fund, doesn't think Blumenauer's bill goes far enough.

"We think the fund should raise $30-35 billion a year, not $10 billion a year," Jones says. "And we want higher taxes on industries that draw on or dispose of their waste in fresh water."

The Water and Wastewater Equipment Manufacturers Association, the National Association of Water Companies, and AWWA are skeptical of a trust fund. A federal subsidy, they say, wouldn't force individuals to reckon with the true cost of water. Moreover, Curtis warns, "Congress would still have to appropriate the money in the trust to water projects," but it wouldn't have to allocate all of it. What's left over is loaned to the general fund, even if it's in a so-called lockbox. "And that money won't be repaid."

Some proponents of a trust fund see an ulterior motive in such objections: should the federal government provide sufficient funding for water infrastructure, goes this line of thinking, utilities may have a harder time pushing for rate hikes at the local level—rate hikes that will enrich large, private water companies. "AWWA and its members want to preserve the ability to argue that rate hikes are necessary," Jones says.

Another idea would be a national water infrastructure bank, a favored choice for big water groups. Capitalized with $10 billion a year from the Treasury Department, it would make very-low-interest loans to water systems both public and private. The existence of an infrastruc-

ture bank and full-cost pricing wouldn't be mutually exclusive. In fact, the bank may insist that a utility hike rates as a condition of making a loan. "Mayors and city managers tell me in private that if someone could make them raise rates, they'd do it," Curtis says. "The bank gives them that political cover."

An infrastructure bank would loan money for projects too large for State Revolving Funds (above $25 million) and could also be used to leverage SRFs. For example, a community could bring its $10 million SRF loan to the infrastructure bank as a down payment on a $50 million loan. Suddenly, the utility can tackle a much larger project, or fund several smaller projects. Among the groups that support a water infrastructure bank are AWWA, WEF, and the Association of Metropolitan Water Agencies, which have circulated proposals around Congress. So far, no legislator has introduced such a bill.

How to Spend It

Perhaps even more important than where we'll find $355 billion over the next two decades is how that money will be spent. Will we continue to build large-scale, centralized projects that encourage communities to use water once before sending it "away"? Or will we replace outdated pipes and plants with more holistic systems that use nature to retain and clean water? While acknowledging that traditional infrastructure has its place, many environmental groups favor smaller-scale retrofits that include permeable pavement, vegetated swales and roofs to store and filter stormwater, decentralized rainwater harvesting, reforestation, and significantly more water reuse and recycling.

No matter how it's funded, smarter, greener infrastructure will deliver far more than tasty tap water. "We'll see huge economic benefits," Jon Scott of Clean Water Action says. "More jobs, more business growth, more livable communities, better public health and recreational opportunities, higher real-estate values, and more energy savings." Considering these synergies, the investment sounds cheap at any price.

Children play in a fountain during Detroit International River Days, a festival centered on the downtown Riverwalk along the Detroit River.

THE
VALUE OF WATER

An Art Exhibition 2011-2012
CATHEDRAL OF ST. JOHN THE DIVINE, NEW YORK CITY

BILL VIOLA
The Messenger, 1996
Video/sound installation
Color video projected on a larger vertical screen
mounted on wall in darkened space; amplified sound
Screen size: 120 x 126 in (305 x 427 cm)
Photo: Kira Perov

Watershed Literacy

BROCK DOLMAN

Watershed, catchment, drainage, basin, cuenca: by any name they function the same, and everyone on the planet lives in one, sailors on the sea the sole exception. Watersheds at all scales are uniquely geomorphic, hydrological, and biological entities

that provide all members of the community a benchmark for judging the wisdom of our past, present, and future land and water use practices.

At the most basic level, a watershed encompasses all of the land surface that collects and drains water down to a single exit point. The continual cycle of erosive water flowing over uplifting and weathering land has sculpted all landscapes into distinct cradlelike entities known as watersheds. Everything we do for work, play, school, shopping, farming, and recreation occurs in a watershed somewhere.

Watersheds can be as large as the Mississippi basin, the fourth-largest in the world, which drains 41 percent of the lower 48 states into the Gulf of Mexico. Or watersheds can be as small as all the land in your neighborhood that flows from your yard, roof, driveway, and streets to the storm drain and out to your local creek, lake, and eventually the ocean.

If you want to understand what a watershed looks like, bring your hands together and cup them, creating a vessel. Imagine the rim of your hands being a water-parting divide with thumb and fingertips as ridgeline spires. Fingers become the mountain slopes, palms the hills and floodplains. Each wrinkle and crease a watercourse conveying flow to the riparian ecotone of adpressed hands, spilling forth toward the mouth of articulated wrists. We all hold the watershed in our hands, and in turn,

A view from space of the Mississippi River Delta. The Mississippi basin is the the fourth largest watershed in the world.

we are all held by the watershed.

The History of Watershed

The word "watershed" has many different meanings and intentions. In its most literal sense, watershed refers to the parting of waters, the actual ridge dividing drainages. In 1852, Charles Darwin referred to the "Line of Watershed dividing inland streams from those on the coast," the Continental Divide of North America being a primary example. In 1878 Thomas Henry Huxley invoked watershed as a landscape entity or catchment basin, stating it is "all that part of a river basin from which rain is collected, and from which therefore the river is fed." This definition encapsulates the basic physical definition of a watershed in common parlance today.

Our challenge is to move beyond a static, hydrologic definition toward a dynamic understanding of the wholeness of watersheds and how they literally underlie all human endeavors. Watersheds at all scales are evolved, living entities that topographically define community. The health of your watershed depends on collaborative relations between neighbors in your shared basin, so ensuring a healthy "basin of relations" is paramount.

In the world of watershed thinking exists the phrase "We all live downstream," implying a deep sense of interconnection between how the behavior of one person can impact the quality of life for someone downstream.

The exciting art and science behind thinking like a watershed nurtures our hearts and sparks our imaginations. I emphasize heart because as a global society, the quality we most urgently need is an open heart, a humility that allows us to perceive the Earth's watersheds not as human commodities but as living communities.

Watersheds in the Mind

Watershed regeneration rests in the hands and hearts of each one of us: the power to restore ourselves by restoring our relationship to the basin where we live. This challenge before us begs our collective capacity to think like a watershed, striving to understand the wisdom of watershed consciousness.

To begin with, we need to learn to read the place we are in. Ecological illiteracy is the single greatest global epidemic we face as a human species today. Effective watershed regeneration must be based in watershed literacy—a literacy of home, a literacy of place.

How do we bring to bear the scientific and professional capacity to convey this information in a manner that pragmatically supports an increasing proficiency of watershed management at all levels of society? The pedagogy of place-based learning is critically dependent on the clarity of being actually able to describe where you live, work, and recreate.

We need to learn to speak of and teach about place in terms that are inclusive to the idea that we are a part of place and not apart from place. Speak with elders in your community about what the river used to look like after a rainstorm or where there used to be big trees or good fishing and hunting. Make a public map of your watershed and engage the community in adding to it points of historical interest or rare resources or issues of concern and pollution. Interview local farmers or public servants on their memories of place and concerns about the future of your watershed. Take guided walks with native plant or wildlife experts, or simply explore places in your watershed you are drawn to, from the ridgeline down to the river mouth.

In what ways can we support a literal sense of embodiment with our watershed? In many ways the body mirrors our watershed. We can imagine the branching patterns of waterways as a macro expression of the same branching patterns of our lungs, capillaries, and neural pathways. Wetlands provide a similar environmental service for watershed health as our livers and kidneys. Soil and skin are both thin and proportionately cover the most surface area. Like our bodies, the life of the watershed is by volume mostly water—in the soil and vegetation such as in our flesh and living tissues. We are actually walking watersheds.

The Threatened Health of Our Watersheds

Our watersheds today are vastly different than they were just centuries ago. The earliest description of North America by Europeans evokes a vision of snow-capped peaks, forested ridges, wooded slopes, rolling prairies, flood plains, riparian jungles, beaver wetlands, and river mouth estuaries brimming with wildlife. It was an ecstatically pervious world that cleansed and cycled and savored its own water to the benefit of unfathomable biodiversity.

Let us dive into that vision for a moment: Rain falling at 30 mph is slowed and sweetened by outstretched leaves; these in turn drip nutrient-laden tea from the canopy to the forest floor. Infused with humus capable of absorbing 10 times its own weight in water, this protective sponge spreads the life-giving liquid over soil shot through with nutrient-grabbing mycorrhizae, the fungal threads connecting all the rooted plants. These vegetated landscapes of yore seeded and combed the aqueous clouds, rehumidified the downwind air, buffered their own climates, and passed on the surplus to recharge groundwater aquifers that sustained the flow of springs, creeks, and rivers.

Now imagine this hydrological wonderland after some centuries of development based on desiccation: Wholesale clearing of forests and draining of wetlands have hardened rivers and streams, the upland capillaries and aquatic arteries of the landscape. Clear-cut logging, mining, overgrazing, plow agriculture, housing, commercial dev-

Greywater Action, Sustainable Water Infrastructure

GREYWATER ACTION BUILDS SMALL-SCALE, low-cost interventions in the urban water system as a strategy for dealing with drought, pollution, and failing water infrastructure. They train people to build simple home greywater and rainwater harvesting systems and waterless toilets to reduce water use and provide nutrients and irrigation to grow food. "Ecological sanitation" solutions reduce water consumption, while at the same time shifting how people view and interact with water, creating a new water culture that conserves and protects both watersheds and communities. For more information visit *greywateraction.org*.

Laura Allen, founding member
of Greywater Action

elopment, road building, and parking lots have all damaged watersheds, making them extremely impervious.

This is where we stand today, with a major challenge ahead of us to restore our water systems, for the sake of our own survival and that of the world around us. Astute ecosystem managers clearly recognize that watershed-scale restoration begins with addressing issues that affect the headwaters of any watershed. To seriously take on this survival challenge, we must first and foremost mitigate the cerebral imperviousness of our own internal "headwaters"—to change the way we think about the natural world and our place in it. Forming collaborative interpersonal and working social relationships between all people who share a watershed rests at the center of our potential for success or failure.

We Face a Future of Thirst

Some will argue that water has never limited human growth and development, that humans have tenaciously applied their technological ingenuity to move water great distances and pump it from deep below the surface to fuel burgeoning growth. It has been said, "Simply bring the water, and the people will come." In the past few centuries, however, this command-control-and-conveyance attitude

toward water has begun to show signs of deepening failure in the U.S. and across the world.

Our societal addiction to the combustion of carbon-based fossil fuels for energy is now understood to cause global climate change due to excessive accumulation of "greenhouse" gases in the atmosphere. These gases thicken the atmosphere's capacity to retain solar energy, leading to an increase in the planet's average surface temperatures. Solid, liquid, and gaseous phase changes by water are the thermal mechanisms through which the planet primarily attempts to regulate its human-induced "fever." Water is manifesting some of the most dramatic expressions of this climate change, with melting polar ice and glaciers, rising sea levels, coastal inundation, ocean acidification, warmer tropical water and air temperatures, slowing of the Gulf Stream, stronger hurricanes, and increased floods and droughts.

Peak Water

As we confront the burgeoning reality of "peak oil"—the knowledge that we are now approaching the halfway point of global petroleum production capacity—we also see a new crisis appearing on the horizon: peak water, which has deep implications for peak food, and consequently

The remains of an old dam, which was inaugurated by Spain's King Alfonso XIII in 1907, peeks out of the reservoir of Santillana . A new dam, which helps provide drinking water for Madrid, was built in 1969 and nearly submerged the first dam.

peak population. Responding in a timely manner to this triangle of energy, water, and food interdependence is one of our challenges. The difference between peak oil and peak water is that, while the total amount of water and oil on the planet is finite, water, unlike oil, cycles infinitely through our lives and watersheds.

Watershed by watershed, functional sustainability will be exemplified by our ability to sustain the integrity and resilience of the water cycle. As the Titanic of cheap energy sinks below the surface, a prudent option would be to perceive our watersheds as living lifeboats and to use the principles of "conservation hydrology" to batten down the hatches. It is incumbent upon us to realize that together we can each work to ensure that all watershed lifeboats float together as a regional raft of resilient stability.

From a Dehydration Model to a Rehydration Model

There are tools, like conservation hydrology, that we can use to begin to restore our watershed and our thinking.

Conservation hydrology utilizes the disciplines of ecology, population biology, biogeography, economics, anthropology, philosophy, and history to guide community-based watershed literacy, planning, and action. It advocates that human development decisions must move from a "dehydration model" to a "rehydration model."

To achieve this goal we must retrofit existing development patterns with new ones based on the principles below. Much like the discussion of our carbon footprint (i.e., the relative relationship of our lifestyle and how it impacts the planet via our consumption of carbon), we can also invoke this same process of inquiry and evaluation to the idea of our water footprint.

Developing a consciousness that appreciates water as the ultimate resource is critical. Thankfully, the federal Clean Water Act now recognizes the "pave, pipe, and pollute paradigm" of past decades as disastrously flawed and hydro-illiterate. These outmoded engineering practices captured, concentrated, and conveyed water away from a site as quickly as possible. The old drain-age

WATER CONSERVATION HAS A CASCADE OF POSITIVE EFFECTS.

is now being replaced by a new retain-age, the key to a healthy watershed.

Balancing Our Water Budget

Our new way of looking at watersheds is a lot like managing money. For a moment, consider water in budgetary terms. Successful businesses must account for income and expenses in order to ensure profitability. Yet how many cities or counties actually have balanced income and expense budgets for their water resources?

In simple fiscal terms, most municipalities are operating deeply in the red, with ecologically and socially damaging hydrological deficits. Typically, the demand or expense side of their water budgets far exceeds their income streams. Impervious surfaces, such as roads, parking lots, and compacted fields, impede water's ability to make deposits that could help recharge groundwater savings accounts.

Ever-increasing reliance on overdrafted groundwater accounts will leave our grandchildren with unrecoverable and undrinkable debts as many of the world's watersheds verge on hydrological bankruptcy. Unlike corporations and people, our watersheds cannot file for Chapter 11 and then just reorganize. Direct deposits of freshly distilled rain and snow are the annual allowance, the only real renewable income source on Earth.

Expenditure of our groundwater trust reserves should be limited to the annual earned interest income of infiltration, with the principal left untapped. All life-forms are shareholders with a fixed interest in ensuring that our watershed economies remain viable and continue to operate in the "blue."

Four R's of Conservation Hydrology

Here's how that budget actually breaks down. The four R's of a water budget are equivalent to income, deposit, savings, and expense. We want the water balance of our watersheds to run in the blue and not in the red. We want to ensure that our liquid assets continually produce a high quality return on investment back into our watershed.

Receive = Income. Watersheds receive water only as snowfall, rainfall, and fogfall. Annual precipitation is the only true source of income to resupply our community's water budget allowance.

Global climate changes are predicted to dramatically alter the frequency, intensity, and type of precipitation events that watersheds can expect to receive. Thus, conservation hydrology advocates the adaptive management of watershed lands to optimize rehydration. Practices such as eco-forestry, holistic rangeland management, organic no-till agriculture, urban forestry, stormwater management with bioswales and rainwater harvesting are but a few examples of land-use practices that can be designed to help rehydrate our watersheds. We must implement and enforce these types of land-use patterns that enhance the receptive capacity of our watersheds in times of excess and in times of scarcity.

Recharge = Deposit. Recharge processes are critical for the water cycle to annually refresh itself via the deposit slip called infiltration. The capacity to make water deposits depends on the watershed's ability to recharge. Precipitation received by our watershed must percolate and be absorbed, or else there is no replenishment of our water savings account. Recharge potential and functions are impaired by the hardening and paving over of natural recharge areas, the disconnection of rivers from their floodplains, the deforestation of native vegetation, and the draining of wetlands. Therefore, to increase recharge, we must limit impervious surfaces and the wholesale conversion of native vegetation.

We must implement stormwater techniques designed to "slow it, spread it, and sink it" so that water seeps back, as a deposit, into the Earth. We must protect open space in known groundwater recharge areas. If site conditions and/or soils are not conducive to recharge, then we install proper biofiltration structures, such as rain gardens or bioswales, to help clean all surface waters prior to their discharge from the site as they are redeposited into

HOW TO HELP PROTECT YOUR WATERSHED

Household Actions

- Use low-flow appliances and fixtures

- Create a stormwater harvesting rain garden

- Focus on the use of drought-tolerant native plants

- Install a rainwater or graywater system for all irrigation

Community Actions

- Form a community watershed group

- Implement habitat restoration projects

- Create watershed literacy curriculum for your local schools

- Know the members of your local, city, county, or regional water board

rivers, streams, wetlands, lakes, estuaries, and oceans.

Retain = Savings. The retention of recharged precipitation is a savings account asset. The storage of water is often the most challenging aspect of water supply management. Conservation hydrology strategies should appropriately slow water down, increasing the residence time of water storage in our watersheds. This will optimize the amount of water available.

We must avoid overdrafting our watersheds. Water should never be extracted from storage in amounts greater than what is annually received and recharged. All sources of water must not be polluted by development, wastewater systems, agricultural runoff, or industrial effluent.

To protect our water savings, we must develop water budgets for all watersheds to ensure that extractions of water do not exceed inputs of water. We must implement groundwater and surface water management programs. We must ensure that surface and groundwater quantity and quality protection programs are funded, monitored, and enforced. And we must continually defend the legally established public ownership of water as a public trust

resource and resist the privatization of water.

Release = Expense. The planet utilizes many ways to release its signature element naturally to the ocean, land, and atmosphere in a process known as the water cycle. Through seasonally melting glaciers, groundwater springs, and seeps, water is returned to creeks and rivers. Solar evaporation and the evapotranspiration of plants help to form clouds and feed the cycle anew. The infinite nature of this cycle is to continually flow and be in flux as the expense of one stage produces income for the next.

Human development practices (creating impervious surfaces, channeling stormwater, etc.) tend to increase the rate and volume of stormwater's return to the ocean via excessive runoff and heightened flood discharges. This directly reduces the landscape's ability to retain water and diminishes the amount of water available for later release during the dry season, when it is most needed.

Therefore the implementation of watershed-scale conservation hydrology practices must be designed to protect reception, amplify recharge, and thus optimize retention. These are the critical steps that can ensure optimal amounts of water will be available for future release.

Watershed issues provide us with many avenues to become involved. Some solutions are small and only require making different choices as an individual or family. These can be done today in your home or yard by using low-flow appliances, creating a stormwater-harvesting rain garden, focusing on the use of drought-tolerant native plants, and installing a rainwater cistern for all irrigation and a greywater system to irrigate a home orchard. Other solutions are more complex, requiring behavioral changes in neighborhoods, communities, or cities, with broad-based participation over some years. Ideas like forming a community watershed group, or implementing habitat restoration projects, or creating watershed literacy curriculum for your local schools are projects that require more group collaboration and planning.

In order to catalyze changes in water security for future generations, we must implement a whole class of democratic opportunities for social policy change at all levels of government. Changes are necessary at the personal, public, and political levels.

On the personal level, practicing water conservation by reducing our demands for water is one of our most powerful acts, individually and collectively. Water conservation has a cascade of positive effects and can influence the overall quantity and quality of available freshwater.

Every gallon of water you choose not to use equals one gallon not taken from your river or aquifer. It means the system does not need that gallon's worth of electricity to pump it nor the chemicals to make it potable. It means that one gallon is not being degraded into "waste" water, which would require additional electricity to pump again, treat, and dispose of in our environment. Choosing not to use water saves water quantity and improves quality. It saves energy and money. It helps reduce demands on our watersheds. And it helps to mitigate climate change-induced water stresses by reducing the collective water footprint of humankind.

On the public level, we are perched on the tipping point of a "watershed moment." From the global scale to the local scale, we are faced with a multitude of issues and decisions that will determine the future world our children will inherit and how to ensure that our watersheds remain healthy in perpetuity.

Viewing your watershed as a shared "basin of relations" allows you and your neighbors to truly define the boundaries of your community and organize around meaningful issues of true and lasting local social security. Each process, like every watershed and its associated community, is unique. Oftentimes you will find that certain local, city, county, state, and federal jurisdictions are ready and waiting to collaborate with these efforts. In the absence of support from the local community, it is often impossible to achieve measurable objectives and resource management goals, especially in areas where the majority of the land is in private ownership.

And politically, when you consider the importance of water, it is essential to involve yourself in the politics of water resources. Do you know the members of your local, city, county, or regional water board? Of your irrigation district, planning commission, board of supervisors, or city council? How about your state and federal legislators? How do they make decisions? Have you ever thought about running for a local office yourself? Answering these questions is critical.

Sustainable Water Policies

Ultimately, lasting change will have to occur via the arenas of politics and democratic decision making. "We the People" are responsible for sane water policies and laws through our legislative, executive, and judicial branches. Metaphorically, you could conceive of these three branches as expressions of social watersheds. At the confluence of these three watersheds, the health of the "mainstream" is only as good as the health of each contributing watershed branch. It is our collective responsibility to make sure each branch of our democratic structure crafts adequate, supportive conditions to care for our

A raindrop-shaped cistern in a home in Victoria, Australia that was designed by Paul Morgan Architects. The tank collects rainwater from the roof and as the rain collects, it provides passive cooling inside the house during summer.

ECOLOGICAL LITERACY IS THE SINGLE GREATEST GLOBAL EPIDEMIC WE FACE.

collective water resources.

The choice is ours whether to move forward to face the challenges head on or not. We do not lack the prescient clarion call of the future or the opportunity to observe the highly degraded state of our watersheds after only a few hundred years of so-called civilized occupation. We do not lack any amount of information or practical knowledge on how to implement regenerative watershed practices.

So, what will it take to motivate us to move in the direction of mitigation and adaptation on behalf of future generations? The ecological literacy of seeing the world through the lens of our watersheds offers communities a realistic scale for feedback.

In ancient Greece, the mathematician and inventor Archimedes said: "Give me a place to stand and a lever long enough, and I will move the world." Several thousand years later, his wise insight offers us a perfect challenge: Are you willing to take a stand for your watershed community? Where strategically will you place yourself and insert your lever against what fulcrum? If you wish to move your watershed world in the direction of resiliency, how many people can you convince to pull on the lever with you? Can you leverage the community willpower to pull on the oars of your watershed lifeboat in a coordinated manner as if your lives depended on it? It is time not just to ask the hard questions but to find the answers, because all of our lives and those of future generations do depend on it.

Acequias: Water Democracy in the U.S.

PAULA GARCIA

Every spring, irrigators in New Mexico's acequia communities look in anticipation at the mountains that are the source of water for the streams and rivers. Like countless generations before, people of the acequias depend on spring runoff to irrigate crops

and pasture that sustain an ancient way of life.

The word "acequia" is of Arabic origin, meaning "quencher of thirst" or "bearer of water." Today, acequias refer to the communal irrigation systems still common in New Mexico and Southern Colorado, which have been the basis for a centuries-old ethic of water sharing, known as the *reparto* or *repartimiento*. These customs guide the distribution of water between families.

Defining an acequia requires both a physical and sociocultural description. From a physical standpoint, an acequia is defined as a system that diverts water from a common source (either a river, stream or spring) and moves water by gravity flow through earthen canals spreading snowmelt and runoff from the upper watershed throughout the valleys of irrigable land via an intricate network of waterways.

The social dimension of the acequia is the community of families who collectively manage, maintain and govern the system. The irrigators, known as *parciantes*, have rights and responsibilities related to the acequia in which permission to use water is conditioned on contributing to cooperative labor for the annual cleaning and adhering to the irrigation schedule set forth by the *Mayordomo* and *Comisionados*, the elected officials of each acequia.

Despite the inevitable tensions and conflicts inherent in sharing a scarce resource, acequia communities continue to be guided by the principle of equity. The water ethic embodied in the acequias is rooted in culture and spirituality in which water is revered as a *don divino*, or divine gift. Acequia traditions of water sharing and participatory

governance have endured for centuries in their respective communities as a cultural practice. Historically, water blessings and processions have contributed to the social glue that emphasizes the common good over any individual getting a disproportionate share of water.

Acequias made their way to the Southwest via Mexico, Spain, and North Africa. By the time of their establishment in New Mexico, acequias were a synthesis of Moorish influences and adaptations learned from Mesoamerica and the Native Americans of the Southwest, who themselves had developed sophisticated water harvesting and distribution techniques.

In the acequia worldview, water is a scarce and precious gift so essential to survival that it must be shared for community well-being. As such, it is governed as a shared resource in which individual families have water rights but also share a common thread of interdependence. This traditional approach stands in sharp contrast with the modern view in which water distribution is more a matter of pumping, piping, and commodification.

In the latter view, water scarcity is not addressed through cultural norms but by "increasing supply" with pipelines or tapping into unseen groundwater reserves. Additionally, water allocation is not guided by an ethic of water sharing but by an emerging water market that values water purely on economic terms. The underlying assumption of this dominant model of water management is that the "water market" will efficiently reallocate water according to the "highest and best" economic use. This is known as the commodification of water.

WHAT HAS BEEN LEARNED SO FAR IS THAT LOCAL WATER

Commodification of Water Rights

In the western United States, water rights are considered property rights that can be bought and sold. The history of the privatization of water in the West is long and complex but its origin is tied to the intent of staking a claim in the westward expansion of the 19th century. Up to the present day, there are essentially no restrictions on the buying and selling of water. Just like any other resource treated as an economic commodity, the ownership of water could be exploited for profit. In extreme scenarios, the ownership of water could be concentrated among the wealthy and corporations.

Treating water as an economic commodity raises many ethical questions: Who decides the allocation of scarce water? How is the fundamental right to water guaranteed if water is an economic commodity? How do poor communities fare in a market system? What are the implications for small-scale, traditional agriculture?

In New Mexico, some of the oldest water rights are in-tertwined with community-based acequias in which individual farmers own water rights that are attached to small parcels of farmland. The day-to-day use and distribution of water is governed through the customs and traditions of each acequia. However, the water rights are administered under the rules of the state, which allow the water to be sold and severed from the land. With increasing pressure from new growth, acequia communities risk losing water through market forces that favor those in economic power such as industry and developers.

While buying and selling are economic transactions, changing the use of a water right, say from agricultural to urban, is considered a "water transfer." Any water transfer that proposes to change the use or location of a water right is the subject of laws that regulate that change from an existing use to a new use. In the West, an agency of the state will decide whether a request to transfer water right will be approved. For New Mexico, water transfers have to be evaluated and approved by the state engineer.

Left, The Bernardo Acequia in New Mexico; *center*, Luminarios line the ditch banks of Albuquerque's South Valley in the annual "Acequia with Lights" holiday celebration; and *right*, an acequia in the Spanish town of Calasparra in the province of Murcia.

GOVERNANCE IS DYNAMIC, COMPLICATED, AND PLACE-SPECIFIC.

Therefore, water transfers are not matters to be driven solely by economics but they are treated in New Mexico law as important public policy decisions. Each decision has to factor three considerations: 1) existing rights; 2) conservation of water; and 3) public welfare. These criteria would seem to ensure that concerns about the environment as well as issues concerning equity, social justice, and fairness would be considered in water transfer decisions.

However, there have been efforts to change state water policy, through legislation or administrative rulemaking, to chip away at these protections. In the early 2000s, New Mexico saw proposed legislation to "expedite water marketing" by deregulating water transfers with amendments to state law. While these attempts failed, other provisions have made their way into administrative rulemaking allowing temporary transfers in certain situations that would circumvent the usual considerations.

Additionally, many new uses of water in New Mexico were enabled by working around the water transfer re-

quirements. State engineers of the past seemed inclined to provide the conditions for New Mexico to continue on its growth trajectory. They got creative with ways to approve applications for water in a manner that deferred the long-term impacts to future generations. In these "pump now, pay later" arrangements, permits to pump groundwater were issued on the condition that the entity would acquire and transfer water rights later, often many years later, when the pumping would begin to affect river flows. Generally, the water rights used as "offsets" to groundwater pumping come from agriculture. Rather than being a movement of an existing use to a new use, these water transfers attempt to put a band-aid on the permanent loss of groundwater.

The overall effect to the water commons is that ancient aquifers are irreversibly pumped and depleted and agricultural water rights are retired to account for the losses these cause to rivers and streams. If one could visualize the finite water supply as a pie, the fraction of the pie dedicated to agriculture is getting smaller. But just as significant, and

- The word "acequia" is of Arabic origin, meaning "quencher of thirst" or "bearer of water"

- They are a communal irrigation system with intricate water-sharing customs that still exist in the Southwest United States

- Acequias are part of an ancient legacy with roots extending back thousands of years to the arid-land peoples of present-day India, the Middle East, and the Americas

- By the time of their establishment in New Mexico, acequias were a synthesis of Moorish influences and adaptations learned from Mesoamerica and the Native Americans of the Southwest

- Their system of water distribution is made possible by communal labor and participation

- The fundamental principle underlying the acequia system of water management is *equidad* (equity)

- The right to use water is attributed to individual families but is contingent upon contribution of cooperative labor

- Because of their resiliency as "water democracies" acequias have earned recognition in the global water movement and they offer some insights for other communities facing chronic water shortages

of great concern to everyone, is that the actual pie is getting smaller when surface water is used to offset the depletions from the pumping of groundwater. Therefore, the commodification of water could just as easily be referred to in this context as "New Mexico's vanishing water."

Resisting the Commodification of Water

Because acequias are concentrated in the communities with some of the highest rates of poverty in the state, they are uniquely vulnerable to market forces pulling water out of their respective communities. At a time when rural communities are embracing small-scale agriculture as a way to rebuild local food systems, the commodification of water threatens to undermine the potential for great local food security. Because acequias depend on a collective of families for mutual support and cooperative labor, water transfers can lead to a piecemeal dismantling of both food and water systems.

For decades, leadership from acequia communities has been critical of water transfers. Since the 1980s, acequias have made passionate and articulate arguments about the significance of water to community well-being. Up until only a few years ago, the only recourse available to acequias in opposing a water transfer was to file an objection with the state. However, the only person with decision-making power on whether to approve water transfers was the state engineer, and in some cases acequia concerns were not fully considered. The growing need to respond to the increasing marketing and transfer of water helped create the New Mexico Acequia Association in 1990.

In 2003, in the culmination of a six year community organizing and legislative campaign, the NMAA with the backing of key legislators passed a new law that fundamentally changed the water transfer process in New Mexico. Before a proposed water transfer can be considered by the state engineer, the application must first go before the acequia community for approval. This was a historically significant change in New Mexico water policy in shifting decisions about water transfers to a local community level.

WATER IS ESSENTIAL TO ALL LIFE AND MUST BE SHARED FOR MUTUAL BENEFIT AND SURVIVAL.

In effect, it re-communitized water and served as a buffer to the increasing commodification of water.

Each acequia is a local government in state law with an elected commission. In order to exercise this authority, an acequia must include certain language in the respective bylaws and rules of that acequia. Hundreds of local acequias have made an affirmative decision to assume this new responsibility of making decisions about water transfers.

For Acequia de la Canada Ancha, an acequia in the historic village of Chimayo in the Espanola Valley, the simple decision to add the water transfer regulatory language to their bylaws was heavily debated due to a pro-transfer member of the community. Over 300 people attended the meeting, and after hearing both sides, the community voted overwhelmingly to enact the water transfer language.

In southern New Mexico, the San Patricio Community Ditch denied a water transfer application to a nearby city. The decision was appealed to district court but the city later dropped the appeal due in large part to the tenacity of the acequia and its shoestring but effective legal defense team who fought to protect the water commons.

In Hernandez, an acequia denied a water transfer to a subdivision development outside the acequia. The decision was appealed and is making its way through the courts. The acequia was recently vindicated in a Supreme Court decision but there are several substantive issues which remain to be considered still.

An acequia in Taos County is considering a request to transfer water rights from the acequia to the drinking water system that serves the same community. The water rights are on agricultural land that has been developed and can no longer be irrigated. Substantial population growth has required an expansion of the community water system. This situation exemplifies the difficult decisions local acequias face in addressing the changing needs in their respective communities.

What has been learned so far is that local water governance is dynamic, complicated, and place-specific. Shifting the decision-making power over water transfers to the local level creates a significant responsibility for local elected officials of acequias, who are usually volunteers. These proceedings heighten awareness in the local community about the high stakes of water decisions and engage community members in decisions that are difficult and sometimes contentious. Water democracy is a tremendous undertaking but worth the effort. From the perspective of the acequia leadership in New Mexico, it was equally important to demonstrate a viable model for community-based decision-making over water transfers as it was to critique the commodification of water.

A Different Way Forward: Local Governance of the Water Commons

For more than four centuries, acequias have endured in New Mexico by upholding the basic principle of equity and by managing the collective resources of the acequia, including the water, the waterways, the irrigation works, and the labor, through a community-based process. These elements collectively constitute a locally governed commons in which individual rights and responsibilities are carefully balanced with the common good. While these characteristics of the acequia are deeply ingrained in the historical practice of sharing irrigation water, the same principles are now being applied in a modern context.

In addressing the growing commodification of water, acequias are putting ancient principles into practice to protect water rights and assert their significance to community well-being. A consciousness grounded in community and culture underpins the contemporary acequia movement, but it is also grounded in a traditional and indigenous environmental ethic. Some of the customs and beliefs that are part of the practice of acequia water governance have emerged from the experience of regulating water transfers in recent years:

Water is connected to and belongs to a place. Traditionally, water was treated as an ephemeral resource and distributed in increments of time to individual families. Water was part of the acequia, an extension of the river, and connected to the farmland through generations of irrigation. The concept of a water transfer, whereby a water right is severed from the land, is antithetical to this fundamental belief that water and land are inextricably intertwined.

Water is essential to all life and must be shared for mutual benefit and survival. This is a fundamental value that runs completely counter to the notion of placing a dollar value on water as an economic commodity that introduces a profit motive into water allocation. When this is the case uses deemed less economically viable, such as sustainable agriculture or a drinking water system in a low-income community, may not be able to compete with resorts or industry for water, thereby presenting major dilemmas for achieving social justice.

Water delivery systems are part of the public domain and should be maintained by the collective. For acequias, a condition of being in good standing with the community and having access to your water is contributing labor and financial assessments (i.e. taxes) to maintain the system. Irrigators are not paying for water as much as they are contributing to the overall system to keep it functioning. Over the long term, water transfers would erode this community-based system that depends on the contributions of the members of the acequia.

Water is finite and how we use it should depend upon its availability. Acequias can only use the water that is provided by nature through snowpack runoff and rainfall. On a seasonal basis, even on a day-to-day basis, an acequia must adjust water allocation accordingly. This is usually done through a rotation. In times of abundance, everyone gets more water. In times of shortage, everyone gets less. In drought, a water right might be reduced to 15-minute increments so that everyone gets something. In a modern context, allocation of scarce water for survival should be a major consideration.

Water governance includes local decision making. Historically, most traditional environmental knowledge that underpinned acequia water allocation was based on generational memory and direct experience. Local knowledge is still important even as the decisions surrounding water management, particularly water transfers, become more complex. In the example of acequias, state law now acknowledges the role of the local community in defining what is the common good. It did not replace state or federal laws covering water, but it created a mechanism for subsidiarity in decisions over water allocation. It is a decentralized model of governance.

Water and Food Sovereignty

Water is integral to food sovereignty: the people's democratic control of the food system, the right of all people to healthy, culturally appropriate food produced through ecologically sound and sustainable methods, and their right to define their own food and agriculture systems. The ability to retain or reclaim water for growing food in accordance with the principles of food sovereignty will be a great challenge facing humanity in coming years. As grassroots movements strive to rebuild local food systems, economic pressures are mounting to move water rights out of agriculture.

In arid regions, access to water is a determining factor in food production. In New Mexico and other areas of the Southwest, there are usually two major categories of agricultural production. The first is large-scale commodity production that is generally made possible through huge federal water reclamation projects or through extensive groundwater pumping. This type of commodity production is part of the industrial food system in that most, if not all, of the product is exported out of the region. Some have

New Mexico's arid climate, like here
along the Rio Chama Road, makes the wise
and democratic use of water in acequias
all the more important for communities.

PHOTOGRAPH BY LESLIE ALSHEIMER

A cornucopia of New Mexico's locally-grown
(and acequia-watered) vegetables.

PHOTOGRAPH BY DEANNA NICHOLS

begun to describe export of food from a region as "virtual water transfers" because the product leaves the area where it was actually grown.

The second type of agriculture is smaller in scale and based on more traditional agricultural methods. In New Mexico, small-scale agriculture is part of an ancient legacy dating back to the Native Americans. It has also been practiced in the centuries-old acequias as well as by more recent migrants since the 1800s. The hallmark of traditional agriculture was community self-reliance, as most food that was eaten in a community could also be grown there. Because of the global restructuring of food production using high energy inputs and policies favoring commodity production, small-scale agriculture has suffered. Many decades of decline are now being replaced with a sense of optimism because of the growing demand for locally grown, affordable, healthy, fresh, and fair food.

Reclaiming food sovereignty will fundamentally change the way communities relate to land and water, the labor needed for cultivating crops, and the whole range of infrastructure needed for growing, processing, and distributing food. With regard to water and farmland, there is a sense of urgency that the remaining farmland and water rights that are in production must be protected from the pressures of urbanization and development. Left to operate unfettered, market forces will continue to erode these essential resources for meeting the increasing need to grow more food at the local and regional level.

The acequia movement in New Mexico has taken some first steps in protecting the water rights that are part of the foundation of small-scale agriculture. Much more remains including building urban-rural solidarity around food systems, protecting farmland, and reinvesting in irrigation works and food system infrastructure. A much greater and also essential task is to build the next generation of acequia irrigators, those who are dedicated to the continuation of the acequia tradition, including growing food and participating in local water governance.

Relationships to Social Justice Movements

A challenge for the future is to proactively address rural-urban tensions surrounding water. The greatest creativity and good faith will be needed to meet our moral imperative to ensure water for all, while also protecting the natural systems intertwined with water and the fundamental need to sustain and regenerate local food systems. An essential ingredient to that process will be to put social justice at the forefront, since the inequities surrounding water are often grounded in historic injustices affecting indigenous peoples, the working poor, and traditional, small-scale farmers.

It is a defining moment in human history. People around the world are taking action to defend water with mass mobilizations and community-based strategies to retain local ownership and decision-making control of water. Like the acequia movement in New Mexico, these movements are integral to other struggles for land rights, human rights, and basic human dignity.

Regardless of the place or context, acknowledging the finite nature of water is crucial. Strategies to address water scarcity should be grounded in local culture and governance, and those strategies should be defined and led by communities with the greatest stake in defending water as a life-giving resource. The refrain that "water is life" is universal and held by peoples throughout the world. Building upon that principle and transforming institutions to reflect it is one of the greatest challenges facing humanity. If recent grassroots struggles are any indication, we have reason to be hopeful. And with acequias, we have a model from which all of us can learn.

Is Conservation Enough?

CHRISTINA ROESSLER

"Those who do not know history are doomed to repeat it."
—EDMUND BURKE

In February 2008, a *New York Times* headline read, "Lake Mead Could Be Within a Few Years of Going Dry, Study Finds." It was grim news for two of the fastest-growing cities in the country. Lake Mead, fed by the Colorado River, provides up to 90 percent of the water

for Las Vegas, and Phoenix gets close to 40 percent of its water from the Colorado.

Of course, this desert area is no stranger to water shortages, but the current condition of the Colorado River, which has seven states gulping from it, could be devastating for the region. It is difficult to imagine what kind of catastrophe that could spell. You have to go back a long ways to find the last major drought in the Southwest that actually sent people packing.

The period from about 1200 to 1300 CE is considered the golden age of the Ancestral Pueblo culture, an ancient civilization of farmers and potters whose ancestors had been living in the Four Corners region of the Southwest for close to 1,000 years. Settlements at that time were increasing in number and size, as evidenced by the magnificent cliff dwellings at Mesa Verde, including the elaborate 150-room Cliff Palace. Agriculture was flourishing at the time and the population was growing.

Then, suddenly, this seemingly stable society collapsed. Mesa Verde and other communities on the Colorado Plateau were abandoned forever. What happened? Tree ring records indicate that the collapse of the Ancestral Pueblo culture coincided with a particularly prolonged period of drought, giving rise to the speculation that a "Great Drought" drove people from the region.

There were other climatological changes as well, including warmer, wetter winters and cooler, drier summers that disrupted the growing seasons and impacted traditional agriculture. Some areas also experienced sharp drops in water table levels.

Sound familiar? This history seems especially relevant today as the Southwestern United States and many other parts of the globe are facing extended periods of drought, increasing temperatures, and dwindling water supplies. The Ancestral Pueblos didn't have the advantage of tree ring studies and climate models, but their rapid decline is still a cautionary tale. The question for us in the 21st century is, can we do better? What will it take for our desert communities and ecosystems to survive?

The Recent Past to Today

The American West, and particularly the Southwest, has been going through a seemingly unstoppable period of population growth for the last several decades. The combined population of the seven Colorado River Compact states—Arizona, California, Colorado, Nevada, New Mexico, Utah, and Wyoming—has grown from just over 21 million people in 1960 to over 48 million people in 2006. Sunny weather, warm temperatures, and lovely landscapes have drawn people from other parts of the country and fed

THE COLORADO RIVER—LIFEBLOOD OF THE REGION, SUPPLYING WATER FOR 30 MILLION PEOPLE IN SEVEN STATES AND MEXICO—IS OVER ALLOCATED.

PHOTOGRAPH BY EDWARD BURTYNSKY

the booming development of the region. At one time the 10 biggest cities in the United States were all located within 500 miles of the Canadian border. Now, seven of the top 10 are in the Sunbelt.

Most of this growth took place during an unusually long, wet period in the history of the West. Rainfall in many parts of the Southwest in the years between 1975 and 2000 were at some of the highest levels the region has seen in 2,000 years, according to tree ring studies.

The West experienced an earlier exceptionally wet period during the 1920s, at the time the Colorado River Compact apportioned Colorado River water to its seven member states. Unfortunately, this means that the allotment of water to these states is based on a calculation of flow in the river that was unusually high in historical terms. The Colorado River—the lifeblood of the region, supplying water for 30 million people in seven states and Mexico—is overallocated in terms of the flow volume we can expect in the future.

In fact, it turns out that the 20th century as a whole was water rich, even by North American standards. We grew accustomed to abundance, and abundance became normal. Now, not even a full decade into the 21st century, we're beginning to recognize that the 20th century was abnormally wet. What we consider drought is largely a return to more typical patterns of precipitation.

Bad as all this sounds, things are almost certainly going to get worse. Climatologists predict that global warming is only going to make the American Southwest hotter and dryer, with precipitation far lower than what we have come to expect. Communities are beginning to recognize they need to plan for a more water-scarce future. Most of the existing surface water is overallocated. Many communities hoping to augment their water supplies with groundwater are discovering that overpumping is already a problem, and water tables in many aquifers have fallen dangerously low.

What we really need are inclusive processes to figure out regional approaches for equitably sharing diminishing water supplies. While necessity may finally get us there, for now rural and urban communities are often pitted against each other as growing urban centers require more and more water. Rural communities are justifiably prickly as they are increasingly pressured to make what they consider their water available for transfer to big cities.

The biggest elephant of all is agriculture, which globally accounts for about 70 percent of water use. Agriculture in the West, and particularly in California, accounts for a significant amount of the food that makes its way to tables all over the United States as well as to other countries. Yet, as we know, growing this food requires massive inputs of water in order to make the desert bloom. The Colorado River alone helps irrigate four million acres of farmland.

Agricultural and urban users alike are going to have to face the fact that, as water becomes scarcer, all of us are going to have to adjust to using less. Changing agricultural practices is a monumental undertaking and is absolutely necessary, but it is not the only culprit. Individuals and families can make a tremendous difference by lowering their water consumption. This will require both becoming more water efficient and also changing our notion of how much water is enough.

Where Do We Go from Here?

As water supplies diminish, we're facing a fundamental supply and demand issue that has to be addressed. Many cities intent on growth are exploring ways to increase supply. However, many of the supply-side solutions are both risky and expensive.

Desalination, for example, poses many challenges. It remains an energy-intensive way to produce fresh water, raising concerns about both cost and the degree to which facilities contribute to climate disruption. There are questions about how to safely dispose of the concentrated salt brine and also about the impacts of the facilities on fragile coastal ecosystems. For these and other reasons California, an obvious place to locate facilities, has been slow to approve the many proposed desalination projects.

Cities are also looking at ways to transfer water from one

THE PROBLEMS WITH SEAWATER DESALINATION

Ocean desalination—a process that converts seawater into drinking water—is being hailed as the solution to water supply problems. Proponents of desalination claim that this technology will create a reliable, long-term water supply, while decreasing pressure on other over–drawn water sources. But desalination facilities have the potential to create more problems than they solve. Here are some reasons why communities need to think twice before embracing ocean water desalination:

1) Alternatives Abound.

Smart water agencies are making great strides in adopting efficient water management practices such as conservation, reuse, and recycling. The Pacific Institute report "Waste Not, Want Not; The Potential for Urban Water Conservation in California" found that California can meet its water needs for the next 30 years by implementing off–the–shelf, cost–effective urban water conservation. Draft guidelines released by the state of Massachusetts found that, "Prior to seeking desalinated water, proponents and communities needing additional water should first achieve savings through efficient use and conservation of existing water." Desalination is an expensive and speculative option that could drain resources away from more practical solutions.

2) It's Expensive.

Ocean desalinated water is among the most expensive ways to supply water. Producing water through ocean desalination costs three or more times what it costs to produce water from traditional supplies. It requires multiple subsidies of both water and electricity to break even, and it entails pricey upfront construction and long–term operation and maintenance costs. California American Water Company has demanded an upfront rate increase to provide for construction of its proposed plant in Monterey, California, before it has even produced a drop of water.

3) It Could Exacerbate Global Warming.

Enormous amounts of energy are needed to force ocean water through tiny membrane filters at a high pressure. Ocean water desalination can be greater than ten times more energy intensive than other supply sources. Ocean desalination proponents, such as private corporations Poseidon Resources and American Water, plan to locate plants alongside existing coastal power plants, thus potentially spurring their emission of global warming pollution.

4) It Creates the Potential for Corporate Control and Abuse.

Ocean desalination provides a new opportunity for private corporations to own and sell water. Currently, there is little regulation of these facilities, creating the possibility that private corporations would rate-gouge thirsty populations—similar to what happened in the Enron energy scheme.

A recent Food and Water Watch analysis compared average water rates charged by publicly and privately owned utilities in four states—California, Illinois, Wisconsin, and New York—and found that privately owned water utilities charge customers significantly higher water rates than their publicly owned counterparts: any-where from 13 percent to almost 50 percent more.

Worse, corporate controlled desalination facilities have performed miserably. Poseidon Resources, whose largest investor is the private equity firm Warburg Pincus, botched a large facility in Tampa Bay, Florida. The facility, at a final price of $158 million, was completed years behind schedule and did not function until the Tampa Bay Water Authority took it over from Poseidon. Poseidon now plans to build several facilities in California, some of which are much larger, including a facility in Carlsbad. Companies like Poseidon view the ocean not as a public resource but as a vast, untapped source of profit, with unlimited potential to supply water to the highest bidder.

5) Fisheries and Marine Environments Will Be Threatened.

Many proposed ocean desalination plants are now planning to rely on "once–through" intake structures—an outdated technology that sucks in ocean water to cool the power plant. These intakes kill fish and other organisms that cannot free themselves from the intakes or that get sucked into the plants.

According to the U.S. Environmental Protection Agency, these intake structures kill at least 3.4 billion fish and other marine organisms annually. This amounts to a $212.5 million loss to anglers and commercial fishermen. California's power plant intake structures, alone, are responsible for the loss of at least 312.9 million organisms each year, resulting in a $13.6 million loss to fishermen.

As power plants begin to shift away from once–through cooling, a real danger exists that some desalination plants will use these intakes, and marine life destruction will continue. Further, the brine, or super salty wastewater

created from the desalination process, also has the potential to upset our delicate coastal ecosystems.

6) It Could Pose a Risk to Human Health.

A number of public health experts have expressed concern about using ocean water as drinking water and the effect that new contaminants have on water quality. Some of these new contaminants include boron, algal toxins (for example, red tide), and endocrine disrupters, all of which are concentrated through the desalination process. Another concern is that ocean desalination draws water from coastal areas with sewage and storm water runoff.

7) It Promotes Environmental and Social Injustice.

Costs may be disproportionately borne by existing low–income communities, both those living near the plant who will not receive the water and those inland whose rates will increase to support the desalination plant, while gaining none of the benefits. In California, most proposed desalination plants would serve affluent communities in Marin County, the Monterey area, Cambria, southern Orange County, and northern San Diego County. Low–income communities located near desalination facilities could be harmed if desalination facilities increase air pollution and limit access to the ocean for subsistence fishing. A proposed desalination plant in Huntington Beach, California would extend the life of a power plant that residents have been struggling to shut down for years.

Source: Food and Water Watch

Conserving Our Way into the Future

By global standards, U.S. residents use a great deal of water per person per day—an estimated 151 gallons. The United States and Canada top the consumption list worldwide. By comparison, people in the United Kingdom use about 31 gallons per person per day, and in developing countries like Ethiopia, that number comes down to three gallons.

Partly this is because we turn on the tap and clean, cheap water comes out. It's just so easy to use more than we really need.

But because issues of water scarcity are not new to people living in the West and Southwest, many cities have robust programs demonstrating that water conservation combined with water efficiency—using enough but not too much—can extend water supplies far more than most people would imagine. These cities can help us see what we are doing wrong and right when it comes to dealing with issues of supply and demand, and the question of how much water is enough.

Las Vegas: The Lush of the Southwest

A good way to take the measure of an area's water culture is to drive around. As you travel through the Las Vegas Valley, it's hard to conceive of a place with a more schizophrenic attitude toward water. On the Strip the message is one of water abundance. Streets are lined with massive palm trees; blocks are punctuated with impressive water displays; people relax outside in 100-degree heat, thanks to overhead misters that cool the air. It's easy to forget that water is a scarce and precious resource in this region.

Drive off the Strip and things get a bit more confusing. In many parts of the valley, desert landscaping is the norm, in keeping with the arid climate (Las Vegas gets about four inches of rain a year). But other areas in the valley are resplendent with emerald green golf courses, gushing fountains, and waterfalls. Raise your eyes a bit, and just above the tops of the palm trees, the landscape is dry as dust.

From the standpoint of demand, Las Vegans have historically used a lot of water per person. In 1994, single-family

place to another. Many of these projects involve multibillion-dollar pipeline systems that have severe environmental impacts and are extremely energy-intensive because of the need to move water long distances. Fast-growing Washington County in southwestern Utah is proposing to build a 158-mile pipeline to bring Lake Powell water to its towns. In Colorado, an entrepreneur is proposing a 400-mile trans-mountain diversion to bring water from the Flaming Gorge Reservoir on the Utah-Wyoming border to Colorado's Front Range.

The reality is that our water supplies are limited and to a great degree overextended. We need to focus less on costly, energy-intensive ways to increase supply and instead concentrate far more on the demand side of the equation. Finally, there is some good news. It turns out that most cities have tremendous water conservation potential. By reducing demand per person, cities can serve more people with the same amount of water, thus eliminating the need for new water supplies. And for the most part, conservation is both less expensive and better for the environment than supply-side alternatives.

residences used 264 gallons of water per person per day. The water profligacy of those days is gone, partially due to the 1992 National Energy Policy Act, which requires the use of water-efficient fixtures in all houses built after 1992. However, Las Vegans still use substantially more water than residents of many other Western cities.

Cities measure water use in different ways, so it is difficult to make accurate comparisons. For this reason, the Western Resource Advocates (WRA) compare cities on the basis of water use in single-family residences—an apple-to-apple comparison. According to a 2007 report by the Pacific Institute and Western Resource Advocates, *Hidden Oasis: Water Conservation and Efficiency in Las Vegas*, residents of single-family residences in Las Vegas consumed 165 gallons per person per day as compared with 110 gallons per day in Albuquerque, New Mexico and 114 gallons in Tucson, Arizona.

Added to high consumption levels is the fact that the Las Vegas valley has been one of the fastest-growing areas in the country for many years. The population in the valley is already about 1.8 million people, and much of the power structure there would like to see the population double by 2030.

In terms of supply, Las Vegas today depends on Lake Mead for 90 percent of its water.

The Southwest is already many years into what is currently considered a drought, and Lake Mead has about half the water it contained 10 years ago.

This mix is clearly a recipe for trouble. Las Vegas has some hard choices to make to either increase supply, reduce demand, or both. And reducing demand can be accomplished by lowering per capita consumption, limiting growth, or a combination.

It probably won't come as a surprise to learn that Las Vegas wants to have it all. Rather than taking a serious look at limiting growth, the valley is avidly pursuing new sources of water. Las Vegas is heavily invested in a supply-side solution to their water woes.

The Southern Nevada Water Authority (SNWA) is propos-

DESERT WATER USE

Which Desert City Is Most Water Conscious?

- **Albuquerque**
110 gallons/person

- **Tucson**
114 gallons/person

- **Las Vegas**
165 gallons/person

ing to build a massive pipeline system that would extract groundwater from a rural area of the state and pump it hundreds of miles to the Las Vegas Valley. Rural residents believe that exporting water from this high desert environment would turn the region into a giant dustbowl and that the farming and ranching communities in the area would be destroyed. They also suspect that, despite promises to the contrary, if the pipeline gets built, the pressure to keep it full will mean that more water will be pumped each year than will ever get replenished. SNWA has never released figures on the cost of the project, but it will certainly be in the billions of dollars.

SNWA would argue that, in addition to supply-side solutions, it has also put tremendous effort and money into promoting water conservation in order to curb demand. While it is true that the authority has instituted water conservation and efficiency programs, the amount of money it has spent on conservation pales by comparison to the amount projected for the pipeline project. For every dollar invested in water conservation efforts, $14 are spent on developing new supplies, and close to 90 percent of water conservation spending has been for turf removal.

What about curbing demand in Las Vegas? Can more comprehensive and aggressive water conservation and efficiency measures meet the needs of a growing city? We have already seen that Las Vegans use substantially higher amounts of water than residents of Tucson and Albuquerque. Why? The simple answer is that Las Vegas is still behind the curve in its adoption of a culture of water conservation and efficiency. A big problem is that the residents of Las Vegas receive mixed messages regarding water. On one hand they're told that Las Vegas is in a water crisis and people need to conserve—but only outdoors. SNWA does nothing to promote indoor water conservation. On the other hand, people are bombarded with visual images of water abundance.

The good news is that Las Vegas can dramatically reduce its overall water use by aggressively pursuing programs that promote both indoor and outdoor conservation. *Hidden Oasis* concludes that if Las Vegas comprehensively adopted readily available water efficiency measures inside and out, it could reduce its water demand by an additional 86,000 acre feet per year—close to a third of its annual allocation from Lake Mead.

Albuquerque: Developing a Culture of Conservation

Driving around Albuquerque, New Mexico it's hard to believe that until the mid-1990s the residential areas, thanks to the profusion of green lawns, looked a lot like parts of the Midwest. Like other places in the West and Southwest, Albuquerque began growing by leaps and bounds in the 1960s. This growth spurt coincided with one of the wettest periods ever recorded in the history of the region. Every year the summer monsoons would come, the winter snows would accumulate as snowpack in the mountains, and it seemed there was water enough for existing residents and more.

The inconvenient truth that Albuquerque did not have boundless supplies of water came as a shock to many of the people living there. Until 1993 the common perception

among city residents was that Albuquerque sat over a vast underground water source that was continually being replenished, largely by water from the Rio Grande. Most of Albuquerque's water came from this underground aquifer, and city officials thought it was virtually limitless.

The city got a rude awakening in 1993 when the United States Geological Survey (USGS) released a report concluding that there was a lot less water than people thought. In fact, water levels in the aquifer had dropped about 160 feet since the 1960s. Not only was the water level dropping, water was not recharging nearly as quickly as people had thought, and water quality was diminishing as water was taken from deeper wells.

When USGS dropped its bombshell about the depleted

Although Albuquerque has reduced water consumption, the city is still growing, and now is relying on water diverted from the Chama River to help meet the city's needs.

aquifer, the city was already in a water crisis; it just didn't know it. The city government had to move very rapidly to change people's perceptions from a sense of bountiful water to an understanding of water scarcity.

In 1994, the city put into motion a process that included extensive citizen participation in order to develop a comprehensive water policy. One of the primary goals of the plan was a 30 percent reduction of per capita water use.

In the next eight years, Albuquerque exceeded its goals and reduced water consumption by 33 percent, moving it from one of the highest per capita users of water in the Southwest to one of the lowest. As of 2006 the average person in a single-family residence in Albuquerque uses 110 gallons of water per day. This stands in stark contrast to

ALBUQUERQUE EXCEEDED ITS GOALS AND REDUCED WATER CONSUMPTION BY 33 PERCENT.

Get rid of your lawn. About 70 percent of water is used outdoors and nice green lawns are a major water guzzler.

Choose an automatic irrigation system. Automatic sprinkler systems can be set to water the lawn for a specified amount of time. A great deal of water can be wasted in short periods of time if sprinklers are left on unnecessarily. Outdoor faucets can flow at rates as high as 300 gallons per hour.

Position sprinklers so that water lands on the lawn or garden, not on areas where it isn't needed, and avoid watering when it's windy—wind causes water to evaporate quickly.

Buy water-efficient appliances. A front-loading washing machine uses one-third less water than a top-loading machine.

Check all faucets, pipes, and toilets periodically for leaks. A faucet drip or invisible leak in the toilet will add up to 15 gallons of water a day, or 105 gallons a week, which adds up to 5,475 gallons of wasted water a year.

Install water-saving showerheads. Low-flow showerheads deliver 2.5 gallons of water per minute or less and are relatively inexpensive. Older showerheads use 5 to 7 gallons.

Install a 1.6-gallon low-flow toilet. Using these could cut indoor water use by as much as 20 percent. Older toilets use 3.5 to 7 gallons per flush.

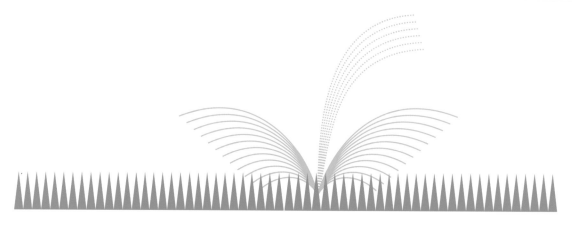

the 165 gallons a day used in Las Vegas.

Albuquerque was able to achieve a remarkable shift in water use in a relatively short period of time. The understanding that the city faced a serious water crisis drove the change, but the city also rose to the challenge. One of the keys was a sizable budget—$1 million per year in the early years of the crisis—for promoting water conservation and developing educational materials.

Anyone visiting Albuquerque today can readily see that residents have adopted a culture of water conservation. Desert landscaping is ubiquitous. In 1995, the city adopted codes limiting the use of turf to no more than 20 percent of irrigable acreage on new private development. Albuquerque also offers rebates to help customers convert from water-intensive turf yards to low-water xeriscape landscaping. In addition, residents receive rebates for replacing high-water-use toilets and washing machines with water-efficient models (together, toilets and washing machines account for over 40 percent of indoor water use in a typical household). These programs and others have been highly

Tucson/Civano: A Leader in Water Conservation

If there's any place in the country that leaps to people's minds when they think of a city with a strong desert aesthetic, it's Tucson. Today almost anywhere you go in Tucson, houses are surrounded not by grass but by cacti and other desert landscaping. In fact, you have to really look to find a house with a green lawn. But it wasn't always that way. Until the 1970s, Tucson was full of lawns. Then there was a crisis: not enough water during periods of peak demand. The city needed to change.

Rather than call for more water, in 1977 Tucson's water department decided to create a highly visible Beat the Peak campaign, encouraging residents to do their outside watering during off-peak periods. It also raised water rates across the board. And it created a new rate structure that made water more costly as consumers used more of it. Studies consistently demonstrate that water demand diminishes as the price of water increases, particularly if the jump in rates is steep. Most cities have adopted a rate structure that is relatively incremental and doesn't send a strong price

UNTIL THE 1970'S, TUCSON WAS FULL OF LAWNS.

effective in helping to reduce Albuquerque's overall water consumption and shift people's consciousness.

However, like Las Vegas, Albuquerque is pursuing a policy of continued growth, which will require difficult choices. The water district has already developed a program to increase supply. In 2008 water from the San Juan and Chama rivers began to augment the city's drinking water, and the San Juan-Chama Drinking Water Project will ultimately supply up to 70 percent of the metropolitan area's future water. To its credit, Albuquerque remains highly ambitious in its efforts to reduce demand and continues to push aggressively for significant reductions in per capita consumption.

signal to customers. Tucson led the way in instituting substantial increases in water prices as consumption went up. While other cities have also raised rates, few have been willing to adopt Tucson's sharp rate increases, which helps to explain why Tucson is consistently at the low end of the spectrum in terms of water consumption.

The combination of approaches proved to be highly effective. Residents changed their habits, and by the early 1980s desert landscaping and a conservation ethic were firmly established. Residents now thoroughly embrace the idea that they live in a desert and should act accordingly. Water conservation is seen as a benefit to the community rather than an individual deprivation.

But some residents of Tucson wanted to demonstrate that even more could be done to reduce water and energy consumption. So, in the 1980s a group of people began meeting to plan a new community in Tucson with a goal of significantly reducing water and energy consumption from the standard levels of the time. Planners were quite ambitious about the kind of community they wanted to create. First of all they wanted homes to be affordable rather than aimed at just the high-end market. And they also wanted it to be "an antidote to urban sprawl's five banes: loss of community, loss of open space, traffic congestion, air pollution, and poor use of resources."

But what made the concept really stand out was the fact that the planners included concrete goals to reduce potable water consumption by 60 percent and home energy consumption for heating and cooling by 50 percent (over the 1995 Tucson model energy code). The way they planned to achieve these goals was not particularly complicated. In terms of energy, it meant building very tight homes (no leaks) with lots of insulation, high standards in terms of the doors, windows, and skylights, and very efficient furnaces and air conditioners. All of the homes have solar panels. The community has been able to reduce water consumption by using water-efficient appliances, strict landscaping standards, small lot sizes, and the use of reclaimed water for outdoor watering.

It took many years to make the dream a reality, but in 2000 the first people began moving into their new homes in what is now known as Civano. Today Civano looks like a lot of other new subdivisions in Tucson—in an odd way, one of the best things about it is that it is unremarkable. This is not a precious retreat for nostalgic baby boomers. Homes average about 1,600 to 1,800 square feet. Lots of retirees live there, but so do lots of people with young children. Only about 10 percent of the homeowners characterize themselves as passionate about the environment. Most residents choose to live here because it's a nice community and the green benefits are an extra perk.

And Civano keeps expanding. Today the homes are built by Pulte, which has been able to build homes that are even more efficient in terms of water and energy consumption than the homes built in the first phase of Civano's development (these had multiple builders). And it's gets better, they're doing it at a price that's only 2 percent higher than comparable homes in the area.

Overall, the houses in Civano consume far less water and energy than "baseline" homes in Tucson. The new Pulte homes use about 47 percent less energy for heating and cooling, 32 percent less energy overall, and 42 percent less potable water than typical Tucson homes. That's really something considering that Tucson's water consumption is already low in comparison to other cities.

Civano's low per-person water and energy consumption is both an inspiration and a ray of hope as we consider our future. This community demonstrates that what constitutes "enough" may be a lot less than we think.

What We Can Learn from Desert Cities
Cities and communities in the Southwest, and all over the developed world, will be forced to rethink their water strategies in the years to come, including taking an honest look at the wisdom of current growth patterns in the face of shrinking water supplies. Rather than increasing supply with infrastructure that can be economically and environmentally costly, we need to focus more on decreasing demand.

All of us from east to west, north to south are facing the impacts of climate change and the possibility of water shortages. It's not going to be easy to reduce our water use; we've become accustomed to abundance. But we're going to have to change our concept of what is enough.

Fortunately, there is ample evidence from cities not only in the West, but all over, that smart water use—including conservation, efficiency, and behavioral changes—is the most cost-effective, least destructive, and most enduring approach to handling diminishing water supplies. Lots of cities, and Civano in particular, have proven that we can do much more to reduce our water use. We just have to make that choice.

The use of xeriscaping, or landscaping with drought-tolerant native plants, has helped residents in desert towns reduce their water use.

THE
VALUE OF WATER

An Art Exhibition 2011-2012

CATHEDRAL OF ST. JOHN THE DIVINE, NEW YORK CITY

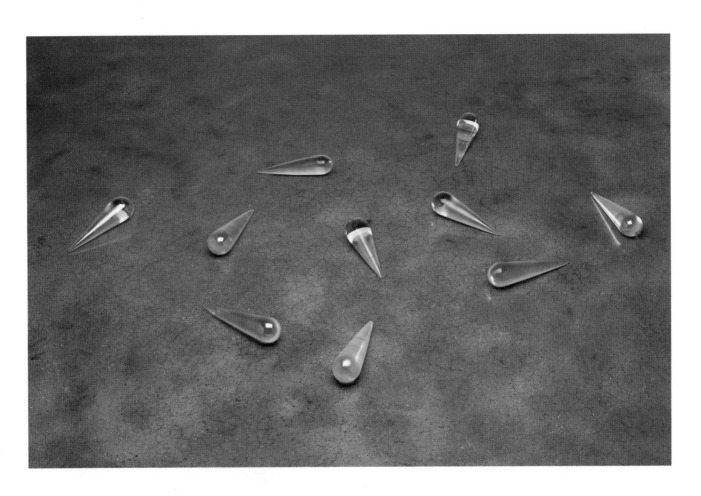

KIKI SMITH
Ten Elements of a Dewbow, 1999
ten elements, from 8" x 2-1/2" (20.3 x 6.4 cm) to 9 x 2-1/2" (22.9 x 6.4 cm) each
72 x 56-1/2" (182.9 x 143.5 cm), overal installed
Photography by G.R. Christmas, courtesy The Pace Gallery
© Kiki Smith, courtesy The Pace Gallery

Working With Nature

ERIN VINTINNER & ELEANOR STERLING

The Mekong River, "Mother of the Waters" in Lao, winds 3,000 miles from its Tibetan Plateau headwaters to its delta, emptying into the South China Sea. The river, along with its feeder streams in Cambodia, China, Laos, Myanmar, Thailand, and Vietnam,

comprise the 300,000-square-mile Mekong River Basin. Approximately 65 million people live in the system, with up to 80 percent supporting themselves with farming and fishing in rural areas. The river system contains almost all of the natural forms fresh water takes on earth—groundwater, lakes, ponds, streams, and wetlands. It is home to over 6,000 known species of vertebrates, and its fish fauna exceeds all but the Amazon and Congo river basins.

During monsoon season, a tributary of the Mekong River reverses direction and flows up into Cambodia's Tonle Sap Lake, advancing shorelines up to 25 miles, nourishing a tremendous diversity of fish and birds, and supporting rice farms. Tonle Sap Lake is the largest freshwater lake in Southeast Asia, with impacts on Cam-bodia's geography, culture, and economy. The rising and falling waters influence nearly everything about life on the lake—houses and entire villages are built on stilts or float on pontoons.

Teeming with biodiversity, the Mekong is one of the most important freshwater ecosystems in the world, and it is one of the world's only major rivers with few mainstream dams. However, upstream hydroelectric dams in Laos, Thailand, and China have begun interfering with the natural water and sediment fluctuations that sustain the river basin's living systems. And more dams are slated for construction in the coming years.

These threats combine with increasing water extrac-

The Tonle Sap Lake in Cambodia is the largest freshwater lake in Southeast Asia.

tions, pollution, invasive species, and overfishing to paint a bleak picture for the basin's future. But these are also the same threats that are affecting freshwater ecosystems around the world, as a growing human population and calls for economic growth make ever-greater demands on our freshwater resources.

As we know, water is essential to the existence and evolution of life on Earth, yet less than 1 percent of the world's water is both fresh and available to humans and all other freshwater-dependent species. As we confront the global water crisis, we must consider both our role and responsibility toward ensuring adequate water for other species and how we can work with nature to find solutions.

While they represent a relatively small area of the planet's total surface, freshwater ecosystems, such as rivers, streams, lakes, ponds, and wetlands (like marshes and swamps), harbor a disproportionate amount of the world's treasured biodiversity.

Freshwater ecosystems contain about 10 percent of all known species, including an estimated 40 percent of the world's fish species and one third of the world's vertebrate species.[1,2] This amazing biodiversity includes everything from the endangered Mekong giant catfish (*Pangasianodon gigas*) that can weigh more than 550 pounds to the tiny 12-spot skimmer dragonfly (*Libellula pulchella*) that lives part of its life in the ponds and lakes of North America. These ecosystems are paramount: They also carry out many important functions that are crucial for the health of the animals and plants that live in them, the terrestrial and marine ecosystems they are connected to, and human

High Impact: There are substantial social, economic, and ecological costs that are often unanticipated. Tens of millions of people have been displaced from their homes by large-scale water projects over the past century. And we regularly neglect the consequences for nonhuman species and ecological systems. Examples of high-impact approaches include:

- Damming and diverting rivers for irrigation, drinking water, flood control, and hydropower

- Altering the natural course of water bodies for navigation

- Directing waste streams into local rivers, lakes, and coastal marine areas

Low Impact: Under a low-impact water regime, the role of management shifts from building and maintaining water-supply infrastructure to providing water services. These include:

- Employing drought resistant landscaping

- Redesigning urban spaces for water conservation and efficiency

- Resusing and recycling water

populations that depend on them.

These functions, also known as "ecosystem services," include cycling water and nutrients throughout the atmosphere and the biosphere, modifying floods and droughts, delivering nutrients to coastal areas and floodplains, and providing habitat for aquatic plants and animals. In addition to benefiting from freshwater ecosystems through all these processes, humans also use these systems more directly for travel and transport routes, energy production through hydropower, harvesting of plants and animals for food, recreation, drinking water, waste removal, and water purification.

It is difficult to calculate a monetary value for all the services provided by freshwater ecosystems, but some scientists have estimated the value of wetlands alone to be in the trillions of U.S. dollars per year. Whatever the exact amount, it is clear that humans and freshwater ecosystems are tightly interconnected, and the health of human populations depends heavily on the healthy functioning of freshwater ecosystems.

And yet, these ecosystems have the highest proportion of species threatened with extinction as they are increasingly besieged by a range of human activities, including water extraction, pollution, and physical alteration.

But there are ways to help save the ecosystems these species and the rest of us depend on for survival. The key is to work with nature, instead of against it, to harness the power of ecosystem services to solve our water woes.

High-Impact Approaches

The history of human civilization has been tightly linked with freshwater resources. Many of the world's greatest cities are sited along lakes and rivers. In order to reap the benefits provided by these resources for human development, societies have taken a utilitarian view: damming and diverting flows for irrigation, drinking water, flood control, and hydropower; altering the natural courses of water bodies for navigation; and directing waste streams into local rivers, lakes, and coastal marine environments.

In 1996 the world's human population was using over half of all the world's renewable fresh water contained in rivers, lakes, and accessible underground aquifers. This percentage is conservatively projected to climb to at least 70 percent by 2025, reflecting human population growth alone, and by much more if per capita consumption continues to increase.[3]

Industrialized societies in particular have been remarkably successful at delivering vast quantities of water whenever and wherever required, by employing large-scale, capital intensive approaches with centralized management, also known as "high impact" approaches,[4] which include large dams and networks of pipes and canals that carry massive amounts of water over long distances.

But the cost for these projects continues to increase with population and the continual upkeep these projects demand. The most-cited estimate of the cost of meeting the world's future infrastructure needs for water is $180 billion per year until 2025 for water supply, sanitation, wastewater treatment, agriculture, and environmental protection. This figure assumes that future global demand for water and water-related services will match the current level of industrialized nations and that high impact approaches will provide those services.[5]

Many of these infrastructure- and energy-intensive high-impact approaches of hydrologic control have benefited millions of people over the last few centuries through reliable access to safe water, improved public health, expanded hydropower generation, agriculture, and reduced risks of seasonal floods and droughts. They focus on the provision of more water to meet growing human demands because planners often equate the idea of using less water with a loss of well-being.[6]

However, there are substantial social, economic, and

WATER LEADER WORKING TO KEEP THE FLOW

Living Technology Institute, Wastewater Recycling

Eric Lohan, research manager for Living Technology Institute

THE LIVING TECHNOLOGY INSTITUTE makes Living Machines®, engineered ecosystems that treat wastewater or stormwater so it can be reused for irrigation, toilet flushing or industrial uses. The patented treatment process uses plants and microorganisms to remove nutrients and solids from wastewater. Aesthetically attractive, the machines have been integrated into landscape and building architecture at schools and universities, office buildings, institutions, military bases, and food processing facilities. Living Machines save water and use a fraction of the energy of competing technologies. For more info visit *livingmachines.com*.

ecological costs that are often unanticipated in the quest for high-impact approaches. Tens of millions of people have been displaced from their homes by large-scale water projects over the past century. And we regularly neglect the consequences for nonhuman species and ecological systems. Over one-quarter of all North American freshwater fauna populations of fishes, mollusks, crayfishes, amphibians, and insects are now considered threatened with extinction.[7] As humankind withdraws and pollutes a growing share of Earth's fresh water, less remains to maintain the vital ecosystems on which we also depend.[8]

In addition to water quantity, water quality is an issue for organisms downstream from us in the water cycle. Wastewater treatment, for example, cannot remove all the impurities that enter waste streams, such as chemicals from pharmaceutical and personal care products. These products, which include prescription and over-the-counter drugs, antibacterial soaps, antiseptic cleaning agents, and cosmetics, contain chemicals that move unchanged through the waste stream, ending up eventually in freshwater ecosystems and coastal areas. For example, Triclosan, the active ingredient in many antibacterial products, is now found in detectable concentrations in bodies of water across the United States. Recent research has shown that this chemical negatively impacts the hormonal system of developing frogs.[9]

Low-Impact Approaches

The limitations of the high-impact approach for water, combined with the sheer social and economic cost of infrastructure, indicate the need for an alternative low-impact approach that focuses on flexible, sustainable solutions that match in scale and geographic distribution to human populations and their needs.[10]

Low-impact approaches are local-scale, efficient, and ecologically sensitive solutions to the problem of water management. According to the Pacific Institute's *The World's Water 2002-2003*, these approaches provide genuine alternatives to the more traditional high-impact

approach of centralized infrastructure. Low-impact advocates strive to improve the productivity of water use rather than seek endless sources of new supply. Society's goal becomes not the use of water, but improved social and individual well-being per unit of water used.[11,12]

Under a low-impact water regime, the role of management shifts from building and maintaining water-supply infrastructure to providing water services, such as new forms of sanitation, drought-resistant landscapes, urban redesign for conservation, and water reuse and recycling. This approach also incorporates constraints that limit the amount of water humans can withdraw so that shortages do not disrupt how ecosystems function. These low-impact alternative approaches offer a comprehensive toolbox of possible solutions.[13]

The Value of Wetlands

A substantial portion of the total fresh water available in the hydrological cycle is needed to sustain natural aquatic ecosystems, such as lakes, rivers, wetlands, and the multitude of species they shelter.[14] For centuries, wetlands were mistreated and misunderstood. Generally called swamps or marshes, they were considered useless, waterlogged, even dangerous land better off filled, farmed, and developed. That's one reason over half the original wetlands in the lower 48 states have been lost and much of the rest degraded. This poses a serious problem.

Wetlands provide key wildlife habitat and are also culturally significant across the world. They are found from the equatorial tropics to the frozen plains of Siberia and are crucial to the planet's well-being.[15] Healthy natural wetlands are indispensable regulators of water quantity and quality. For example, flood plain wetlands soak up and store water when rivers flood their banks, reducing downstream damage. Wetlands also filter pollutants and sediments, and provide valuable products, such as food, medicinal plants, fuel sources, fiber, and timber. Fortunately we are beginning to realize the value of these environmental services to humankind is immense.

Residents of the Megma Valley in Nepal use nets to strain fog. The system provides water for the community and means women no longer have to walk long distances to gather water.

PHOTOGRAPH BY BRENT STIRTON

Across the world, and in the United States, people are coming to appreciate wetlands for what they offer and take advantage of their ability to purify both wastewater effluent and stormwater overflows.

For example, the Carolina Bay Natural Land Treatment Program relies on a natural wetland as the final treatment stage for wastewater effluent that has already undergone primary and secondary treatment to remove solids and treat biological matter at a nearby facility.[16]

Similar systems exist in many states, from California to Florida. Especially in urbanized areas where construction and paving have increased the amount of impervious surface area, rainfall cannot percolate into the soil and is converted into overflow runoff that washes urban pollutants into nearby bodies of water or sewage systems. Excess runoff can exceed the drainage capacity of existing wastewater treatment systems, and during heavy storms cities regularly have to direct untreated wastewater into nearby streams and rivers. Across the U.S, over 700 cities and communities with about 40 million people rely on these "combined sewer systems."[17] In New York City, overflow from this combined system results in 270 billion gallons of untreated wastewater flowing into New York Harbor annually.[18]

Using Rainwater as Resource

Relatively clean rainwater that is directed into sewers makes little sense if alternatives exist, such as redirecting rain water into parks or wetlands (though it is important to ensure that the waste stream is managed so as not to degrade the wetlands). Another low-impact alternative is the use of permeable pavement, which is a pavement system that allows water to seep through the surface, permitting natural filtration of water through soil, rather than runoff into storm drains.

Green roofs are a further example of a low-impact solution to the problem of stormwater runoff. Various green roof designs exist, but the fundamental principle involves layering of waterproofing materials, soil support system, and appropriately chosen drought-resistant plants. Besides the ability of green roof systems to absorb rain and moderate against pulses of storm runoff, the thermal insulation provided by the soil layer can provide energy savings over conventional roofing. One such system was installed in 2002 on top of the Justice Center in Seattle, Washington, as part of the city's sustainable building program. This green roof requires minimal maintenance and is estimated to reduce annual storm water runoff from the building by 50 to 75 percent.[19] Given the extensive costs of high-impact

THE USE OF LOW-IMPACT WATER TREATMENT OPTIONS MAKES ECOLOGICAL AND ECONOMIC SENSE.

wastewater and storm water treatment, exploring the use of low-impact water treatment options makes ecological and economic sense.

The Growing Field of Ecological Design

The Environmental Protection Agency notes that constructed wetlands are also being used to treat petroleum refinery wastes, landfill leachates, and pretreated industrial wastewaters, such as those from pulp and paper mills. A large number of wetlands have been constructed to treat drainage from active and abandoned coal mines, particularly in Appalachia.[20]

The emerging fields of ecological design and ecological engineering are informing the practice of wetland construction. Ecological designers use appropriate technology and ecological principles to engineer low-impact solutions to environmental problems. One remarkable ecologically designed installation transformed a canal in Fuzhou, China, that was polluted with sewage. The artificial wetland constructed on the site, called an "eco machine," used a combination of plants, microorganisms, and an aeration system to restore the canal.

Today, the canal has reduced floating solids and odors, and it no longer negatively impacts downstream aquatic ecosystems.[21] Another such facility in South Burlington, Vermont, is using the principles of ecological design and constructed wetlands to successfully treat 80,000 gallons of wastewater diverted daily from the city's conventional waste treatment plant.[22]

Wastewater Is Not Always a Waste

Wastewater recycling is another potential low-impact solution to the growing problem of water management. This approach emphasizes the value of wastewater as not just a "waste" product but as a potential source of water that can be put to use. In some cases, treated wastewater effluent can be used for irrigation or in situations where the use of nonpotable water is acceptable, such as for flushing toilets. However, the utility of recycled wastewa-

ter may also be extended to drinking water sources in carefully designed systems. In order to address the challenge of meeting the water needs of the growing city of Aurora, Colorado, water managers have developed an innovative solution known as the Prairie Waters Project, slated to begin operation in 2011.

For this project, the city will continue to draw water from its current source, the South Platte River. Once the water enters the waste stream, it is returned to the river after passing through a treatment facility. About 20–30 miles downstream, the city has drilled wells to pull water up from the riverbed, using the gravel and sand as a natural filter.

This extracted water will then be pumped back to Aurora (along the way, treated with chemicals and UV light to soften the water and remove any microbial contaminants picked up during the journey and then filtered), approximating a closed loop of recycled water.[23] A drop of water used by a resident would find its way back to the city's taps as a half-drop in 45 to 60 days, a quarter-drop 45 to 60 days after that, and so on.[24] Innovative approaches, such as the Prairie Waters project, will be increasingly necessary as water stress increases in areas such as the southwestern United States due to increasing population and demand on a finite resource.

Reviving the Ancient Practice of Rainwater Harvesting

One of the oldest recorded hydrological techniques, rainwater harvesting is another example of a sustainable low-impact approach to water management. Since rainwater is relatively clean in comparison with many surface waters, it makes both economical and ecological sense to use rainwater as a resource. On smaller household scales, rainwater harvesting is practiced across the world.

In Southeast Asian countries, rainwater jars are made of durable materials and may hold as much as several thousand liters. Gutters funnel rain from the roof into the mouth of the jar, which is covered with mesh to screen out leaves and other debris. The water can then be drawn from a tap at the bottom of the jar. Collecting rainwater in this way is a popular technique throughout the region, where rainfall patterns vary greatly throughout the year.

The idea is catching on. In the United States and the United Kingdom, rainwater-harvesting systems have been increasingly used in households, gardens, and even commercial venues. Academic institutions, community groups, government agencies, and cooperatives such as the Texas Cooperative Extension hosted by Texas A&M University are actively promoting rainwater harvesting as a sustainable way to augment water supplies and reduce demand on municipal water systems. California offers a tax credit for household rainwater harvesting systems. Residents in Australian cities such as Sydney and Brisbane can receive a rebate for installing rainwater-harvesting systems for household use.[25,26]

On larger scales, some municipal systems have even incorporated rainwater harvesting. For thousands of years, arid Yemen has relied on large cisterns to collect rainwater for public use. In some United States cities, such as Seattle, Tucson, and Austin, rainwater systems are increasingly being used in larger buildings, public facilities, and schools to irrigate landscaping and supply restroom facilities.

Xeriscaping with Appropriate Plants

Another example of a water management technique that can work synergistically with nature is the practice of xeriscaping, or landscaping that does not require additional watering or irrigation to maintain. Over 50 percent

of the total water used in households in the United States is used outside the home to water lawns and gardens, and to maintain pools.[27] The EPA estimates that over 7 billion gallons per day are used in landscape irrigation alone in the United States. Especially in hot and dry climates of many parts of the country, water-intensive lawns and gardens are unnecessarily consuming vast amounts of precious water resources.

Xeriscaping typically involves the use of appropriate plant species that tolerate or avoid water stress, the practice of hydrozoning (grouping plants with similar watering requirements), and conserving water by using garden designs and soil types that minimize evaporation. Oftentimes, these drought resistant plants and turf are native to the area and are accustomed to the local climate. There are numerous advantages to xeriscaping, including water conservation, reduced water costs and lawn and garden maintenance, and flexibility during times of water restriction or drought.

Examples of How Investing in Natural Systems Pay Off

Technological solutions to our water woes will always capture our imagination, but they often solve one problem while creating another and carry high costs, both monetary and environmental. Oftentimes, there are natural, intact ecosystems that continue to offer the numerous benefits humankind depends upon.

The Nakivubo Swamp, Uganda

The largest wetland in Uganda's Kampala district, the Nakivubo Swamp, is a prime example of the vital ecosystem services that natural wetlands provide. Many of the city's residential settlements and some of its industrial facilities are not connected to Kampala's sewage system, and as a result, the wetland receives contaminated water flows that drain from the city's central business area, industrial district, and residential settlements.[28] The Nakivubo swamp purifies the discharge before it enters

Thanks to a Living Machine®, visitors to the El Monte Sagrado resort in Taos, New Mexico are treated to a lush cascade of water features, hydroponic plants, and engineered wetlands, all of which are constantly working to cleanse wastewater and rainwater for re-use.

Lake Victoria, which in turn serves as a drinking water source for Kampala.[29,30]

The originally extensive Nakivubo wetland has become severely degraded over recent years and is particularly threatened by the spread of agriculture and industrial and residential developments. The areas surrounding Nakivubo, and the wetland itself, are regarded as prime sites for urban expansion for many reasons: their proximity to the city center, land shortage in higher areas of Kampala, and relatively cheap land prices as compared to other parts of the municipality.[31]

Yet, studies conducted by the World Conservation Union and the United Nations' World Water Assessment Program have estimated the cost of replacing just the wetland's wastewater processing services with high impact technologies. The study found that the infrastructure required to achieve a similar level of wastewater treatment to that provided by the wetland would incur costs of up to U.S. $2 million a year in terms of extending sewerage and treatment facilities. [32,33] If residents lose this resource, they lose a vital environmental and economic asset. Investment in and protection of the Nakivubo wetland is essential for the residents of Kampala.

New York City's Water Source

The case of the New York City water supply system is an excellent example of the tremendous benefits of investing in natural systems. The main sources of drinking water for the nine million people of NYC are the Catskill and Delaware watersheds in upstate New York. The city water supply system from these watersheds is the largest unfiltered system in the world.

Since 1997, NYC has worked with upstate communities to protect and invest over $1.5 billion in the natural water purification services provided by these watersheds. This investment has allowed the city to maintain the high quality of the water from the watersheds and, as a result, avoid the prospect of having to build a multibillion-dollar water filtration plant.

HUMANS AND ALL OTHER SPECIES ARE CONNECTED BY THE GLOBAL WATER CYCLE, AND WE ARE TRULY EACH DOWNSTREAM FROM ONE ANOTHER.

NYC compensates residents of upstate watershed communities, who are significantly impacted by restrictions on their development activities, for their vital work in ensuring the quality of the water. Compensation avenues include a residential septic rehabilitation and replacement reimbursement program. This case demonstrates that stewardship of water is not an altruistic act, but a rational one of self-preservation; the goods and services that freshwater ecosystems provide are absolutely central to our quality of life. It also demonstrates the hard work it takes to arrive at effective compromises across different stakeholder groups when it comes to investing in natural systems.

Reasons To Be Hopeful

Beyond the story of the New York City water supply system, there are hopeful signs that keeping freshwater habitats intact and healthy is becoming a top global priority. Initiatives by the United Nations, such as the Millennium Ecosystems Assessment and the Ramsar Convention on Wetlands, seek to recognize and preserve the vital functions provided by freshwater ecosystems.

The remarkable Mekong River Basin is one example of such a natural system that deserves investment and protection, as it is one of the world's least degraded river systems. Several transboundary initiatives that may help balance the needs of people and wildlife are emerging between the six nations that share the Mekong. Political mechanisms, such as the Mekong River Commission, are moving toward more holistic management that takes into account environmental health and sustainability, though these political mechanisms are dependent on the support of their member governments.

Becoming Water Stewards

Humans and all other species are connected by the global water cycle, and we are truly each downstream from one another. This interconnectedness brings with it responsibility to properly steward our freshwater resources. In doing so, we can invest in natural systems to help us navigate our coming water crisis. There are numerous examples of how nature can help—from investing in natural and constructed wetlands for wastewater purification and storm water control, to employing the principles of ecological design, to local-scale water conservation measures such as rainwater harvesting.

The study of ecosystem services as they relate to water is still developing. Scientists are working to understand how resilient freshwater ecosystems truly are to modification without compromising essential functions. Accurately valuing water, human impacts on water, and the functions of freshwater ecosystems, is a constant challenge, as is clarifying the tradeoffs inherent in confronting the water crisis.

Although restoration and regeneration are possible, they are costly and require long-term commitment. Our best option is to preserve healthy functioning ecosystems and the natural services they provide. Actions we take today to reduce or mitigate human impacts on rivers, lakes, wetlands, and all our waterways, can ensure their health for generations to come.

The spillway for the Neversink Reservoir in upstate New York, which provides drinking water for New York City.

Water in Myth and Religion

WILLIAM WATERWAY

In my boyhood I served as an altar boy in the Catholic Church. Even though I no longer practice the Catholic religion, I recall with fascination the rituals and beliefs surrounding water. Making the sign of the cross with fingers moistened with holy water, the

use of water in baptism by anointing the head or by immersion; the sprinkling of water with an aspergillum on the congregation during certain ceremonies; the use of holy water as a sacrament to protect against evil.

Today, after decades of researching and experimenting with water, I have come to see and feel water as a religious experience. This feeling manifests itself in realms of the physical, emotional, mental, and spiritual.

For instance, each time I submerge myself into a hot tub; enter a hot spring; sit or stand beneath a waterfall; wash my feet after a long day of hiking; quench my thirst from a bubbling spring; wash my sore hands after a hard day's labor; or enter into a body of water, there is a sense of well-being that emotionally moves me to quietly give thanks.

During backcountry travels across America and Sahara Desert on horseback, and by foot across remote regions in other countries, I've lived each moment with a heightened awareness of connecting with water—for my survival, health, and peace of mind.

Throughout ancient history, nomadic people almost always traveled along waterways, oftentimes following the trails of animal herds. All of our early ancestors knew that their daily existence was dependent upon the waters that supported the natural world surrounding them. It is for this reason that we find prehistoric places of worship and healing that were established near special bodies of water such as springs, waterfalls, or at the confluence of rivers.

It is through our ancient ancestors that we find the first connections of water with the mysteries of life and death; creation and destruction; death and rebirth; health and illness; good and evil; the known and unknown.

As I continue to evolve, I find it interesting to attend the services of various religions. As a result, I am intrigued how almost every service offers the presence of water or something about water as ritual or in prayer. This use of water predates today's institutionalized religions and has survived for untold thousands of years.

Why is this? Over and over again the answer flows from the mystery of water itself.

Could it be that water, the common denominator connecting all life, is also the common denominator connecting all religions? And, if this is true, through water will we soon discover new knowledge about our spiritual connection to each other?

Perhaps, this will happen much in the same way that water continues to reveal information to us about the interconnectedness of all life. Water may serve as an important factor in our finding a common ground to neutralize religious and water conflicts. If two or more theocratic governments are negotiating water rights, they may recognize their preexisting enjoyment of common water rituals and reconcile.

It is no coincidence that water scarcity often serves as the undercurrent for diplomacy in order to avoid conflict.

Tens of thousand of people make the annual journey to Ville-Bonheur, Haiti for the Saut D'eau festival. The Virgin Mary is said to have appeared at this remote waterfall during the mid 1800s.

PHOTOGRAPH BY KIRSTEN LUCE

IN ALMOST EVERY FORM OF MYTHOLOGY WATER IS PRESENTED AS A NECESSARY INGREDIENT FOR THE CREATION OF THE WORLD.

The Mystery of Water in Science

Another theme we find in various religions is the concept of the "trinity," whereby the "three" are actually "one."

For instance, we find that Brahma is the Hindu god associated with the formation of the universe and is one of the three important Hindu gods, along with Vishnu and Shiva.

In the Christian belief system, the Bible teaches us about God the Father, God the Son, and God the Holy Spirit. The riddle to there being three gods is resolved in the "doctrine of the Trinity," which simply states, "God is simultaneously both Three and One."

As an analogy, we often find water being used as an example of how three entities may exist as one.

However, as we explore the structure of water today using our high-tech tools and modern computers, we have discovered a mystery in the structure of water. A mystery whereby the trinity structure of water presents a myriad of ever-changing configurations that have thus far baffled all fields of modern science.

Among the more than 15 million chemical species we presently know—water possesses indecipherable properties that make it unusual and mysterious. Water—as a trinity of two hydrogen chemical elements and one oxygen chemical element—breaks all the rules that normally apply to our physical dimension. Just the fact that water exists as a liquid, solid, and gas (another trinity) makes it unique. Especially, when we learn that as a solid, water is lighter than its liquid form.

Using sophisticated computer molecular modeling simulations, we now know that the hydrogen bonds of water connect and disconnect at over a trillion times each second. In other words—the structure of water is constantly and dynamically changing in a disorderly fashion that is influenced by variables beyond our ability to quantify and identify.

It is also because of this unique behavior, that whenever water touches our skin—it changes its form to accommo-

date the shape of our body. Water can do this because its hydrogen and oxygen molecules are rapidly connecting and disconnecting at over one trillion times each second.

Just the simple act of submerging one's body into a bathtub, pond, lake, ocean, or river is an impressive feat of physics. How amazing it is to feel the energy of shifting water molecules massaging and pressing themselves against our skin.

It is also because of this mysterious fact that we and other life forms have the gift of motion. As we move, the connecting and disconnecting molecular bonds of water inside our bodies change form to allow us to experience motion as a "living" being. This unsolvable mystery of the molecular structure of water may be one reason why water is often affiliated with the mystical realms of religion.

Water Worship

In his book *Patterns in Comparative Religion*, Mircea Eliade explains how water "precedes all forms and upholds all creations." In exploring the religious use of various water rituals, Eliade tells us, "Immersion in water symbolizes a return to the pre-formal, a total regeneration, a new birth, for immersion means dissolution of forms, a reintegration into the formlessness of pre-existence; and emerging from the water is a repetition of the act of creation in which form was first expressed."

Eliade's words echo the fact that in almost every form of mythology, both recorded and oral, water is presented as a necessary ingredient for the creation of the world and of humankind. Recognition of this fact may be seen as the source or essence of many rituals involving water. For this reason, we find many gods and prophets being quoted as

A baptism taking place in the Jordan River on the border of Israel, the Palestinian territories, and Jordan.

they speak with reverence about water. Water also plays a vital part in many of the rituals and sacred writings that have evolved through time.

In the *Encyclopedia of Religion* we read that in addition to its generative powers, water can heal and prolong life:

> *As vital principle, water allows people to ward*
> *off illness and to keep death away.*
> *Because water makes the plants of pharmacopoeia grow,*
> *or because of the effects of its intrinsic qualities,*
> *the Veda associates it with the origin of medicine.*
> *Water is even capable of conferring immortality ...*
>
> *There is a more enigmatic aspect of water:*
> *it possesses wisdom and knowledge.*
> *Water seeks the truth, we read in the Vedas.*
> *The Mesopotamian water god Ea,*
> *full of wisdom, dispenses counsel to the gods*
> *[and] resembles Proteus, who knows the present,*
> *the past, and the future ...*
> *But perhaps the wisdom of the water gods is*
> *a function of their age. In the Hellenic world,*
> *the wisest among them are called*
> *"the old men of the sea."*

The thought of water possessing knowledge that is transferred to humans is a foundation stone in the belief system of the Ijaw, a tribe that lives along the Niger River and has long believed that the Niger transmits knowledge and information to its people.

This is a similar idea to the Sufi practice of "imitation." According to old Sufi teachings, there is a purpose to knowledge that is passed along by certain teachers, even though the teachers mostly imitate the words and rituals relating to water. This imitation of ancient worship was once commented on by the great Sufi Master Jalaluddin Rumi shortly before his death in 1273. One of his last messages was, "The imitator is like a canal. It does not itself drink, but may transmit water to the thirsty."

This translates to other religions where there are many examples of the ritualistic use of water—John the Baptist cleansing people of their sins through the sacrament of baptism; Jesus Christ washing feet; Pontius Pilate washing his hands before turning Jesus over for crucifixion; a Greek Orthodox priest using an aspergillum to sprinkle holy water over the altar before beginning the ceremony; using water to exorcise demons; the use of a mikvah for monthly cleansing by orthodox Jewish women; Japanese Kamikaze pilots using hand-painted cups to drink from a

Left, Prayer bells at Lake Manosaravar, Tibet. *Right,* The Shinto practice of Misogi Harai is performed to cleanse impurity.

common bowl before flying off to their deaths; the blessing of wedding rings in a Catholic ceremony; the washing of hands by Moslems before reading the Koran; and the washing away of sins by millions of worshipers in the Ganges River each year.

Today, the symbolic and physical presence of water for washing, healing, sprinkling, drinking, pouring, anointing, and worshiping remains an important practice.

Water and Religion

Even though the reasons many water rituals were originally created may be forgotten, they remain a vital part of ongoing worship.

In Eastern religions, the sacredness of water receives great emphasis. For example, according to Hindu teachings, the "waters of life" bring humankind the life force itself. This idea is prevalent elsewhere.

The sacredness of water was expressed clearly in the early Hindu writings of India known as Vedas (Veda means "knowledge"). These Vedas were written in ancient Sanskrit and include the psalms, incantations, hymns, and formulas of worship practiced by the faithful. In the ancient Vedas water is called "matritamah" (most maternal).

In India, there is an extensive temple complex known as Rameshvaram. This complex is located near the seashore in Tamil Nadu in South India. Within this elaborate temple are 22 sacred bathing pools. These pools receive over 10,000 pilgrims each day and are famous for their miraculous healings. The pilgrims immerse themselves in the water fully clothed before going on to pray in another part of the temple complex. According to the explorer, anthropologist and photographer Martin Gray, who has visited over 600 sacred sites in 40 countries, the Rameshvaram temple is one of the most visited and vital sacred sites of all of Asia.

Another major theme in Eastern thought is the Dao concept of yin and yang. In the book *Eastern Wisdom,* edited by C. Scott Littleton, it says that water is thought to represent the Dao:

> *"Nothing is softer than water,*
> *yet it is stronger than anything when it attacks*
> *hard and resistant things. Gentleness prevails*
> *over hardness; weakness conquers strength";*
> *"The highest good is like water.*
> *Water benefits the myriad creatures*
> *without contending with them and*
> *comes to rest where none wishes to be.*
> *Thus it is close to the Dao."*

A variation on this water theme can be seen at every Shinto shrine in Japan. Each shrine has a water bowl decorated with sacred images. Those who enter the shrine are required to dip water from the bowl and wash their hands and clean out their mouths. This ritualistic cleaning is an ancient practice of purifying the spirit and body before worship. Shintoists also believe that departed spirits return to the flowing water of rivers as a way of traveling home to the next world.

The Japanese are also known to use cold spring water for healing, as evidenced by their famous Moon Washing Spring. Another form of mind, body, and spirit purification is practiced by Zen monks who sit beneath a cold waterfall in order to try and cleanse and heal themselves of this world's defilements.

The use of cold water for healing can also be found in India. As an ancient practice, yogis dive into cold water to help induce wakefulness of the body, mind, and spirit. On a similar note, the Brahman rainmaker has to bring himself into union with water three times a day, as well as on various special occasions.

Elsewhere in Asia in the far western region of Tibet, rising over 22,000 feet above sea level, is the holy Mount Kailash. This mountain, and its sacred Lake Manosaravar, have been worshipped long before the dawn of recorded history, and are considered sacred by the religions of Buddhism, Hinduism, Jainism, Ayyavazhi, and the Bön faith. These five religions have a following of about 1.3 billion people around the globe.

Buddhism, Hinduism, and Jainism all have origin myths that include stories of Mount Kailash and its holy water. The believers see the water that comes from this mountain as the birthing place of all things and the ongoing center of the world.

To the Hindus, Mount Kailash is the pillar of the world; is the center of the world mandala; and is located at the heart of six mountain ranges symbolizing a lotus. They believe the four rivers flowing from Kailash flow to the four quarters of the world and divide the world into four

regions. In fact the Indus, Brahmaputra, Sutlej (a major Indus tributary), and the Karnali (a major Ganges tributary), all flow from the mountain—indeed making it the hydrographic nexus of South Asia.

To date, there have been no recorded attempts to climb Mount Kailash; it is considered off limits to climbers out of respect to its sacred nature. Because of this Mount Kailash is the most significant peak in the world that has not seen any known climbing attempts.

Water Beliefs of Indigenous Peoples

Just like the ancient Sumerians and Egyptians, the American and Australian natives also had a body of knowledge that was passed along orally for thousands of years before the written word.

In what is now the United States, the Kwakiutl tribes of the Northwest, the Algonquin tribes of the East, and the Taos Indians of the Southwest all shared the similar belief that in the beginning of all things there was only water.

The Taos Pueblo Indians of New Mexico to this day believe that Blue Lake is the center of the universe, the source of all created humans, and the home of all departed souls. Blue Lake is an ancient spring-fed lake high in the nearby Sangre de Cristo or Rocky Mountains. According to local mythology, the waters of Blue Lake are believed to possess mystical properties that sustain the well-being of the Taos Pueblo on many levels, as well as sustaining the ongoing reality of all of creation. Each summer for centuries beyond memory, every able-bodied person in the tribe has made a pilgrimage to the lake to give thanks and pray for the universe.

Holding a similar belief, several aboriginal coastal clans in Australia believe they were led to their locations long ago by individuals called Wandjina. These clans believe that after death each Wandjina was represented by a painting on a cave or rock shelter in the clan's country and that the Wandjina spirits went into a "water-place." As a result, the Wandjina spirits are associated with coastal rains, the rainbow, the sky, and therefore the cycle of seasons. Every

ALL OF OUR EARLY ANCESTORS
KNEW THAT THEIR DAILY EXISTENCE
WAS DEPENDANT UPON THE WATERS
THAT SUPPORTED THE
NATURAL WORLD AROUND THEM.

Photograph by Gabriel Muñiz Buendía

Millions of devout Hindus take a dip in the Ganges during Kumbh Mela, a festival celebrated every three years and sometimes described as the world's largest religious gathering.

year as the wet season approaches, each clan retouches the rock paintings, thus making sure they continue to exist. In this way, the dream spirits that bring rain become operative, as they were in the days when the Wandjina lived on Earth, thus ensuring that the wet season will come, vegetation will grow, and animal and bird life will be plentiful.

Another living example of the passing along of ancient information concerning water is provided by the Kogi Indian tribe in Colombia. The Kogi live in the remote mountains and represent one of the few surviving pre-Columbian civilizations. Due to the geographical barriers of the Andes on one side and the Caribbean on the other, the Kogi, until recently, had lived undisturbed for thousands of years.

Living high atop the mountains, the Kogi began to notice changes in the vegetation and wildlife, and in the snow and ice formations. It did not take them long to realize that these destructive changes were caused by modern human activities. For this reason, the Kogi decided to come forth from isolation to warn all humankind that the water of our Earth must soon be nurtured back to health.

It is no surprise for us to learn from the Kogi, that their word for water is the same as their word for spirit, and that all of creation was born from "water thinking."

The Kogi warn that humankind must change its ways, or else a great catastrophe will soon come to pass. The Kogi's respect and love for water is an integral part of their culture. For untold thousands of years they have lived their lives according to ancient customs.

We should heed their words. Indeed, without respect for water, there cannot be respect for the forms of life it creates. Without respect for life, I believe the human race will not survive to evolve to its fullest potential. It is as simple and as complex as that. In time, we may learn that it is in the sharing of common beliefs about water that hope for all life on Earth springs.

Why We Need a Water Ethic

SANDRA L. POSTEL

Now for the million dollar questions: Why has so much of modern water management gone awry? Why is it that ever greater amounts of money and ever more sophisticated engineering have not solved the world's water problems? Why, in so many places

on this planet, are rivers drying up, lakes shrinking, and water tables falling?

The answer, in part, is simple: We have been trying to meet insatiable demands by continuously expanding a finite freshwater supply. In the long run, of course, that is a losing proposition. It is impossible to expand a finite supply indefinitely, and in many parts of the world, the "long run" has arrived.

For sure, measures to conserve, recycle, and more efficiently use water have enabled many places to contain their water demands and to avoid or at least delay an ecological reckoning. Such tried-and-true measures as thrifty irrigation techniques, water-saving plumbing fixtures, native landscaping, and wastewater recycling can cost-effectively reduce the amount of water required to grow food, produce material goods, and meet household needs. The conservation potential of these measures has barely been tapped.

Yet something is missing from this prescription, something less tangible than drip irrigation lines and low-flow showerheads but, in the final analysis, something more important. It has to do with modern society's disconnection from nature's web of life and from water's most fundamental role as the basis of that life. In our technologically sophisticated world, we no longer grasp the need for the wild river, the blackwater swamp, or even the

Establishing a water ethic will mean reconnecting to nature's web of life.

diversity of species collectively performing nature's work. By and large, society views water in a utilitarian fashion— as a "resource" valued only when it is extracted from nature and put to use on a farm, in a factory, or in a home.

Overall, we have been quick to assume rights to use water but slow to recognize obligations to preserve and protect it. Better pricing and more open markets will assign water a higher value in its economic functions and breed healthy competition that weeds out wasteful and unproductive uses. But this will not solve the deeper problem. Instead what is needed is a set of guidelines and principles that stops us from chipping away at natural systems until nothing is left of their life-sustaining functions, which the marketplace fails to value adequately, if at all. In short, we need a water ethic—a guide to right conduct in the face of complex decisions about natural systems that we do not and cannot fully understand.

The essence of such an ethic is to make the protection of freshwater ecosystems a central goal in all that we do. This may sound like an idealistic prescription in light of our ever more crowded world of needs and aspirations. Yet it is no more radical a notion than suggesting that a building be given a solid foundation before adding 30 stories to it. Water is the foundation of every human enterprise, and if that foundation is insecure, everything built upon it will be insecure, too. As such, our stewardship of water will determine not only the quality but the staying power of human societies.

The adoption of such a water ethic would represent a historic shift away from the strictly utilitarian approach to

PHOTOGRAPH BY LYNSEY ADDARIO/VII NETWORK

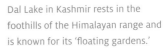
Dal Lake in Kashmir rests in the foothills of the Himalayan range and is known for its 'floating gardens.'

water management and toward an integrated, holistic approach that views people and water as interconnected parts of a greater whole. Instead of asking how we can further control and manipulate rivers, lakes, and streams to meet our ever-growing demands, we would ask instead how we can best satisfy human needs while accommodating the ecological requirements of freshwater ecosystems. It would lead us, as well, to deeper questions of human values, in particular how to narrow the wide gap between the haves and have-nots while remaining within the bounds of what a healthy ecosystem can sustain.

Embedded within this water ethic is a fundamental question: Do rivers and the life within them have a right to water? In his famous essay, "Should Trees Have Standing? Toward Legal Rights for Natural Objects," legal scholar Christopher D. Stone argued more than 35 years ago that yes, rivers and trees and other objects of nature do have rights, and these should be protected by granting legal standing to guardians of the voiceless entities of nature, much as the rights of children are protected by legal guardians.

Stone's arguments struck a chord with U.S. Supreme Court Justice William O. Douglas, who wrote in a famous dissent in the 1972 case *Sierra Club v. Morton* that "contemporary public concern for protecting nature's ecological equilibrium should lead to the conferral of standing upon environmental objects to sue for their own preservation.... The river, for example, is the living symbol of all the life it sustains or nourishes—the fish, aquatic insects, water ouzels, otter, fisher, deer, elk, bear, and all other animals, including man, who are dependent on it or who enjoy it for its sight, its sound, or its life. The river as plaintiff speaks for the ecological unit of life that is part of it."

During the next three decades, U.S. courts heard cases brought by environmental groups and other legal entities on behalf of nature and its constituents. In water allocation, concepts such as "instream flow rights" began to take hold, although these rights often received too low a priority to offer meaningful protection of river health. With freshwater life being extinguished at record rates, a more fundamental change is needed. An ethical society can no longer ignore the fact that water-management decisions have life-or-death consequences for other species. An ethically grounded water policy must begin with the premise that all people and all living things be given access to enough water to secure their survival before some get more than enough.

On paper, at least one government has grounded its water policy in precisely such an ethic. South Africa's 1998 water law establishes a water reserve consisting of two parts. The first is a nonnegotiable water allocation to meet the basic drinking, cooking, and sanitary needs of all South Africans. (When the government changed hands, some 14 million poor South Africans lacked water for these basic needs.) The second part of the reserve is an allocation of water to support ecosystem functions. Specifically, the act says that "the quantity, quality, and reliability of water required to maintain the ecological functions on which humans depend shall be reserved so that the human use of water does not individually or cumulatively compromise the long-term sustainability of aquatic and associated ecosystems." The water determined to constitute this two-part reserve has priority over licensed uses, such as irrigation, and only this water is guaranteed as a right.

At the core of South Africa's policy is an affirmation of the "public trust," a legal principle that traces back to the Roman Empire and says that governments hold certain rights and entitlements in trust for the people and are obliged to protect them for the common good. In addition to the public trust, another rule fast becoming essential for freshwater ecosystem protection is the "precautionary principle," which essentially says that given the rapid pace of ecosystem decline, the irreversible nature of many of the resulting losses, and the high value of freshwater ecosystems to human societies, it is wise to err on the side of protecting too much rather than too little of the remaining freshwater habitat.

The utilitarian code that continues to guide most water management may fit with prevailing market-based socioeconomic paradigms, but it is neither universal nor unchanging. The American conservationist Aldo Leopold viewed the extension of ethics to the natural environment as "an evolutionary possibility and an ecological necessity." More recently, Harvard biologist Edward O. Wilson noted in his book *Consilience* that ethical codes historically have arisen through the interplay of biology and culture. "Ethics, in the empiricist view," Wilson observes, "is conduct favored consistently enough throughout a society to be expressed as a code of principles."

In other words, ethics are not static; they evolve with our social consciousness. But that evolution is not automatic. The extension of freedom to slaves and voting rights to women required leaders, movements, advocates, and activists that collectively pulled society onto higher moral ground. So it will have to be with the extension of rights to rivers, plants, fish, birds, and the ecosystems of which they are a part.

As societies wrap their collective minds around the consequences of global environmental change—rising temperatures, prolonged droughts, chronic water shortages, disappearing species—it may well be that a new ethic will emerge, one that says it is not only right and good but necessary that all living things get enough water before some get more than enough. Because in the end, we're all in this together.

AN ETHICAL SOCIETY CAN NO LONGER IGNORE THE FACT THAT WATER-MANAGEMENT DECISIONS HAVE LIFE-OR-DEATH CONSEQUENCES FOR OTHER SPECIES.

PHOTOGRAPH BY ED KASHI/VII

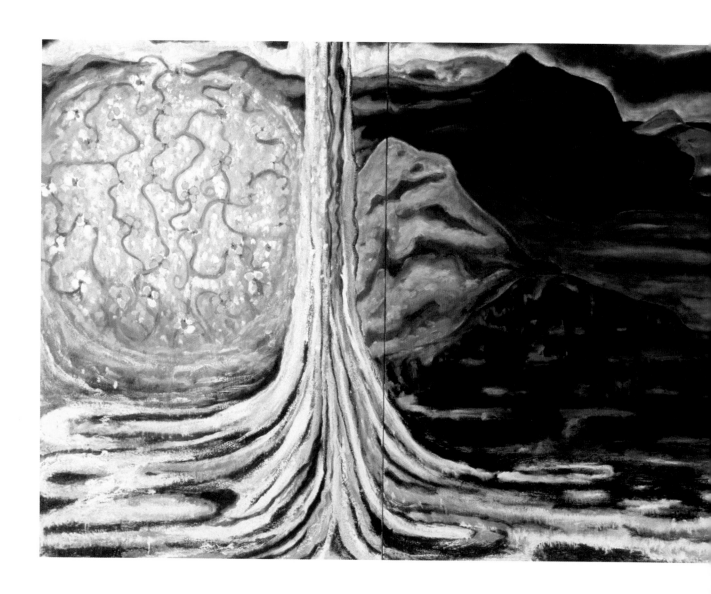

THE
VALUE OF WATER

An Art Exhibition 2011-2012
CATHEDRAL OF ST. JOHN THE DIVINE, NEW YORK CITY

GREGORY AMENOFF
Arbor II, 2000
Oil on canvas, 72" X 144"
Courtesy the Artist and Alexandre Gallery NYC

We've read the facts and the grim statistics, and we've also learned what we can do about it. It's time to get to work and begin living these solutions. We've only got one planet Earth and we can't get by without it. Neither can all the other living things that call this place home, and yet we're living past our means when it comes to integral resources like water.

Carl Sagan, the author and astrophysicist, said, "Anything else you're interested in is not going to happen if you can't breathe the air and drink the water. Don't sit this one out. Do something. You are by accident of fate alive at an absolutely critical moment in the history of our planet."

This should be our mantra, our rallying cry. The magnitude of this situation calls for action at every level. We need people to rethink how we use water—not just watering the lawn less, but rethinking the kinds of foods we eat and where our energy comes from. This also means pushing for change at every level of government—becoming involved in your community watershed, working for federal laws to improve water quality and create a trust fund for clean water, and fighting on the international level to make sure water is a fundamental human right for all of us. We can do this. We have to do this.

Not all of these solutions may sound glamorous but they are necessary. What can you do today, right now, to begin helping out at this critical moment? Looking at a global water crisis as a whole can be overwhelming, but not if we break it down. There are thousands of solutions to pressing water issues, from new technology being developed to purify water to community groups teaching each other how to recycle rainwater. The list goes on and on. If we dig into one small piece of this problem we can create a ripple.

And we're going to need each and every one of us to dig in, toss a stone into the water, create a ripple that will resonate and inspire our friends and neighbors to join us in working for change—personal, political, planetary. In Maude Barlow's essay about the fight for the human right to water she recounted the story of how Bolivia's ambassador to the United Nations spoke before the U.N.'s historic vote on recognizing water as a fundamental human right. He referenced a new report showing that every 3.5 seconds a child in the Global South dies because of dirty water. Barlow writes, "Then he held up his fingers and counted—1, 2, 3 ..."

That's the best summation of this crisis: Every second counts. Now, let's get to work.

THE
VALUE OF WATER

An Art Exhibition 2011-2012
CATHEDRAL OF ST. JOHN THE DIVINE, NEW YORK CITY

DIANE BURKO
1) Grinnell, 1938 after Hileman, GNP archives; 2) Grinnell, 1981 after Carl Key;
3) Grinnell, 1998 after Dan Fagre; 4) Grinnell, 2006 after Karen Holzer
Oil on canvas, each 88" x 55"

14 ACTIONS
You Can Take to Protect Our Water

1) Find out how much water you use.
Visit the Water Calculator and see what you can do to cut back. *www.h2oconserve.org*

2) Stop drinking bottled water.
Choose tap water over bottled water whenever possible. Create a bottled water free zone in your classroom, campus, workplace, union, community center, city hall, environmental organization or faith-based group. *www.thinkoutsidethebottle.org*

3) Help create a clean water trust fund.
Support public control of water resources and increased funding for public drinking water by signing a petition urging Congress to create a Clean Water Trust Fund. *www.foodandwaterwatch.org/water/trust-fund*

4) Conserve water inside.
Retrofit with efficient appliances and fixtures, take shorter showers, check faucets for leaks and drips. *www.awwa.org/waterwiser*

5) Conserve water outside.
Reduce lawn size and choose drought-tolerant xeriscapes. You can also recycle municipal water and on-site greywater, or harvest rainwater to use in the garden. *www.greywateraction.org*

6) Don't pollute our watershed.
Stop using toxic cleaners, pesticides, and herbicides. Properly dispose of pharmaceuticals and personal care products. *www.ewg.org/ourwater*

7) Learn about your watershed.
Form a watershed group. River Keeper organizations, Friends of Creeks groups, and watershed councils are springing up all over the country. *www.riverkeeper.org*

8) Help keep your watershed healthy.
Support or start water-quality monitoring programs. Citizen-based water-quality monitoring is an accessible and meaningful way to understand the health of your waterways. *www.healthywater.org*

9) Clean up agriculture.
Buy local and organic food. Help with the implementation of on-farm water conservation and protection programs. *www.nrcs.usda.gov/programs*

10) Protect groundwater from depletion and degradation.
Help ensure legislation to manage and protect all groundwater. Unlike our system of surface-water rights, the extraction of unlimited quantities of groundwater is largely unregulated. *www. groundwater.org*

11) Learn about dams in your area.
Oppose construction of new dams and always ask if any planned dams are really necessary or if there are better, less destructive ways of conserving water, preventing floods or generating power. *www.internationalrivers.org*

12) Reduce your energy use.
Producing electricity uses lots of water. You can figure out how much energy you use at Low Carbon Diet. *www.empowermentinstitute.net/lcd/index.html*

13) Support the right to water for everyone.
Learn more about grassroots movements for water democracy and the right to water. *www. blueplanetproject.net*

14) Help spread the word.
Visit *AlterNet.org/watermatters* for more information or to buy a copy of the book for a friend.

HOW MUCH WATER DO YOU USE?

Take the Water Calculator Quiz

THE H2O CONSERVE WATER CALCULATOR is designed to help you measure how much water you use, better understand the ways you use water in your daily life, and get you thinking about what you can do to use less.

This lets you know what your "water footprint" is. In other words, it gives you an estimate of the total amount of water you use. Your water footprint takes into account not only the water used in your home, but also the water that is used to produce the food you choose to eat and the products you buy. Your water footprint also includes other factors such as the water used to cool the power plants that provide your electricity, and the water that is saved when you recycle. You may not drink, feel, or see this water, but it makes up the large majority of your water footprint.

It is important to recognize that the H2O Calculator relies on national averages and approximations, and since not everyone's lifestyle is "average," your results should be considered an estimate of your water use and not a scientifically accurate assessment. Regardless, this calculator does provide a general assessment of your water use, as well as the quantity of water used daily by the average American to give you an idea of where you stand in terms of your daily water use.

You can find a more detailed version online at *H2OConserve.org*.

1) How many people are in your household?   _____

2) In which state do you live?
Give yourself the corresponding number of points. Kentucky,
Louisiana, North Dakota, Wyoming, West Virginia   **18 points**   _____

All other U.S. states and Washington, D.C.   **6 points**

3) Water used for power generation:
Multiply the points from your state by the number
of people in your household.   _____

4) Domestic water use:

A. BATHS
How many baths per week does your
household take?
Multiply the number of baths by 5   _____
(*Average bath uses 35 gallons H_2O*)

B. SHOWERS
On average, how many minutes does a person in your
house take a shower?
Multiply the number of minutes by 3.
Multiply that by the number of people in
your household
(*Average shower uses 3 gallons H_2O per minute*)   _____

C. TOILETS
Multiply the number of people in your household by 12
(*Average person uses 12 gallons per day flushing*)   _____

D. SINKS
On average, how many minutes does a person
in your household use the sink?
Multiply the number of minutes by 3.
Multiply that by the number of people in your household
(*Average sink uses 3 gallons H_2O per minute*)   _____

E. LAUNDRY

How many loads of laundry per week does your household do?

Multiply the number of loads by 4

(Average load uses 30 gallons)

_____

F. DISHES

How many loads of dishes per day does your household do?

Multiply the number of loads by 10

(Average load of dishes uses 10 gallons)

_____

5) Lawn and Garden

On average, how many times each week do you water your lawn or garden?

Multiply the number of times per week by 171

(Based on 1/4 acre yard, watered once per week, 1200 gallons used)

_____

6) Pool

If you have a pool, give yourself **52 points**

If you don't cover your pool, give yourself an additional **16 points**

_____

7) Automobile

A. GAS

Give yourself **5 points** per car.

(Based on 20 gallons per week per car, 1.75 gallons of water per gallon gasoline)

_____

B. CAR WASHING

If you wash your car, give yourself **21 points** per car.

(Based on 1 car wash per week per car, 150 gallons water per car wash)

_____

8) Diet

A. MEAT EATING

Give yourself **446 points** for each vegan in your household.

Give yourself **516 points** for each vegetarian in your household.

Give yourself **1032 points** for each meat eater in your household.

B. BOTTLED WATER

Multiply the number of people in your household by 1.5

(Based on 1 bottle per day per person, 1.5 gallons used per bottle)

_____

9) Recycling

A. PAPER

Multiply the number of people in your household by 5
(Recycling some paper saves you 5 gallons per day per person)

_____

B. PLASTIC

Multiply the number of people in your household by 3
(Recycling some plastic saves you 3 gallons per day per person)

_____

C. CLOTHING

_____

Multiply the number of people in your household by 5
(Recycling some clothing saves you 5 gallons per day per person)

10) Greywater and Rainwater

(these values are subtracted from your total)

_____

A. GREYWATER

Does your household reuse greywater?
Multiply the of people in your household by 40
(Based on reusing 40 gallons per person per day)

_____

B. RAINWATER

Give your self 9 points if your household collects rainwater
(Based on saving and using 9 gallons of water per day)

_____

Total Household

(add your values for 3-8; subtract your values for 9 and 10)

_____

Total Individual

divide the total household value by the no. of people in your household)

_____

Find out what your
score means >

What Does Your Score Mean?

The score for the average American is 1,190.

900 and below: Water Warrior

Congratulations, you are doing better than most Americans! Give yourself a pat on the back for being water conscious. You have a thing or two to teach your neighbors, but there may still be ways to cut back on your water use.

901 -1,300: Water Activist

Not too shabby! Your water consumption is typical of most Americans. But as we know, Americans are among the highest water users worldwide. The good news is, there are many ways to use less water and decrease your footprint.

1,301 and above: Water Enthusiast

Time for a water-use makeover! Your household is a thirsty one, even by American standards. Now is a great time to think of ways to cut back on your water use— whether it is in the home, outside your home or in your consumption habits.

For more ideas on conservation, read the Learn to Conserve tips or visit *www.H2OConserve.org*

Learn to Conserve

Here are some tips for cutting down on water use.
For a more detailed list visit www.H2oConserve.org.

Put a bucket in the shower while you're waiting for the water to warm up, and use the water you catch for watering plants or cleaning.

To check for a toilet leak, put dye or food coloring into the tank. If color appears in the bowl without flushing, there's a leak that should be repaired.

Fix those leaky faucets. You may think that a constant drip is just annoying, but it's also a huge waste of water (you can lose about 20 gallons of water per day from a single drippy faucet!).

Use the garbage disposal less and the garbage more (or even better, start composting!).

Install a low-flow showerhead. It may cost you some money up front, but your water conservation efforts will save you money down the road.

Use the water left over from boiling to water your plants (just let it cool down first!).

Eat meat and dairy foods fewer times a day, or just in smaller portions. The amount of water used to produce animal products far exceeds the amount used for growing vegetables and grains.

Use your laundry machine only when it's full.

Use a pool cover! You'll keep leaves and bugs out of the pool, and save thousands of gallons of water from evaporation.

If your family wants to play with the hose or the sprinkler, make sure they do it in a dry part of the lawn that can use the water.

Use a drip irrigation system instead of a hose or sprinkler to water your garden.

Xeriscape! Plant native species that don't require additional watering around your house. Grassy lawns make sense in wet climates, but in dry areas like the southwest they're huge water-wasters. In dry climates, try landscaping with rock gardens, cacti, and native trees and plants that won't require watering.

Buy re-usable products for you home instead of disposables.

Your trash is someone else's treasure! Make sure to donate or re-sell your old stuff instead of just throwing things out.

Set up a rain barrel under a rain gutter outside your house. You can catch hundreds of gallons to use for watering the lawn, washing the car, etc. Just don't drink it, and make sure to keep it covered with a screen so it doesn't breed mosquitoes. Check your local municipal regulations to see if a rain barrel is allowed.

If you're building a new house, or re-doing the plumbing in your old house, **consider setting up a graywater system**. These systems allow you to re-use the water from your sinks, laundry machine and dishwasher for watering plants and flushing toilets. Check your local municipal regulations to see if a graywater system is allowed.

WATER: H2O = LIFE

American Museum of Natural History

YOU CAN ALSO LEARN ABOUT WATER issues interactively. *Water: H$_2$O = Life* is an exhibit that illuminates some of the many challenges related to humanity's sustainable management and use of the life-giving, but finite, resource—water. It explores the ways that water shapes life on Earth and makes our planet livable and also suggests actions people can take to help preserve our planet's water.

Exhibition Organization and International Tour

Water: H$_2$O = Life is designed and produced by the American Museum of Natural History's Department of Exhibition under the direction of David Harvey, Vice President for Exhibition and curated by Eleanor Sterling, Director of the American Museum of Natural History's Center for Biodiversity and Conservation (and a contributor to *Water Matters*).

The exhibit is organized by the American Museum of Natural History, New York (www.amnh.org), and the Science Museum of Minnesota, St. Paul (www.smm.org), in collaboration with Great Lakes Science Center, Cleveland; The Field Museum, Chicago; Instituto Sangari, São Paulo, Brazil; National Museum of Australia, Canberra; Royal Ontario Museum, Toronto, Canada; San Diego Natural History Museum; and Singapore Science Centre with PUB Singapore.

The exhibit showed at the American Museum of Natural History from November 3, 2007 until May 26, 2008, when it began an international tour. Its next stops include:

- Fernbank Museum of Natural History, Atlanta, GA (October 2, 2010—January 10, 2011)
- Palazzo Bonacquisti, Assisi, Italy (October 10, 2010—May 15, 2011)
- Royal Ontario Museum, Toronto, Canada (March 12, 2011—September 5, 2011)
- ADACH, Abu Dhabi, UAE (September 18, 2011—January 5, 2012)
- Prairiefire Cultural Center, Overland, KS (March 2014—July 2014)

The Exhibition

Water: H$_2$O = Life examines the beauty and essential nature of our planet's lifeblood using imaginative presentation techniques, including a 68-inch globe displaying composite satellite images of Earth and three-dimensional video, as well as live animals and walk-through dioramas that give visitors a firsthand experience of the power and importance of water. The exhibition also addresses the most compelling issues facing societies and ecosystems around the globe related to water quality and availability. Learn more at *amnh.org/water*.

End Notes

CHAPTER 3

1   Upper Chattahoochee Riverkeeper, www.ucriverkeeper.org/Ourriver5.htm/.

2   Georgia Department of Natural Resources, Environmental Protection Division, "Chattahoochee River Basin Watershed Protection Plan," 1997, 3-11.

3   Sidney Lanier, "Song of the Chattahoochee," in Thomas R. Lounsbury, editor, *Yale Book of American Verse*, (New Haven: Yale University Press, 1912), p. 480.

4   Consent decree, *Upper Chattahoochee Riverkeeper, Inc., et al. v. City of Atlanta*, Case No. 1:95-CV-2550-FMH, (N.D. GA 1997). See also new, $4 billion pricetag, Eric Stirgus, "Atlanta wants more time to finish sewer work, pay for it," *The Atlanta Journal-Constitution*, May 3, 2010.

5   Sam D. Hamilton, regional director, Southeast Region, U.S. Fish and Wildlife Service, Department of the Interior, testimony, House Transportation and Infrastructure Committee, Subcommittee on Water Resources and the Environment, March 11, 2008, p. 3.

6   Joe and Monica Cook, *River Song: A Journey Down the Chattahoochee and Apalachicola Rivers* (Tuscaloosa: The University of Alabama Press, 2000), 258.

7   *Ibid*.

8   Alex Pearlstein, "Metro Atlanta Tops U.S. Population Growth," *The Atlanta Journal Constitution*, April 5, 2007.

9   "North Georgia Water Supply and Water Conservation Management Plan," May 2009. Section 3, Water Demand Forecasts. Overall water-use figures are on page 3; toilet-flushing figures on page 9. http://www.northgeorgiawater.com/files/Sec3_WaterDemandForecasts_WSWC_May2009.pdf

10   Amanda K. Brown, "The Real Thing," *Atlanta Magazine*, June 2008, p. 78.

11   James A. Miller, U.S. Geological Survey, "Groundwater Atlas of the United States: Alabama, Florida, Georgia and South Carolina," HA 730-G, see "Floridan aquifer system and Southeast Coastal Plain aquifer system." http://pubs.usgs.gov/ha/ha730/ch_g/index.html

12   John M. Hefner and James D. Brown, U.S. Fish & Wildlife Service, "Wetlands Trends in the United States," Wetlands, Volume 4, Number 1, December 1984.

13   Lester M. "Buddy" Blain, former general counsel, Southwest Florida Water Management District, interview by Julian Pleasants, University of Florida Samuel Proctor Oral History Program, February 17, 2003.

14   ABC News, video, "Georgians Pray for Rain—Literally," November 13, 2007.

15   *Ibid*. Gov. Perdue is quoting Psalm 65, *The Holy Bible*, New King James version, lines 9-10.

16   For an overview of the "Comprehensive Everglades Restoration Plan" and cost estimates, see http://www.evergladesplan.org. The $30 billion figure has emerged in the wake of Florida's plan to purchase restoration land from U.S. Sugar Corp., see Curtis Morgan, "Charlie Crist's downsized U.S. Sugar deal under siege," *The Miami Herald*, March 7, 2010.

17   U.S. District Judge Paul A. Magnuson, Memorandum and Order in re Tri-State Water Rights Litigation, Case No. 3:07-md-01, U.S. District Court, Middle District of Florida, p. 94.

18   Bill Rankin, "Court allows Georgia to appeal water ruling," *The Atlanta Journal-Constitution*, January 21, 2010.

19   Patricia Metz and Matthew Cimitile, U.S. Geological Survey, "Peace River in Florida Loses as Much as 11 Million Gallons a Day to Sinkholes and is Vulnerable to Running Dry," USGS Sound Waves, January/February 2010. http://soundwaves.usgs.gov/2010/02/research.html.

20   Douglas Jehl, "Arkansas Rice Farmers Run Dry, and U.S. Remedy Sets Off Debate," *The New York Times*, November 11, 2002.

21   *The Holy Bible*, King James version, Psalm 46, lines 4-5.

CHAPTER 5

1   Gustave Leven, Chairman of the Board, The Perrier Corporation of France, quoted in P. Betts, "Bubbling Over in a Healthy Market," *The Financial Times*, January 13, 1988.

2   Eskenazi, Stuart. "The Biggest Pump Wins," *Dallas Observer*, November 19-25, 1998, http://www.dallasobserver.com/1998-11-19/news/the-biggest-pump-wins/.

3   Gleick, Peter H. *The World's Water 2004-2005: The Biennial Report on Freshwater Resources*. Island Press, 2004, p. 17.

4   Flynn, Sean and Kathryn Boudouris. "Democratizing the Regulation and Governance of Water in the U.S.," Excerpt from *Reclaiming Public Water: Achievements, Struggles and Visions From Around the World*, Transnational Institute and Corporate Europe Observatory, January 2005.

5   Fishman, Charles. "Message in a Bottle," *Fast Company*, July 2007; "Bottled Water: More than just a story about sales growth," Press Release International Bottled Water Association, April 9, 2007, http://www.bottledwater.org/public/2007_releases/2007-04-09_bevmkt.htm. Note: I used to use an $11 billion figure (you may see it on some materials) from Beverage Marketing Corporation (pulled from the same press release above), which refers to wholesales, which are slightly different from retail sales–the prices people actually pay for water. However, retail sales figures tend to track just over wholesale figures over time, so we can be confident that people spent at least $11 billion on bottled water, if not more. The *Fast Company* article, which cites *Beverage Digest*, another respected beverage market research firm for the $15 billion figure, provides that revised figure, while the BMC release correlates with the $11

billion figure and the consumption figure.

6   U.S. Environmental Protection Agency. "Analysis and Findings of The Gallup Organization's Drinking Water Customer Satisfaction Survey," August 6, 2003.

7   Eskenazi, *Ibid.*; Farhrenthold, David A. "Bottlers, States and the Public Slug It Out in Water War," *Washington Post*, June 12, 2006. http://www.washingtonpost.com/wp-dyn/content/article/2006/06/11/AR2006061100797_pf.html.

8   "The Clean Water and Drinking Water Gap Analysis." Office of Water, U.S. Environmental Protection Agency, Sept. 30, 2002. http://www.epa.gov/safewater/gapreport.pdf.

9   Vega, Cecilia, M. "City pays big for bottled water," *San Francisco Chronicle*, January 27, 2006. http://www.sfgate.com/cgi-bin/article.cgi?f=/c/a/2006/01/27/MNGBEGUHCJ1.DTL.

10   Chura, Hilary. "$7.7 billion industry: Water war bubbling among top brands," *Advertising Age*, July 7, 2003.

11   Bloom, Jonah ed. "Ad Age Annual," *Ad Age*, January 1, 2007.

12   Bauers, Sandy. "Bottled water's environmental backlash," *Philadelphia Inquirer*, November 3, 2007. http://www.philly.com/philly/news/20071103_Bottled_waters_environmental_backlash.html.

13   Press Release. "The U.S. Conference of Mayors Announces 2007 City Water Taste Test Winners, "USCOM Annual Meeting, June 25, 2007. www.usmayors.org/75thAnnualMeeting/pressrelease_062507b.pdf.

14   Harris Interactive, "How Green Are We?" Harris Poll, October 13, 2009, http://www.harrisinteractive.com/vault/Harris-Interactive-Poll-Research-Going-Green-2009-10.pdf.

15   Beverage Marketing Corporation, "The U.S. Liquid Refreshment Beverage Market Declined by 3.1% in 2009," press release, March 24, 2010. http://www.beveragemarketing.com/?section=pressreleases.

16   Scanlon, Jessie. "Buy Water, Help Children: Interview with Peter Thum," *BusinessWeek* Online, March 22, 2006. http://www.businessweek.com/investor/content/mar2006/pi20060322_252796.htm.

17   "Nestle Waters Global Business Review," Presented by Kim Jeffery, President and CEO, Nestle Waters North America at the Morgan Stanley Global Consumer and Retail Conference, November 15, 2007, New York City, NY. http://www.nestle.com/Resource.axd?Id=89D1A0C8-4355-41F0-8A99-AB505CE3D6F3 .

18   Carlton, Jim. "Can a Water Bottler Invigorate One Town?" *Wall Street Journal*, June 9, 2005.

19   Indar, Josh. "Drinking Problem," *Sacramento News and Review*, August 18, 2005.

20   Indar, *Ibid.*

21   "Nestle In McCloud: The Costs," Memo from original McCloud Watershed Council website, McCloudWater.com. Website has subsequently been updated to www.mccloudwatershedcouncil.org.

22   McCloud Watershed Council, *Ibid.*

23   McCloud Watershed Council, *Ibid.*

24   Indar, *Ibid.*

25   Indar, *Ibid.*

26   Suzanne Hurt, "Bottled Water Foes May Join Forces; AG to consider review," *Sacramento Press*, October 4, 2009. http://www.sacramentopress.com/headline/14879/Bottled_water_foes_may_join_forces.

27   Gladwell, Malcolm. *Blink: The Power of Thinking Without Thinking.* Little, Brown & Company, 2005.

28   CBS Poll, http://cbs2chicago.com/video/?id=37419@wbbm.dayport.com.

29   Olson, Erik. "Bottled Water: Pure Drink or Pure Hype?" Natural Resources Defense Council (NRDC), March 1999, http://www.nrdc.org/water/drinking/bw/exesum.asp.

30   Britton, Charles R., Richard K. Ford and David, E.R. Gay. "The Market for Bottled Water in a "Water Rich" State," *The Forum of the Association for Arid Lands Studies*, Volume XXII, 2006.

31   Gleick, Peter H. *The World's Water: The Biennial Report on Freshwater Resources*, Vols. 4 and 5. Island Press, 2004/2006.

32   Mercer, Chris. "US: Bottled water pulled in bromate scare," BeverageDaily.com, August 14, 2006. http://www.beveragedaily.com/news/ng.asp?n=69827-wegmans-bromate-bottled-water.

33   Basu, Moni and Scott Leith. "Villagers to Coke: 'Go away,'" *Atlanta Journal Constitution*, May 29, 2005.

34   Simons, Craig. "Report looks at Coke water use in India," *Atlanta Journal Constitution*, January 14, 2008. http://www.ajc.com/business/content/business/coke/stories/2008/01/14/cokeindia_0115.html.

35   Basu, *Ibid.*

36   "Water privatisation to be a key issue in elections," *The Hindu*, January 23, 2004, http://www.thehindu.com/2004/01/23/stories/2004012305921200.htm.

37   Basu, *Ibid.*

38   Date Vidyadhar. " Villagers blame Coca Cola for water woes in Thane district," *Times of India*, June 5, 2003. http://timesofindia.indiatimes.com/articleshow/6753.cms.

39   Basu, *Ibid.*

40   Jeff Seabright, Vice President, Environment & Water Resources Remarks at the Center for Strategic & International Studies & Sandia National Laboratory—Global Water Futures Workshop: Water Sustainability and Corporate Responsibility, Washington D.C., February 9, 2005. http://www.thecoca-colacompany.com/presscenter/viewpoints_environmental_csis.html.

41   Coca-Cola Company Press Release, June 5, 2007; http://www.thecoca-colacompany.com/presscenter/nr_20070605_tccc_and_wwf_partnership.html.

42   UN-Water. "Fact Sheet on Water and Sanitation," International

Decade for Action: Water for Life, 2005-2015, http://www.un.org/waterforlifedecade/factsheet.html.

43   "California considers new bottled-water rules," *U.S. Water News Online, May 2003.* http://www.uswaternews.com/archives/arcquality/3calcon5.html.

44   International Bottled Water Association Press Release, June 5, 2003. http://www.bottledwater.org/public/2003_Releases/CorbettAB83.htm.

45   Geissinger, Steve. "Schwarzenegger OKs bills on gay rights, toxic toys," *Oakland Tribune*, October 15, 2007; Editorial. "Bottled Water Mystery: Consumers need more information," *Sacramento Bee*, April 26, 2007. http://www.sacbee.com/110/story/161153.html, Lazarus, David. "What the heck is in those water bottles?" *San Francisco Chronicle*, May 4, 2007. http://www.sfgate.com/cgi-bin/article.cgi?f=/c/a/2007/05/04/BUGUSPKP6D1.DTL.

46   "Executive Directive 07-05: Permanent Phase-Out of Bottled Water Purchasesby San Francisco City and County Government." Office of the Mayor, City and County of San Francisco, June 21, 2007. http://sfwater.org/Files/Pressreleases/Bottled%20Water%20Executive%20Order.pdf.

47   USCOM Business Council Website.

48   Swanson, Stevenson. "Some would like to play taps for bottled water," *Chicago Tribune*—reprinted by *The Seattle Times*, July 26, 2007. http://seattletimes.nwsource.com/html/nation-world/2003806269_water26.html.

49   U.S. Conference of Mayors 2007 Adopted Resolutions. Resolution #90: "The Importance of Municipal Water." http://usmayors.org/uscm/resolutions/75th_conference/environ-ment_02.asp.

50   For example: The International Bottled Water Association is a member of the National Uniformity for Food Coalition (http://www.uniformityforfood.org/aboutthecoalition.htm), a group comprised of food companies and food industry associations that lobbied for the passage of H.R 4167 the National Uniformity for Food Act in 2005 and 2006. Contrary to industry assertions, this bill would have weakened regulatory standards for food and beverages, including bottled water, at the state level. For more information, refer to the Consumers Union website: http://www.consumersunion.org/pub/core_food_safety/003230.html.

51   Container Recycling Institute's Bottle Bill Resource Guide – Opponents of Bottle Bills. http://www.bottlebill.org/about_bb/opponents.htm#spending.

52   Gitlitz, Jennifer and Pat Franklin. "Water, Water Everywhere: The growth of non-carbonated beverage containers in the United States." Container Recycling Institute, February 2007.

53   O'Donnell, Maureen. State of Illinois Department of Central Management Services Memorandum, October 29, 2007. http://thecapitolfaxblog.com/Watermemo.pdf.

54   Credeur, Mary Jane. "PepsiCo Adds `Public Water Source' to Aquafina Label," Bloomberg.com, July 26, 2007. http://www.bloomberg.com/apps/news?pid=20601205&refer=consumer&sid=aiqSSi38Zp6E.

CHAPTER 7

1   Hoekstra, A.Y. and A.K. Chapagain, "Water Footprints of Nations: Water Use by People as a Function of Their Consumptive Pattern," *Water Resource Management, Vol. 21*, 2007 at 38.

2   World Bank. *World Development Report 2008* at 64. Organization of Economic Co-operation and Development. Environmental Performance of Agriculture in OECD Countries Since 1990. 2008 at 95. While agriculture is not the majority of water withdrawn in the United States, it is the majority of water that is used up, because most irrigation water evaporates instead of returning to the watershed where it could be reused. As a result, agriculture represents more than four fifths of U.S. water consumption. See USDA Economic Research Service. "Agricultural Resources and Environmental Indicators, 2006." July 2006 at 25; Hutson, Susan S. et al. U.S. Department of the Interior, U.S. Geological Survey. "Estimated Use of Water in the United States in 2000." Circular 1268. 2004 at 7. Food & Water Watch calculation based on the share of water withdrawals for end-use consumption by sector taken from Solley, Wayne B., Robert R. Pierce and Howard A. Perlman. U.S. Department of the Interior, U.S. Geological Survey. "Estimated Use of Water in the United States in 1995." Circular 1200. 1998 at 19.

3   Hendrickson, Mary and Bill Heffernan. Department of Rural Sociology, University of Missouri-Columbia. "Concentration of Agricultural Markets." April 2007.

4   Whoriskey, Peter. "Monsanto's dominance draws antitrust inquiry." *Washington Post.* November 29, 2009; Hendrickson and Heffernan.

5   Clapp, Stephen. "Monsanto to charge up to 42% more for next generation seeds." *Food Chemical News.* August 24, 2009; "Pioneer seed sales up." *Feedstuffs.* June 29, 2009; Kaskey, Jack. "DuPont Raises Corn, Soybean Seed Prices Most Ever." *Bloomberg.* June 12, 2009.

6   Rosegrant, Mark W., Ximing Cai and Sarah A. Cline, International Food Policy Research Institute and International Water Management Institute, "Global Water Outlook to 2025: Averting an Impending Crisis," September 2002 at 6; Cosgrove, William J. and Frank R. Rijsberman, World Water Council, "World Water Vision," 2000 at 7.

7   Cosgrove, William J. and Frank R. Rijsberman, World Water Council, "World Water Vision," 2000 at 8.

8   USDA National Agricultural Statistics Service. Farm and

Ranch Irrigation Survey 2008. AC-07-SS. February 2010 at 17.

9   USDA National Agricultural Statistics Service. Farm and Ranch Irrigation Survey 2008. AC-07-SS. February 2010 at 17 and 32.

10   Organization of Economic Co-operation and Development. Environmental Performance of Agriculture in OECD Countries Since 1990. 2008 at 92.

11   USDA National Agricultural Statistics Service. Farm and Ranch Irrigation Survey 2008. AC-07-SS. February 2010 at 17.

12   World Bank, Independent Evaluation Group, "Water Management in Agriculture: Ten Years of World Bank Assistance, 1994-2004," 2006 at xiii.

13   Yang, H., L. Wang, K.C. Abbasour, and A.J.B. Zehnder, "Virtual Water Trade: An Assessment of Water Use Efficiency in the International Food Trade," *Hydrology and Earth System Sciences*, Vol. 10, 2006 at 447.

14   Rosegrant, Mark W., Ximing Cai and Sarah A. Cline, International Food Policy Research Institute and International Water Management Institute, "Global Water Outlook to 2025: Averting an Impending Crisis," September 2002 at 5.

15   World Bank. *World Development Report 2008* at 64.

16   USDA National Agricultural Statistics Service. Farm and Ranch Irrigation Survey 2008. AC-07-SS. February 2010 at 70.

17   Keeney, Dennis and Mark Muller, Institute for Agriculture and Trade Policy, "Water Use by Ethanol Plants: Potential Challenges," 2006.

18   Dennehy, Kevin F. USGS. "High Plains regional ground-water study." USGS Fact Sheet, FS-091–00. 2000.

19   Gurdak, Jason J. et al. United States Geological Survey. "Water Quality in the High Plains Aquifer, Colorado, Kansas, Nebraska, New Mexico, Oklahoma, South Dakota, Texas, and Wyoming, 1999–2004." Circular 1337. 2009 at 10.

20   U.S. Geological Survey. "Estimated Use of Water in the United States in 2005." Circular 1344. 2009 at 26.

21   Key and McBride (2007) at 5.

22   Key and McBride (2007) at 5; USDA NASS. 2007 Census of Agriculture. 2009 at Table 20.

23   Van Heugten, Eric. "Water Intake of Pigs." North Carolina Cooperative Extension Service, North Carolina State University. *Swine News*, February 1999; Almond, Glen. "Water: Optimizing performance while reducing waste." Department of Farm Animal Health & Resource Management, North Carolina State University. 2002.

24   Looper, Michael L. and Waldner, Dan N. "Water for dairy cattle" (Guide D-107). Cooperative Extension Service, New Mexico State University College of Agriculture and Home Economics. February 2002 at 1; Weida, William J. "A Citizen's Guide to the Regional Economic and Environmental Effects of Large Concentrated Dairy Operations." Department of Economics at the Colorado College, Colorado Springs, CO, and The Global Resource Center for the Environment, New York, N.Y., November 19, 2000; USDA Agricultural Research Service. Research Project: New Water Management Economies to Sustain Rural Economies—Texas A&M University. 2008 Annual Report.

25   UN Food & Agriculture Organization. *The State of Food and Agriculture 2009: Livestock in the Balance*. 2009 at 27.

26   USDA ERS, *Environmental Resources and Environmental Indicators 2006*, at Chapter 2.2.

27   USDA Economic Research Service. U.S. Consumption of Plant Nutrients. Available at www.ers.gov/data/FertilizerUse/.

28   Trautmann, Nancy M. et al. "Nitrogen: The Essential Element." Cornell Cooperative Extension. Available at: http://pmep.cce.cornell.edu/facts-slides-self/facts/nit-el-grw89.html.

29   McCasland, Margaret, et al. "Nitrate: Health Effects in Drinking Water." Cornell Cooperative Extension. Available: http://pmep.cce.cornell.edu/facts-slides-self/facts/nit-heef-grw85.html.

30   Knobeloch, L et al. "Blue babies and nitrate-contaminated well water." *Environmental Health Perspectives*. Vol. 108, No. 7. July 2000 at 675.

31   Knobeloch, L et al. "Blue babies and nitrate-contaminated well water." *Environmental Health Perspectives*. Vol. 108, No. 7. July 2000 at 678.

32   "Eutrophication." United States Geological Survey, Toxic Substances Hydrology Program. Available at: http://toxics.usgs.gov/definitions/eutrophication.html.

33   Brasher, Philip. "U.S. study says Iowa among main Gulf polluters." *Des Moines Register*. January 30, 2008.

34   USDA Economic Research Service. "Agricultural Resources and Environmental Indicators, 2006." July 2006 at 108.

35   U.S. Geological Survey. "Pesticides in the Nation's Streams and Ground Water, 1992-2001. Circular 1291. February 15, 2007 at 91.

36   *Ibid.* at 96, 104.

37   UN Food and Agriculture Organization. FAOSTAT, ResourceState database. Available at http://faostat.fao.org.

38   World Bank. *World Development Report 2008* at 58-59.

39   Jeyaratnam, J. "Acute pesticide poisoning: a major global health problem." *World Health Statistics Quarterly*. Vol 43, Iss 3. 1990 at 139-44.

40   Thakur, J.S. et al. "Epidemiological Study of High Cancer Among Rural Agricultural Community of Punjab in Northern India." *International Journal of Environmental Research and Public Health*. Vol. 5, Iss. 5. December 2008.

41   Pew Commission on Industrial Farm Animal Production. "Putting meat on the table: industrial farm animal production in America." April 2008 at 23.

42   Starmer, Elanor. Report to the Campaign for Family Farms and the Environment. "Industrial Livestock at the Taxpayer

Trough: How Large Hog and Dairy Operations are Subsidized by the Environmental Quality Incentives Program." December 2008 at 11-12.

43 Gurian-Sherman, Doug. "CAFOs uncovered." Union of Concerned Scientists. April 2008 at 4.

44 Boenning & Scattergood, *B&S Water Digest*, December 1, 2008 at 1-2.

45 Chapagain, Ashok K. and Arjen Y. Hoekstra, "The Global Component of Freshwater Demand and Supply: An Assessment of Virtual Water Flows Between Nations as a Result of Trade in Agricultural and Industrial Products," *Water International*, Vol. 33, No. 1, March 2008 at 22.

46 Chapagain, Ashok K. and Arjen Y. Hoekstra, "The Global Component of Freshwater Demand and Supply: An Assessment of Virtual Water Flows Between Nations as a Result of Trade in Agricultural and Industrial Products," *Water International*, Vol. 33, No. 1, March 2008 at 22.

47 Galloway, James N., Marshall Burke, G. Eric Bradford, Rosamond Naylor, Walter Falcon, Ashok K. Chapagain, Joanne C. Gaskell, Ellen McCullough, Harold A. Mooney, Kirsten L. L. Oleson, Henning Steinfeld, Tom Wassenaar and Vaclav Smil, "International Trade in Meat: The Tip of the Pork Chop," Royal Swedish Academy of Sciences, Ambio, Vol. 36, No. 8, December 2007.

48 Borlaug, Norman E. "The Green Revolution and the Road Ahead." Special 30th Anniversary Lecture. The Nobel Institute. Oslo. September 8, 2000 at 5, 7.

49 Gurian-Sherman, Doug. Union of Concerned Scientists. "Failure to Yield." April 2009.

50 International Assessment of Agricultural Knowledge, Science & Technology for Development. Press release. "Major agriculture report: 'Business as usual is not an option.'" 2009.

51 UN Environment Programme. "Organic Agriculture and Food Security in Africa." 2008.

52 Badgley, Catherine et al. "Organic Agriculture and the Global Food Supply." *Renewable Agriculture and Food Systems*. Vol. 22, Iss. 2. 2007.

CHAPTER 8

1 Ken Kirk, Executive Director, National Association of Clean Water Agencies, presentation at EPA funding conference, "Paying for Sustainable Water Infrastructure," Atlanta, GA, March 2007, as cited in Food & Water Watch, The Case for a Clean Water Trust Fund, 2007, 2.

2 Duhigg, C. (2009a, December 8). Millions in US Drinking Dirty Water, Records Show. *New York Times*.

3 U.S. Environmental Protection Agency. (1984). *Environmental Equity: Reducing Risk for All Communities, Volume 1*. Washington: U.S. Environmental Protection Agency.

4 Mather, M. (2004). *Housing and Commuting Patterns In Appalachia*. Washington: Population Reference Bureau.

5 Federal Reserve Bank of Texas n.d. *Texas Colonias: A Thumbnail Sketch of the Conditions, Issues, Challenges and Opportunities*. Retrieved August 2, 2009, from: http://www.dallasfed.org/ca/pubs/colonias.html.

6 http://www.santafenewmexican.com/Local%20News/ Mysterious-firm-s-water-plan-draws-protests, accessed, 6.11.10.

7 http://www.thefirstpost.co.uk/47372,news-comment,news-politics,aaron-millions-green-river-pipe-dream-is-an-opening-shot-in-the-water-wars.

8 http://www.businessweek.com/magazine/content/08_25/ b4089040017753.htm, accessed 6.26.10.

9 Hall, David, Lobina, Emanuele, Corral, Violeta, Hoedeman, Olivier, Terhorst, Phillip, Pigeon, Martin, and Kishimoto Satoko, *Public-Public Partnerships in Water*, Transnational Institute, Public Services International Research Unit, March, 2009.

10 Vibhu Nayar and V. Suresh, Global water crisis: Partnerships for the future, *The Hindu*, 2 November 2008.

11 Sean Flynn and Kathryn Boudouris, Democratising the Regulation and Governance of Water in the US, in Reclaiming Public Water, 79.

CHAPTER 15

1 Dudgeon, D. et al. 2006. Freshwater biodiversity: importance, threats, status and conservation challenges. *Biological Reviews* 81(1):163-182.

2 Strayer, D.L. and D. Dudgeon. 2010. Freshwater biodiversity conservation: recent progress and future challenges. *Journal of the North American Benthological Society*: 29(1): 344-358.

3 Postel, S., G.C. Daily, and P.R. Ehrlich. 1996. Human appropriation of renewable fresh water. *Science* 271: 785-788.

4 Brooks, D.B. 2005. Beyond greater efficiency: The concept of water soft paths. *Canadian Journal of Water Resources* 30(1): 1-10.

5 Gleick, P. 2003. Global Freshwater Resources: Soft-Path Solutions for the 21st Century. *Science* 302:1524-1528.

6 Brooks, D.B. 2005. Beyond greater efficiency: The concept of water soft paths. *Canadian Journal of Water Resources* 30(1): 1-10.

7 Dudgeon, D. et al. 2006. Freshwater biodiversity: importance, threats, status, and conservation challenges. *Biological Reviews* 81(1):163-182.

8 Gleick, P. 2003. Global Freshwater Resources: Soft-Path Solutions for the 21st Century. *Science* 302:1524-1528.

9 Veldoen, N. et al. 2006. The bactericidal agent triclosan modulates thyroid hormone-associated gene expression and disrupts postembryonic anuran development. *Aquatic Toxicology* 80(3):217-227.

10 Lovins, A. 1976. Energy strategy: The road not taken? *Foreign*

Affairs 6(20): 5-15.

11   Gleick, P. 2003. *The World's Water 2002-2003: Biennial Report on Freshwater Resources*. From: http://www.islandpress.com/bookstore/details5dc2.html?prod_id=985.

12   Gleick, P. 2003. Global Freshwater Resources: Soft-Path Solutions for the 21st Century. *Science* 302:1524-1528.

13   Brandes, O. and D. Brooks. 2007. Ingenuity trumps hard tech: the water soft path is the best bet for Canada's public and ecological needs. *Alternatives Journal* at http://goliath.ecnext.com/coms2/gi_0199-6935073/Ingenuity-trumps-hard-tech-the.html.

14   Hinrichsen, D., B. Robey, and U.D. Upadhyay 1998. Solutions for a Water Short World, *Population Reports Series* M, Number 14. From: http://info.k4health.org/pr/m14edsum.shtml.

15   WWF. 2010. Wetlands. From: http://wwf.panda.org/about_our_earth/about_freshwater/intro/.

16   US Environmental Protection Agency. 1993. *Constructed Wetlands for Wastewater Treatment and Wildlife Habitat*. From: http://www.epa.gov/owow/wetlands/pdf/ConstructedWetlands-Complete.pdf.

17   US Environmental Protection Agency. 2007. Combined sewer overflows. From: http://cfpub.epa.gov/npdes/faqs.cfm?program_id=5.

18   Riverkeeper. 2009. Sewage and Combined Sewer Overflors. From: http://www.riverkeeper.org/campaign.php/pollution/the_facts/986.

19   Greenroofs.com. 2010. Seattle Justice Center. From: http://www.greenroofs.com/projects/pview.php?id=311 and http://www.psat.wa.gov/Publications/LID_studies/lid_natural_approaches.pdf.

20   US Environmental Protection Agency. 1995. *Handbook of Constructed Wetlands*. From: http://www.epa.gov/owow/wetlands/pdf/hand.pdf.

21   John Todd Ecological Design. 2010. City of Fuzhou case study. From: http://toddecological.com/files/case-studies/Baima_Case_Study.pdf.

22   John Todd Ecological Design. 2010. City of South Burlington case study. From: http://toddecological.com/files/case-studies/SBLM_Case_Study.pdf.

23   Prairie Water Project. 2010. From http://www.prairiewaters.org/overview.htm.

24   Gertner, J. Oct. 2007. "The Future is Drying Up." *New York Times*.

25   Sydney Water. 2010. In your garden. From: http://www.sydneywater.com.au/Water4Life/InYourGarden/.

26   Rainharvesting.com. 2010. Rainwater tank rebates. From: http://www.rainharvesting.com.au/rainwater_tank_rebates.asp.

27   Ofwat. 2000. Worldwide Water Comparisons. From: http://www.ofwat.gov.uk/legacy/aptrix/ofwat/publish.nsf/AttachmentsByTitle/worldwide_water_comp9900.pdf/$FILE/worldwide_water_comp9900.pdf.

28   Emerton, L., L.Iyango, P. Luwum, and A. Malinga. 1999. The Present Economic Value of Nakivubo Urban Wetland, Uganda IUCN—The World Conservation Union, Eastern Africa Regional Office, Nairobi. From: http://www.iucn.org/places/earo/pubs/economic/nakivubo.pdf. Emerton, L. and E. Bos. 2004. *Value—Counting Ecosystems as Water Infrastructure*. From: http://europeandcis.undp.org/WaterWiki/images/c/ca/VALUE.pdf.

29   World Health Organization/Water, Sanitation and Health Protection and the Human Environment. 2005. *Water Safety Plans: Managing drinking-water quality from catchment to consumer*. From: http://www.who.int/water_sanitation_health/dwq/wsp170805.pdf.

30   AWE (Air, Water, Earth) Limited. 2005. Why Lake Victoria pollution levels are rising. From: http://www.awe-engineers.com/lake_victoria_pollution.php.

31   Emerton, L., L.Iyango, P. Luwum, and A. Malinga. 1999. The Present Economic Value of Nakivubo Urban Wetland, Uganda IUCN—The World Conservation Union, Eastern Africa Regional Office, Nairobi.

32   Emerton, L., L.Iyango, P. Luwum, and A. Malinga. 1999. The Present Economic Value of Nakivubo Urban Wetland, Uganda IUCN—The World Conservation Union, Eastern Africa Regional Office, Nairobi. Emerton, L. and E. Bos. 2004. Value—Counting Ecosystems as Water Infrastructure. From: http://europeandcis.undp.org/WaterWiki/images/c/ca/VALUE.pdf.

33   UNESCO World Water Assessment Programme. 2006. National Water Development Report: Uganda. From: http://unesdoc.unesco.org/images/0014/001467/146760e.pdf.

Contributors

Evan Abramson is a self-taught photographer and filmmaker based in New York City. Evan's work has appeared in *The Guardian Weekend Magazine, The Atlantic Monthly, National Geographic Adventure, Newsweek, The New York Times, The Washington Post, The Sunday Times, FT Weekend, Daylight Magazine, NACLA Report on the Americas, Visura Magazine,* and *Courier Japan.* Clients include UNICEP, Oxfam America, CHF International, The Legatum Foundation, Vassar College, and The Children Affected by AIDS Foundation.

Lynsey Addario was born in 1973, and is an American photojournalist based in Istanbul, Turkey, where she photographs for *The New York Times, The New York Times Magazine,* and *National Geographic,* among others. Lynsey started photographing conflict in 2000, when she traveled to Afghanistan under Taliban rule to document life and oppression under the Taliban. She has since covered the war in Afghanistan for the *New York Times Magazine,* and the wars in Iraq, Lebanon, Darfur, and Congo for *The New York Times, The New York Times Magazine,* and *Time.* Lynsey has been the recipient of numerous awards, including the 2009 Pulitzer Prize for International Reporting as part of the *New York Times* team covering the war in Afghanistan and Pakistan for the magazine cover article "Talibanistan," published Sept. 7, 2008.

Leslie Alsheimer, author of *Black and White in Adobe Photoshop CS4 and Lightroom,* is an internationally published and award-winning author, educator, and photographer dedicated to documenting the human condition worldwide. Her work—spanning editorial, fine art, and documentary genres—celebrates the beauty and splendor that can be found in humanity—regardless of circumstance. Leslie's images and unique perspectives have been published and exhibited worldwide. Along with numerous awards, including honors with the Professional Journalism Award of Distinction, Vincent Versace Award for Photographic Excellence, and six International Photography LUCIE Awards, her work has also appeared in numerous publications including *National Geographic, Black & White Magazine, PDN, National Geographic Traveler,* and featured with Photolucida's Critical Mass Top 50, and NPR's "The Picture Show."

Maude Barlow is the National Chairperson of the Council of Canadians and chairs the board of Washington D.C.-based Food and Water Watch. She is also an executive member of the San Francisco–based International Forum on Globalization and a Councilor with the Hamburg-based World Future Council. Barlow is the recipient of ten honorary doctorates as well as many awards, including the 2005 Right Livelihood Award (known as the "Alternative Nobel"), the Citation of Lifetime Achievement at the 2008 Canadian Environment Award, and the 2009 Earth Day Canada Outstanding Environmental Achievement Award. In 2008/2009, she served as Senior Advisor on Water to the 63rd President of the United Nations General Assembly. She is also the best selling author or co-author of 16 books, including the international best seller *Blue Covenant: The Global Water Crisis and the Coming Battle for the Right to Water.*

Cynthia Barnett is the author of *Mirage: Florida and the Vanishing Water of the Eastern U.S.* She is a long-time journalist whose awards include a national Sigma Delta Chi prize for investigative magazine reporting; a gold medal for best nonfiction in the Florida Book Awards; and eight Green Eyeshades, which recognize outstanding reporting in the southeast U.S. Barnett earned a bachelor's in journalism and master's in environmental history, both from the University of Florida, and spent a year studying water supply as a Knight-Wallace Fellow at the University of Michigan. She lives in Gainesville, Florida, with her husband and two water-conscious grade-schoolers. Her second book, working title *Blue is the New Green: An American Water Ethic,* is forthcoming from Beacon Press.

Peter Bennetts was born in 1967 in Sydney, Australia. He studied photography at the Royal Melbourne Institute of Technology. His initial pursuit of environmental reportage assignments has led Peter to photograph features all over the world. He has particularly focused his camera on the island nation of Tuvalu, whose coral atolls are especially vulnerable to a changing climate. His work regularly features in the Australian publications *Architecture Australia, Artichoke, Inside, AR*, and *Monument* and he is a frequent contributor to *Wallpaper*, Frame, Mark, Dwell, Domus, Casabella*, and other international publications. His photography has appeared in numerous books including four monographs and the two volumes of the *Phaidon Atlas of Contemporary World Architecture*. Peter lives in Melbourne, Australia with his wife; architect Rowena Hockin, and their two young sons.

Edward Burtynsky is known as one of Canada's most respected photographers. His remarkable photographic depictions of global industrial landscapes are included in the collections of over fifty major museums around the world. Born in 1955 of Ukrainian heritage in Ontario, Burtynsky is a graduate of Ryerson University (Bachelor of Applied Arts in Photography) and studied Graphic Art at Niagara College in Welland. In 1985, Burtynsky founded Toronto Image Works, a darkroom rental facility, custom photo laboratory, digital imaging, and new media computer-training centre catering to all levels of Toronto's art community. Burtynsky's visually compelling works have recently been exhibited in solo and group exhibitions across Canada, in the United States, Europe, and Asia. He is an active lecturer on photographic art and his images have appeared in various periodicals. His distinctions include the TED Prize, The Outreach Award at the Rencontres d'Arles, The Flying Elephant Fellowship, *Applied Arts Magazine* book award(s), and the Roloff Beny Book Award. In 2006 he was awarded the title of Officer of the Order of Canada and given an honorary degree; Doctor of Laws, from Queen's University, Kingston, Ontario, Canada.

Jeff Conant is a writer, journalist, and educator whose work focuses on ecological and social justice. He is the author of *A Community Guide to Environmental Health*, a grassroots educational manual currently being translated into numerous languages, and *A Poetics of Resistance: The Revolutionary Public Relations of the Zapatista Insurgency*, about the cultural politics of the Zapatista movement of Chiapas, Mexico. He won a 2010 Project Censored Award for his coverage of the World Water Forum in Istanbul, Turkey. He is a Fellow with the Oakland Institute, an active member of La Red VIDA (the InterAmerican Network for the Defense of the Right to Water), and a permaculturalist, and sits on advisory boards of several non-profit organizations.

Paul Corbit Brown was born and raised in the coalfields of West Virginia and is the first male in his family to not be a coal miner. He has photographed humanitarian issues throughout the United States, Mexico, Kenya, Jamaica, Russia, Israel, Laos, Thailand, Rwanda, Indonesia, Haiti, and Northern Iraq. He has had significant gallery exhibitions in Washington DC; Baltimore, Maryland; Columbus, Ohio; Minneapolis, Minnesota; and West Virginia. In 2009 he was chosen by Frontline Human Rights Defenders as one of their top one hundred human rights defenders in the world. He is committed to two long-term projects: stopping the devastation of mountaintop removal coal mining in Appalachia and documenting the aftermath of the Rwandan Genocide.

Robert Dawson has long been interested in how photography can be used to understand our relationship with the environment. His photographs have been recognized by a Visual Artists Fellowship from the National Endowment For the Arts, a Ruttenberg Fellowship from The Friends of Photography, a Photographer's Work Grant from the Maine Photographic Workshops, a James D. Phelan Award through the San Francisco Foundation, and a Dorothea Lange-Paul Taylor Prize from the Center For Documentary Studies at Duke University. He served as a Panelist for the Visual Arts Fellowship in Photography for the National Endowment For the Arts in Washington, DC. Dawson's photographs have been widely exhibited and are

in the permanent collections of many institutions. Dawson was born in Sacramento, California in 1950. He received his B.A. from the University of California at Santa Cruz in 1972 and his M.A. from San Francisco State University in 1979. Dawson served as a member of the Board of Directors of San Francisco Camerawork and later of the Friends of Photography. He is a founding member and continues to serve on the Board of PhotoAlliance. He has been an Instructor of Photography at San Jose State University since 1986 and is now an Instructor of Photography at Stanford University since 1996.

Brock Dolman is the director of Occidental Arts and Ecology Center's WATER Institute and Permaculture Design Program, and he co-directs the Wildlands Biodiversity Program. He co-instructs Basins of Relations and permaculture-related courses. He also co-manages the center's biodiversity collection, orchards, and 70 acres of wildlands. His experience ranges from the study of wildlife biology, native California botany and watershed ecology, to the practice of habitat restoration, education about regenerative human settlement design, ethno-ecology, and ecological literacy activism towards societal transformation.

J Henry Fair is best known for his "Industrial Scars" series, in which he researches our world's most egregious environmental disasters and creates images that are simultaneously stunning and horrifying. Fair's work has been featured in segments on the "TODAY Show," CNN, FOX News, and WDR German TV, as well as in most major publications, including *National Geographic, TIME, New York Magazine, Harper's Magazine,* and *GQ.* Additionally, his work travels around the world in fine art exhibitions at major museums, galleries, and educational institutions. J Henry Fair is co-founder of the Wolf Conservation Center in South Salem, NY, dedicated to the protection of and education about the world's wolf population. His book, *The Day After Tomorrow: Images of Our Earth in Crisis* will be released in January, 2011, published by powerHouse Books. His work is represented by Gerald Peters Gallery. For more information, please visit *jhenryfair.wordpress.com.*

Paula Garcia is the executive director of the New Mexico Acequia Association. She is a community leader, political activist, and aspiring farmer who dedicates her time to family and community. During her years of service to the NMAA, acequia communities have built a movement around the principle that "el agua es la vida" (water is life), and have achieved major policy changes locally and statewide. The association also launched campaigns and programs to involve youth in agricultural traditions and to increase cultivation of foods of spiritual and cultural significance to native and traditional communities in New Mexico.

Laurent Goldstein was trained to be an architect, but then he became the designer and the art manager of several high fashion companies in Paris, London, and Milan, before settling in India in order to launch a household linen label. Along the Ganges, relationships with people are different and Laurent carries on this human adventure through photography, which allows him to extend his glance to the world and to show many aspects of the Indian society sometimes deeply devoted to its traditions or on the contrary forward-looking. Laurent has prepared a beautiful art book with a French editor for publication in March 2011 and will be featured in a French film.

Tim Griffith has been photographing architecture and design related images for over twenty-five years. Melbourne born and working from bases in San Francisco and Singapore, he travels extensively on assignments in Asia, Europe, and North America for a number of the world's leading design firms. His inventive and graphic images are widely published in a diverse range of international design journals, housed in several private and public collections and sought after by architectural, corporate, and advertising clients around the world.

Barbara Grover, a self-taught photographer began her career as a political consultant where she created and executed image-driven campaigns to affect social change. She started working as a freelance photojournalist and documentary photographer in the late 90's after winning the prestigious Ernst Haas award in photojournalism for her images of the Los Angeles Riots. Driven to projects that break down stereotypes and unveil an

unexpected side of everyday issues, Barbara has traveled to over 40 countries to put a face—and give a voice—to the homeless, refugees, and children of war. Her work has appeared internationally in various print and online publications including *Time*, CNN, *Stern*, and several Rizzoli publications. Her current assignments include nonprofits and international humanitarian organizations ranging from the Los Angeles Free Clinic and Common Ground to The Jerusalem Foundation, Whole Child International, and Jewish World Watch. She has exhibited in solo and groups shows throughout the U.S. A world traveler who is based in her native Los Angeles, Barbara is currently working on a multimedia series about homeless youth in Santa Monica, California.

Wenonah Hauter is the executive director of Food and Water Watch. She has worked extensively on water, food, energy, and environmental issues at the national, state, and local level. From 1997 to 2005 she served as Director of Public Citizen's Energy and Environment Program, which focused on water, food, and energy policy. From 1996 to 1997, she was environmental policy director for Citizen Action, where she worked with the organization's 30 state-based groups. From 1989 to 1995 she was at the Union of Concerned Scientists where as a senior organizer, she coordinated broad-based, grassroots sustainable energy campaigns in several states. She has an M.S. in applied anthropology from the University of Maryland.

Knut-Erik Helle works for the Norwegian magazine *Folkevett* as an assistant editor, journalist, and photographer.

Nigel Holmes studied at the Royal College of Art in London and then freelanced for magazines and newspapers for 12 years before coming to America in 1978 to work for *Time Magazine*. He became graphics director and stayed there for 16 years. His business, Explanation Graphics, explains all sorts of things for clients like American Express, The Smithsonian Institution, and United Healthcare, and for publications such as *The Atlantic*, *National Geographic*, and the *New York Times*. He has written six books including *Wordless Diagrams* and *Nigel Holmes on Information Design*. His first book for children, *Pinhole and the Adventure to the Jungle*, was published in 2010. With his son Rowland, he makes short animated films. Clients have included the TED conference, *Fortune Magazine* conferences and *Good* magazine. You can find more at *nigelholmes.com*.

Dick Johnson (aka rovingmagpie) lives with his wife in the mountains east of Albuquerque, New Mexico. Retired corporate minions (aka engineers), their favorite place is "somewhere new."

Ed Kashi is a photojournalist dedicated to documenting the social and political issues that define our times. In addition to editorial assignments, film making and personal projects, Kashi is an educator who instructs and mentors students of photography, participates in forums, and lectures on photojournalism, documentary photography, and multimedia storytelling. Along with numerous awards, including honors from Pictures of the Year International, World Press Foundation, *Communication Arts* and *American Photography*, Kashi's images have been published and exhibited worldwide, and his editorial assignments and personal projects have generated six books.

Barbara Kingsolver's 13 published books include fiction, poetry, and creative nonfiction. Her most recent novel is *The Lacuna*, published in 2009.

Alex Leong is a Malaysian photographer and photojournalist.

Jacques Leslie writes narrative nonfiction about the world's most pressing environmental issues. His 2005 book, *Deep Water: The Epic Struggle Over Dams, Displaced People, and the Environment*, won the J. Anthony Lukas Work-in-Progress Award and was named one of the top science books of the year by *Discover Magazine*. A former *Los Angeles Times* foreign correspondent, he has won numerous literary and journalism awards including the Drunken Boat Panliterary Award in nonfiction, the Sigma Delta Chi Distinguished Service Award for Foreign Correspondence, and an Overseas Press Club citation. For more information go to *jacquesleslie.com*.

Tara Lohan is a senior editor at AlterNet and heads up the Environment, Food, and Water special coverage sections. She is the editor of *Water Consciousness: How We All Have to Change to Protect Our Most Critical Resource* from AlterNet Books. She has worked as a writer and editor on environmental and social justice issues for over ten years. She has a master's in Literary Nonfiction from the University of Oregon and bachelor's in English and Environmental Studies from Middlebury College.

Kelle Louaillier has been with Corporate Accountability International for more than two decades, serving as director of international outreach, campaign director, development director, and associate director before becoming the organization's executive director in 2007. Under her leadership, Corporate Accountability International (formerly Infact) helped move General Electric out of the nuclear weapons business, spearheaded grassroots efforts behind the passage of the global tobacco treaty, and launched the nationwide "Think Outside the Bottle" campaign. Prior to joining the organization, Louaillier taught math in the Central African Republic and worked to empower homeless youth in Seattle. She holds degrees in French, philosophy, and mathematics from Seattle University.

Kirsten Luce is a photojournalist based in New York City. She is a regular contributor to the *The New York Times*. While attending the University of Georgia, she traveled to Haiti to document an anthropologist's fieldwork. She then interned at the *Birgmingham News* in Alabama and has been primarily photographing for newspapers since then. She freelanced in Atlanta and Mexico City and also worked as a staff photojournalist for *The Monitor* in McAllen, TX, on the Mexican border. She is also the Coordinator of the Foundry Photojournalism Workshop, a non-profit workshop for emerging photojournalists that is held in a different developing country each year. For more info, please go to *foundryphotoworkshop.org.*

Bill McKibben is a scholar in residence at Middlebury College, and the founder of 350.org global warming campaign. He is the author of a dozen books, most recently *Eaarth: Making a Life on a Tough New Planet*.

Pierre Montavon was born in 1970 and lives in Delemont, Switzerland. His first major documentary project as a photographer was about the approach to psychiatry in Vietnam, Belgium, and Benin. This work was made into a book that was published in 1994. He then trained as a cameraman and did news reporting for Swiss television before coming back to his profession as a photographer. From 1995 to 2004 he followed a cathedral-building monk. He has won several awards, including the 1996 Kodak Award for his portraiture. In recent years, he has been working on a long-term documentary on the subject of environmental refugees and is preparing a book on the region of Three Gorges in China.

Gabriel Muñiz Buendía of Madrid, Spain has been working as a photographer for 20 years, with a special interest in rural culture and peoples. He recently completed a project about towns in Spain that are now underwater.

Deanna L Nichols has lived in Albuquerque, New Mexico since 1995. She finds photographic inspiration in the urban of natural landscapes of Los Ranchos, Albuquerque, New Mexico, and the Southwest. Her images have appeared in Southwest publications including *New Mexico Magazine, Cowboys and Indians*, and the annual *New Mexico Treasures Engagement Calendar.* The acequias of the Rio Grande valley are much more than photographic inspiration: They carry the lifeblood of her home. You can find more of her work at *dnicholsphotos.com.*

Sandra Postel directs the independent Global Water Policy Project, as well as the Center for the Environment at Mount Holyoke College. She is author of *Pillar of Sand: Can the Irrigation Miracle Last?* and of *Last Oasis: Facing Water Scarcity.* She is also co-author (with Brian Richter) of *Rivers for Life: Managing Water for People and Nature.* Postel has served as advisor to the Division on Earth and Life Studies of the U.S. National Research Council as well as to American Rivers. She has served on the Board of Directors of the International Water Resources Association, and on the editorial boards of Ecosystems, Water Policy, and Green Futures. She received a B.A. in geology and political science at Wittenberg University and an M.E.M. with emphasis on resource economics and policy at Duke University. She has also received two honorary Doctor of Science degrees.

Christina Roessler is a consultant and writer working on water issues in the western United States. Before becoming a consultant she was the founding director of the French American Charitable Trust.

Tina Rosenberg is a Pulitzer Prize-winning journalist and author, and the recipient of a MacArthur Fellowship 'genius award.' She is a frequent contributor to the *New York Times Magazine* and the author of the books *Children of Cain: Violence and the Violent in Latin America* and *The Haunted Land, Facing Europe's Ghosts After Communism*.

Elizabeth Royte is the author of *Bottlemania: Big Business, Local Springs, and the Battle Over America's Drinking Water*; *Garbage Land: On the Secret Trail of Trash*; and *The Tapir's Morning Bath: Solving the Mysteries of the Tropical Rain Forest*.

Victoria Sambunaris received her MFA from Yale University in 1999. Each year, she structures her life around a photographic journey crossing the American landscape. She is currently following the US/Mexican border photographing the intersection of geology, politics, and culture along the volatile international boundary. She has received fellowships from the Center for Land Use Interpretation and the Lannan Foundation. Her work is held in the collections of the Museum of Modern Art, the Museum of Fine Arts Houston, the National Gallery of Art, the San Francisco Museum of Modern Art, and the Lannan Foundation.

George Steinmetz, best known for his exploration photography, sets out to discover the few remaining secrets in our world today: remote deserts, obscure cultures, the mysteries of science and technology. Since 1986, George has completed 18 major photo essays for *National Geographic* and 25 stories for *GEO* magazine in Germany. His expeditions to the Sahara and Gobi deserts have been featured in separate National Geographic Explorer programs. In 2006 he was awarded a grant by the National Science Foundation to document the work of scientists in the Dry Valleys and volcanoes of Antarctica. He has won numerous awards for photography during his 25-year career, including two first prizes in science and technology from World Press Photo. He has also won awards and citations from Pictures of the Year, Overseas Press Club and *Life Magazine*'s Alfred Eisenstadt Awards. Born in Beverly Hills in 1957, George graduated from Stanford University with a degree in geophysics. His current passion is photographing the world's deserts while piloting a motorized paraglider. George lives in Glen Ridge, New Jersey, with his wife, *Wall Street Journal* editor Lisa Bannon, their daughter, Nell, and twin sons John and Nicholas.

Eleanor Sterling is the Director of the American Museum of Natural History's Center for Biodiversity and Conservation. She received her B.A. from Yale College and a joint Ph.D. in physical anthropology, and forestry and environmental studies from Yale University. Sterling has more than 25 years of field research experience in Africa, Asia, and Latin America. She has served as an adjunct professor at Columbia University since 1997, and has served as the Director of Graduate Studies for Columbia University's Department of Ecology, Evolution, and Environmental Biology since 2003. Sterling is the Deputy Chair of the Society for Conservation Biology's Education Committee.

Brent Stirton is the senior staff photographer for the assignment division of Getty Images, New York. Getty Images is the largest photographic agency in the world. He specializes in documentary work and is known for his alternative approaches. He travels an average of nine months of the year on assignment. Brent's work is published by: *National Geographic Magazine*, *National Geographic Adventure*, *The New York Times Magazine*, *The London Sunday Times Magazine*, *Smithsonian Magazine*, *The Discovery Channel*, *Newsweek*, *Le Express*, *Le Monde 2*, *Figaro*, *Paris Match*, *GQ*, *Geo*, *Stern*, *CNN*, and many other respected international titles and news organizations. He also photographs for the Global Business Coalition Against AIDS,

Tuberculosis, and Malaria. He has been a long time photographer for the World Wide Fund for Nature. He works for the Ford and Clinton Foundations, the Nike foundation and the World Economic Forum. He was appointed one of 200 Young Global leaders in 2009 by the World Economic Forum. He has received numerous awards, most recently a gold award from China International photographic awards, as well as awards from the National Press Photographers Association, *Graphis*, *American Photography*, and *ASME* magazine publishers award for photojournalism for his work in the Democratic Republic of Congo.

Dieter Telemans is a freelance photographer based in Brussels. He's a member of the photo agency Panos Pictures (*www.panos.co.uk*). For his first long term project, *Heart of Dance*, he focused on the positive sides of African countries by photographing the music scene. His project *Troubled Waters* started with a reportage on the disaster of the shrinking Aral Sea in Uzbekistan. From floods in Bangladesh to drought in the North-East of Kenya, he visited regions where the Millennium Goals are words never heard of. His work has been published in amongst others, *The New York Times*, *The Independent*, *National Geographic*, *Libération*, *Le Monde*.

Erin Vintinner is Program Coordinator and Biodiversity Specialist at the Center for Biodiversity and Conservation (CBC) at the American Museum of Natural History. She provides research and writing support for various CBC projects and contributes content to the Network of Conservation Educators and Practitioners. Prior to coming to the CBC, she served as research and expedition coordinator for the "No Water No Life" nonprofit photodocumentary project in the Columbia River Basin. She also previously served as a fisheries technician with the USDA Forest Service in Sitka, Alaska and the Bureau of Land Management in Eugene, Oregon. She holds a M.A. in conservation biology from Columbia University's Department of Ecology, Evolution and Environmental Biology and a B.A. in biology from Boston University.

Stephen Voss is a Washington DC-based editorial photographer. His clients include *Smithsonian*, *BusinessWeek* and National Public Radio among others. His documentary work covers environmental and globalization issues worldwide, and U.S. politics. He is currently working on a project on his native state of New Jersey exploring the intersections of development and environment.

George Waldman has spent 30 years photographing the Detroit streets, boardrooms, sports arenas, government corridors, and the people who move there. He's worked street corners and executive suites, weddings and political conventions, Super Bowls, and Detroit Tigers baseball games. He does editorial photography, assignments for portraits, news events, and feature stories, specializing in social issues: education, environment, labor, health, family, and urban affairs including landscape, architecture, and city scenes.

William Waterway was raised on an organic farm and is an award-winning water researcher, author, poet, and Native American flutist. He has traveled to over fifteen countries doing water research. While in college he investigated fish kills and industrial polluters. He resigned his job as Senior Environmental Analyst for the city of Newark to live outside for two-years while undertaking a 7,000 mile horseback trek across America. He founded Martha's Vineyard's first state-certified water testing laboratory, and Vineyard Environmental Research Institute. His water research has been featured in CNN, MSNBC, MVTV, CBS, NBC, ABC, NPR, UPI, New Zealand National Radio, AP, *New York Times*, *The Water Encyclopedia*, AlterNet, Care2.com, MaximsNews, and other media. He is also the author of essays published in magazines and books such as National Geographic's *Written in Water*, and is author of *The Holy Order of Water, Healing Earth's Waters and Ourselves*; publisher of the United Nations' affiliated, *Water Voices from Around The World*; author of *The History of Wind Power on Martha's Vineyard*, and founder of *Martha's Vineyard Magazine* and *Nantucket Magazine*.

Jim West has been an editorial photographer, based in Detroit, for more than 25 years. His work focuses on social issues and the labor movement and has been published in major news magazines in the U.S. and abroad, in newspapers from the *New York*

Times to *Los Angeles Times*, by religious organizations, environmental groups, labor unions, textbook publishers, and trade magazines. Jim is a member of the American Society of Media Photographers, International Labor Communications Association, Stock Artists Alliance, and Editorial Photographers. His work is distributed by several photo agencies, including The Image Works, Alamy Images, PhotoEdit, Imagebroker, Zuma Press, and Sipa Press.

Herbert Wong is passoniate about traveling and capturing the world in photographs. He enjoys the exhilaration in the shadows of majestic mountains, the intimacy of quiet secluded lakes, the timeliness of ancient beauty and age-old lifestyle preserved in forgotten corners of the earth. He is similarly awed by the religious fervent of devoted pilgrims, the warm and unforgettable hospitalities and cultures of ethnic minorities around the world. Photography is a means for him to define and capture such experiences and unforgettable moments to be shared. His photography also attempts to retain those magical spectacles before they disappeared forever in the name of developments.

The Value of Water: An Art Exhibition
Cathedral of St. John the Divine, New York City

Gregory Amenoff is a painter who lives in New York City and Ulster County, New York. He is the recipient of numerous awards from organizations including the American Academy of Arts and Letters, National Endowment for the Arts, New York State Council on the Arts, and Tiffany Foundation. He has had over 50 one-person exhibitions in museums and galleries throughout the U.S. and Europe. His work is in the permanent collections of more than 30 museums, including the Whitney Museum of America Art, the Museum of Fine Arts in Boston, the Museum of Modern Art in New York, and the Metropolitan Museum of Art. He served as President of the National Academy of Design from 2001-2005. He is a founding member of the CUE

Art Foundation where he serves on the Board and as the Foundation's Curator Governor. Amenoff has taught at Columbia for the last 15 years, where he holds the Eve and Herman Gelman Chair of Visual Arts and is currently the Chair of the Visual Arts Division.

Diane Burko is an artist who paints on canvas and also makes archival inkjet prints. Her canvases are usually large visceral responses to monumental environments. Her photographs have a more intimate reading, capturing unconventional views of natural spaces, with detailed structures. Both mediums formally locate in the balance between abstraction and representation. "Politics of Snow" is currently an on-going series where her practice as a painter serves to document the rapidity of change in our natural icons such as the Matterhorn, as well as the shrinking of glaciers in America and Iceland. In a series of diptychs of historical visual comparisons, she is contrasting past and present situations of glacial activity.

Fredericka Foster describes moving water using oils applied in many layers of complex color. Her practice begins with photographing the interaction of light and water. Out of the hundreds of photographs she makes, several inspire each painting. In October of 2009, she had a solo exhibit at the Fischbach Gallery in New York City. This was her fourth "Waterway" show with the Gallery since 2001. She has been exhibiting since 1972.

April Gornik lives and works in New York City and in North Haven, Long Island, NY. Born in Cleveland, Ohio, in 1953, she received a BFA from the Nova Scotia College of Art and Design, Nova Scotia, Canada. She has work in the Metropolitan Museum of Art, NY; the Whitney Museum of American Art, NY; the Museum of Modern Art, NY; the National Museum of American Art in Washington, DC; the National Museum of Women in the Arts in Washington, DC; the Cincinnati Museum; the High Museum of Art, Atlanta; the Modern Art Museum of Fort Worth; the Orlando Museum of Art; and other major public and private collections. She has shown extensively, in one-person and group shows, in the U.S. and abroad.

The Rev. Thomas Miller is Canon for Liturgy and the Arts at the Cathedral of St. John the Divine in New York City. A graduate of the University of Pittsburgh with degrees from both Union and General theological seminaries, he has worked in the theatre as an actor, writer, and producer. At Lincoln Center for the Performing Arts he managed the Meet-the-Artist program and he was Lyricist-in-Residence at the Williamstown Theatre Festival. In 1999, Tom founded the Woodstock Cycle, an annual new works arts festival in Woodstock, New York.

Samantha Scherer was born in New Jersey in 1970 and grew up in Columbia, MO. She attended the Kansas City Art Institute in the early 90s, graduating with a BFA in Printmaking in 1994. Samantha moved to Seattle in 1995 to study for an MFA in Printmaking at the University of Washington, which she completed in 1997, and has remained in Seattle ever since. She currently shows at Davidson Galleries and has exhibited locally at Wright Exhibition Space, Kirkland Arts Center, SOIL Art Gallery, and NW Museum of Arts & Culture in Spokane. She has also shown nationally in Los Angeles, Denver, and Kansas City. Samantha has been featured in several local and national arts publications and is the recipient of three Artist Trust GAP awards. She currently lives and works in the Greenwood neighborhood of Seattle with her artist husband and infant daughter.

Kiki Smith was born in 1954 in Nuremberg, Germany. The daughter of American sculptor Tony Smith, she grew up in New Jersey. As a young girl, one of Smith's first experiences with art was helping her father make cardboard models for his geometric sculptures. This training in formalist systems, combined with her upbringing in the Catholic Church, would later resurface in Smith's evocative sculptures, drawings, and prints. The recurrent subject matter in Smith's work has been the body as a receptacle for knowledge, belief, and storytelling. In the 1980s, Smith literally turned the figurative tradition in sculpture inside out, creating objects and drawings based on organs, cellular forms, and the human nervous system. This body of work evolved to incorporate animals, domestic objects, and narrative tropes from classical mythology and folk tales. Life, death, and resurrection are thematic signposts in many of Smith's installations and sculptures. Smith received the Skowhegan Medal for Sculpture in 2000, the Athena Award for Excellence in Printmaking from the Rhode Island School of Design in 2005, the 50th Edward MacDowell Medal from the MacDowell Colony in 2009, and has participated in the Whitney Biennial three times in the past decade. In 2005, Smith was elected to the American Academy of Arts and Letters, New York. Smith's work is in numerous prominent museum collections. She lives and works in New York City.

Bill Viola has been instrumental in the establishment of video as a vital form of contemporary art, and in so doing has helped to greatly expand its scope in terms of technology, content, and historical reach. For over 35 years he has created videotapes, architectural video installations, sound environments, electronic music performances, flat panel video pieces, and works for television broadcast. Viola's video installations—total environments that envelop the viewer in image and sound—employ state-of-the-art technologies and are distinguished by their precision and direct simplicity. They are shown in museums and galleries worldwide and are found in many distinguished collections. His single channel videotapes have been widely broadcast and presented cinematically, while his writings have been extensively published, and translated for international readers. Viola uses video to explore the phenomena of sense perception as an avenue to self-knowledge. His works focus on universal human experiences—birth, death, the unfolding of consciousness—and have roots in both Eastern and Western art as well as spiritual traditions, including Zen Buddhism, Islamic Sufism, and Christian mysticism. Using the inner language of subjective thoughts and collective memories, his videos communicate to a wide audience, allowing viewers to experience the work directly, and in their own personal way.

Stock Credits

Page 14, frogs
Getty Images/PIER

Page 24, Lake Lanier
Atlanta Journal Constitution, Rich Addicks

Page 27, sinkhole
Unknown

Page 29, Gov. Perdue
AP/Atlanta Journal Constitution, Rich Addicks

Page 47, water bottle
© Ugurhan Betin/istockphoto.com

Page 59, Feliciano dos Santos
Goldman Environmental Prize

Page 66, KickStart
KickStart

Page 86, BP spill
US Coast Guard

Page 97, Mehta Patkar
Goldman Environmental Prize

Page 111, (center) Philippines protest
Keith Bacongco, flickr.com/photos/kitoy

Page 111, (bottom) UK protest
Peter Mulligan, flickr.com/photos/nagillum

Page 114, water pipe
Sir Mildred Pierce

Page 144, Lake Mead
© Digital Hallway/istockphoto.com

Page 149, ocean icons (altered)
© Paul Pantazescu/istockphoto.com

Page 157, xeriscaping
© ivanastar/istockphoto.com

Page 74, food shopping icons (altered)
© sasimoto/istockphoto.com (strawberry)
© Ryan Putnam/istockphoto.com (shopping cart)

Page 177, Shinto ritual
Wikimedia Commons, Takeski Ueki

Page 182, boy fishing
© Roberto A Sanchez, Vetta Collection/istockphoto.com

Page 203, fog curtain
American Museum of Natural History

Page 205, ice cubes
© Evgeny Terentev/istockphoto.com

Pages 207/232, water splash
© Okea/istockphoto.com

Page 209, sign (altered)
© Amanda Rohde/istockphoto.com

Page 211, elephant
© victor zastol`skiy/istockphoto.com

Page 212, umbrella
© Sharon Kaasa/istockphoto.com

Page 214, baby duck standing
© Sascha Burkard/istockphoto.com

Page 215, baby duck smelling
© Kevin Russ/istockphoto.com

Page 217, dirty/clean water
© Peter Brutsch/istockphoto.com

Page 219, lizard
© Oleg Mitiukhin/istockphoto.com

Page 223, hot water bottle
© Scrambled/istockphoto.com

Page 224-225, ladybugs
© Tomasz Zachariasz/istockphoto.com

Page 226, bottle with faucet
© Ljupco/istockphoto.com

Page 229, fish
© Eric Isselée/istockphoto.com

Acknowledgments Don Hazen

It is very exciting to see the tide shifting on the national debate on the water issue. The public consciousness is being transformed as more and more people, from everyday citizens to world leaders, recognize the importance of clean water for everyone. Many more people under-

stand the challenges we face, the need for education and conservation, and the realization that we have a serious crisis on our hands, both in the U.S. and across the world.

We like to think that AlterNet's water program has played an important role in building momentum on this crucial issue. Two years ago, we published *Water Consciousness*—the forerunner to *Water Matters*, the book in your hands—and we launched our special coverage of the issue on *AlterNet.org/water* over three years ago.

Since then, we're grateful to see media interest growing. In the past year, *the Economist, National Geographic* and *Yes!* Magazine all produced special reports or issues on water. The social action Web site Change.org sponsors Blog Action Day each year where participating bloggers

from more than 150 countries vote on a single pressing issue that requires global attention. In 2010 voters chose water, a striking indication of the increasing interest in water as an issue worldwide. Thousands of bloggers wrote about water issues on Blog Action Day 2010, held on October 15.

If *Water Consciousness* helped kick-start a growing movement, *Water Matters* takes us to the next level—an energized call to action. Although people are beginning to recognize the importance of water and its connection to energy and food, we still need to start implementing changes. Water is not a partisan issue; everyone needs a clean and reliable source of freshwater. The United Nations General Assembly recently voted to make water a human right. (Sadly, the U.S., along with a few others like the United Kingdom and Canada, abstained from voting. But 122 nations did affirm this important principle.)

Tara Lohan, AlterNet's environment editor, is most responsible for the creation of the book and its contents, as she was with *Water Consciousness*. She has emerged as one of the top journalists and advocates for changing water policy, and she works with a broad array of leading authors, analysts, and photographers. She recruited some of the best writers in the world on the topic, organized the material, facilitated the powerful graphics generously created by Nigel Holmes, and did everything necessary to bring a beautiful and influential book to press.

Enormous thanks goes to the Panta Rhea Foundation and its visionaries—founder Hans Schoepflin and executive director Diana Cohn. As much as anyone in philanthropy and policy advocacy, these two saw the extent of the water crisis in front of us, and they acted without hesitation in dozens of ways, to make sure that water is on the map of priorities for citizens and activists alike. We're also indebted to the Park Foundation, especially to Adelaide Gomer and Amy Panek, for their generous support of our water program.

Plaudits and appreciation go to art director Robin Terra of Terra Studio, San Francisco, whose talents are showcased in this book. She worked long and hard to ensure that the book is a work of great creativity while being solidly grounded in the need for action. Robin wrangled photos from top artists, and often these creative people were extremely generous in helping us produce a book that didn't break the bank. The same appreciation goes for our writers, a fantastic array of thinkers, journalists, and advocates, whose hearts have long been engaged in solving the water crisis. We are proud to be publishing their words and we look forward to working with them long into the future.

The origins of both of AlterNet's water books are linked to the powerful exhibit "Water: H2o = Life," which opened in the fall of 2007 at the American Museum of Natural History. This exhibit is traveling the globe over a 10-year period, helping to educate hundreds of thousands of people about the miracles of water, and the perilous path ahead as we work to protect this valuable resource. Eleanor Sterling, who has contributed to both our water books, was one of the masterminds of the exhibit, and we owe a lot to her vision and her collaboration as we moved our water effort forward.

We were also fortunate this time to gain an incredible partner in New York's Cathedral of St. John the Divine. An exhibition of leading artists, on view at the Cathedral beginning in the fall of 2011, will further deepen our water consciousness, and several of the artists volunteered their work to be featured in this book. Special thanks to exhibit curator and contributing artist Fredericka Foster; vice president of events, marketing and communications Lisa Schubert; and the Reverend Canon Thomas Miller, who all helped make our partnership with the Cathedral a reality.

Thanks also goes to Island Press for recognizing our book as one they wanted to see in the hands of many people. They embraced the opportunity to distribute the book, and they have helped publicize its message.

On the AlterNet staff, this effort would not have been possible without the help from our associate publisher Roxanne Cooper, our communications and development associate Kristen Lee, our finance manager Mari Ordonez-Branstetter, and the whole AlterNet editorial team. And an additional thanks goes to the invaluable efforts of proofreader Debra Gates and indexer Ken DellaPenta.

Indeed, it takes a village to publish a book, and we are truly grateful for the one that we are a part of. We look forward to strengthening this community as we continue to grow a movement for change.

Resource List

Advocacy, Public Education, Research

350.org
San Francisco, California
350.org
350.org is an international campaign that's building a movement to unite the world around solutions to the climate crisis.

Amigos Bravos
Taos, New Mexico
(575) 758-3874
amigosbravos.org
A river conservation organization guided by social justice principles and dedicated to preserving and restoring the ecological and cultural integrity of New Mexico's rivers and watersheds.

Blue Planet Project
Ottawa, Ontario, Canada
(613) 233-2773
blueplanetproject.net
An international civil society movement begun by The Council of Canadians to protect the world's fresh water from the growing threats of trade and privatization.

Corporate Accountability International
Boston, Massachusetts
(617) 695-2525
stopcorporateabuse.org
A nonprofit challenging corporate abuse for more than 30 years, including water privatization.

Food & Water Watch
Washington DC
(202) 683-2500
foodandwaterwatch.org
A nonprofit consumer organization that challenges the corporate control and abuse of our food and water resources.

Global Water Policy Project
globalwaterpolicy.org
Promotes the preservation and sustainable use of Earth's fresh water through research, writing, outreach, and public speaking.

GRACE
New York, New York
(212) 726-9161
gracelinks.org
A non-profit environmental organization that promotes sustainable solutions for American's food, energy, and water systems.

Greywater Action
California
Greywateraction.org
A collaborative group of educators, designers, builders, and artists who educate and empower people to build sustainable water culture and infrastructure.

International Rivers
Berkeley, California
(510) 848-1155
internationalrivers.org
An international nonprofit opposing destructive dams, protecting rivers, and defending communities that rely on rivers.

KickStart
Nairobi, Kenya and San Francisco, California
kickstart.org
KickStart's mission is to help millions of people out of poverty by developing and promoting technologies that can be used by dynamic entrepreneurs to establish and run profitable small scale enterprises.

Living Machines
Charlottesville, Virginia
(434) 973-6365
livingmachines.com
A company dedicated to developing environmentally sustainable wastewater treatment technologies.

Michigan Citizens for Water Conservation
Mecosta, Michigan
savemiwater.org
A group helping Michigan's citizens protect community water supplies.

New Mexico Acequia Association
Santa Fe, New Mexico
(505) 995-9644
lasacequias.org
Works to protect the acequia system and water as a community
resource.

Occidental Arts and Ecology WATER Institute
Occidental, California
(707) 874-1557
oaecwater.org
Promotes the understanding of healthy watersheds through
advocacy and policy development; training and support;
education and demonstration; and research.

Pacific Institute
Oakland, California
(510) 251-1600
pacinst.org
An independent, nonpartisan think-tank that conducts
research on water, community strategies for sustainability
and justice, and globalization.

People's Water Board Coalition
Detroit, Michigan
peopleswaterboard.blogspot.com
A coalition of organizations (labor, social justice,
environmental, conservation) working together to protect our
water from pollution, high water rates, and privatization.

Polaris Institute
Ottawa, Ontario, Canada
(613) 237-1717
polarisinstitute.org
Helps citizen movements fight for democratic social change,
including in the area of water democracy.

Exhibits, Media, Resources

AlterNet.org and AlterNet Books
San Francisco, California
(415) 284-1420
alternet.org
An award-winning news magazine, online community, and
book publisher that focuses on progressive issues, including the
environment and water.

H2O Conserve Water Calculator
H2OConserve.org
An online tool that enables people to calculate their water
footprint and find ways to reduce their consumption.

Snitow-Kaufman Productions
Berkeley, California
(510) 841-1068
snitow-kaufman.org
A nonprofit that produces film, video, and educational media
for the general public on social issues from race relations
to globalization, including *Thirst*, about water privatization.

The Value of Water: An Art Exhibition
Cathedral of St. John the Divine
New York, New York
(212) 316-7490
stjohndivine.org
A vast exhibition that includes a range of programs including
visual art, multi-media, poetry, music, liturgy, drama, con-
versations and storytelling will be at the Cathedral of St. John
the Divine—often referred to as the Green Cathedral—from
September 2011—March 2012. The Cathedral of St. John
the Divine is the Cathedral of the Episcopal Diocese of New York.

Water: H2O=Life
amnh.org/exhibitions/water
An exhibit organized by the American Museum of Natural
History, New York, and the Science Museum of Minnesota,
St. Paul, in collaboration with Great Lakes Science Center,
Cleveland; The Field Museum, Chicago; Instituto Sangari,
São Paulo, Brazil; National Museum of Australia, Canberra;
Royal Ontario Museum, Toronto, Canada; San Diego
Natural History Museum; and Singapore Science Centre
with PUB Singapore.

Index